WHARTON ON
MAKING
DECISIONS

WHARTON ON MAKING DECISIONS

Editors
STEPHEN J. HOCH
and
HOWARD C. KUNREUTHER
with
ROBERT E. GUNTHER

WILEY

John Wiley & Sons, Inc.

Published by John Wiley & Sons, Inc., Hoboken, New Jersey.
Published simultaneously in Canada.

For general information on our other products and services please contact our Customer Care Department within the United States at (800) 762-2974, outside the United States at (317) 572-3993 or fax (317) 572-4002.

Wiley also publishes its books in a variety of electronic formats. Some content that appears in print may not be available in electronic books. For more information about Wiley products, visit our web site at www.wiley.com.

Library of Congress Cataloging-in-Publication Data:

Wharton on making decisions : edited by Stephen J. Hoch and Howard C. Kunreuther with Robert E. Gunther.
    p.   cm.
   Includes bibliographical references (p.) and index.
   ISBN 0-471-38247-7 (alk. paper); 0-471-68938-6 (pbk.)
   1. Decision making. 2. Group decision making. 3. Decision making—Social aspects. I. Hoch, Stephen J. (Stephen James), 1952– II. Kunreuther, Howard C. III. Gunther, Robert E., 1960–

HD30.23.W5   2001
658.4′03—dc21   00-053369

Printed in the United States of America.

10 9 8 7 6 5 4 3 2 1

PREFACE

In the early 1970s, a group of faculty members and PhD students in various departments at the Wharton School of the University of Pennsylvania organized an informal weekly workshop in Decision Processes. We invited faculty members from here and other universities to present their current research on decision making and choice behavior. This Workshop has continued with active participation from faculty and students not only at Wharton but also in the Psychology Department, the Engineering School, and the Medical School. The seminar complements much of the research activity of the Wharton Risk Management and Decision Processes Center and served as a stimulus for writing *Wharton on Making Decisions*.

This book brings together the decision-making research of 16 University of Pennsylvania faculty members (and their coauthors), all of whom play an active role in the Decision Processes area at Wharton. We feel very fortunate to have their talents and unique perspectives on decision making and choice behavior represented in this book.

Each chapter in the book is motivated by a set of real-world problems at either the individual, group, organizational, or societal level. We asked each author to discuss what factors influence individuals and groups in their decision-making process, why they may be costly to the individual and/or organization, and how the choice process can be improved. All the papers address these questions and provide valuable guidance on making better decisions in the future.

We hope this book provides a multifaceted view of decision making and opens up doors for new ways of evaluating this behavior. If the book provokes readers to be more aware of the factors that influence their decisions and provides the motivation to take remedial actions, then we have succeeded. Here's to better decision making!

STEPHEN J. HOCH
HOWARD C. KUNREUTHER

ACKNOWLEDGMENTS

We want to thank all of the organizations and firms who provided empirical data on which the studies of choice are based. The illustrative examples from these firms provide an appropriate platform to understand more fully the difficulties that consumers and managers have in making choices when there is uncertain information.

A special note of appreciation goes to Robert E. Gunther who has played a key role in pulling this book together. He provided masterful critiques of the chapters at an early stage of the process after the group convened for a day and a half retreat where preliminary outlines of papers were presented. He edited the penultimate versions of the papers and provided constructive feedback to all the authors. He also helped organize the photos and cartoons that illustrate key concepts in each of the chapters.

We also wish to acknowledge the research, editorial work, and many other contributions of Martha Carroll Vollmer. Our thanks to Kate Fang and Anne Stamer of the Wharton Risk Management and Decision Processes Center who coordinated the challenging process of communicating with all the authors. The yeoman contributions of Amy Myers were also invaluable. Our thanks also to Wiley editors Larry Alexander and Matt Holt for carrying this process forward and the staff of Publications Development Company for many improvements to the manuscript.

Finally, we wish to acknowledge the continual support and encouragement of our spouses, Judy Tschirgi and Gail Loeb Kunreuther.

S. H.
H. K.

CONTENTS

CHAPTER 1

A COMPLEX WEB OF DECISIONS

STEPHEN J. HOCH
The Wharton School

HOWARD C. KUNREUTHER
The Wharton School

What is the cost of poor decisions? The accumulated trading losses of over $1 billion by Barings Bank trader Nick Leeson led to one of the most spectacular collapses in banking history. But while one rogue trader was at the heart of the disaster, it was actually the result of a complex web of decisions—personal, managerial, and societal.

He who has a choice has trouble.
Danish proverb

As a manager, every day you face a myriad of decisions from the time you wake up in the morning until the time you go to sleep at night. Some of these decisions are fairly mundane, but others have a significant impact on the future of your life, your organization, and your career. Making the right choices is crucial. While the impact of anyone's decisions is far-reaching, managers' decisions have particular significance because they affect all the people who report to them and the businesses they manage. For this reason, making better decisions is a key concern of managers and their organizations.

Most of us do not make great decisions, and few of us are aware of this fact. We think we are making excellent decisions, and as long as the results are good, we don't look too closely at our decision processes. For long periods, we may be fortunate that the world is forgiving and some poorly made decisions lead to positive outcomes. We congratulate ourselves for walking along the cliff's edge and not falling, but do not fully appreciate how close we may have come to disaster. It usually is only when we have a spectacular failure that we sit back and look at our decision processes. We then ask the questions we should be asking every day: What are my goals and objectives? What are my assumptions? What are the potential pitfalls? How could I make better decisions? It is usually only when we look at our failures that we actually improve our decision making.

We have an opportunity to be more proactive. We need to make these decision processes conscious, to be aware of when we are cutting corners and when we need more thorough analysis. Building this awareness of the process—especially given the new complexities of decision making in our modern age—is crucial to successful management. We cannot always guarantee positive outcomes; many factors that affect these outcomes are out of our control. This awareness, however, ensures that we follow a coherent and conscious process that leads to better decisions.

The goal of this book is to build this awareness of the intricacies of the decision-making process. For the most part, efforts to improve managerial decision making have relied on formulas and frameworks for systematically making choices. This is an important first step, because a systematic approach can help avoid imprecision in the decision process. Our book, however, takes a different approach, drawing on several decades of research into the psychological, interactive, and temporal aspects of decision making. We reflect the insights of researchers who studied how people make decisions and how they can make better ones. This book offers research-based insights on diverse aspects of making better decisions rather than simplistic formulas for making decisions.

This book looks at decision making from various levels. First, you make decisions as an individual. The decisions are often influenced by emotions, intuitions, and a focus on present versus future consequences. How do these factors influence decision making? How can we use these personal assets and foibles to make better decisions? Second, we make decisions in our role as manager. We may be more concerned in this role with using models to set up decision processes in our organization, balancing speed and reflection, dealing with complexity and reframing questions to break out of traditional mind-sets. Third, we make decisions in the context of negotiations and other multiparty interactions. Learning across several rounds of interaction, the power of reputations, deception in negotiations and the impact of e-mail and the Internet on bargaining are critical issues. At the broadest level, we need to consider how societal decisions on issues such as environmental protection, risks from catastrophes, and health care coverage can be managed. Decisions about these issues involve a mix of personal and collective values and reflect quirks in how we prepare for high-impact, low-risk events such as earthquakes. We also tend to like to keep our options open, to follow the crowd even when it is going in the wrong direction, and, surprisingly, we sometimes have very different approaches to our public and private decisions.

Effective decisions at all these different levels can produce outstanding outcomes. Yet, the right decisions are by no means easily discernible at the time the decision is made. When managers decided to launch the ill-fated Challenger space shuttle, the concerns about the O-rings that ultimately led to the explosion were buried in a vast sea of thousands of other decisions and concerns leading up to the launch. Poor decisions at different levels may lead to disastrous consequences. A venerable banking institution and an obscure—but soon to become infamous—trader named Nick Leeson learned this lesson the hard way, illustrating how complex webs of decisions can lead to success or failure.

A MOMENT OF DECISION

Nick Leeson was a bit nervous about the new trader he hired at the Barings Futures Singapore (BFS) office. He tried sticking close by her when the trading opened. But the day was crazier than usual and that was impossible. At the end of the day, he discovered she'd made a terrible mistake: She'd *sold* contracts when she should have *bought* them. Making good to the client would cost the firm 20,000 pounds sterling. Leeson had only been in the job a few months, and was thousands of miles from the home office in an exotic city.[1]

Nick Leeson faced a seemingly minor decision on the evening of Friday, July 17, 1992. Should he reveal the error to his superiors or conceal it? He decided to hide the mistake. What he justified initially as a desire to protect one of his employees snowballed into a habitual hiding of his own trading errors in the derivatives market—deceptions that three years later brought down one of the world's oldest financial institutions. How did a back office clerk in his twenties become responsible for bankrupting one of the world's oldest merchant banks? The answer: many bad decisions.

Leeson alone didn't bring down Barings. There were decisions at multiple levels—complex webs of decisions—that either encouraged his actions or created the holes through which he slipped. Beyond Leeson's own personal mistakes, there were managerial decisions that caused his supervisors to fail to challenge his actions, there were negotiations on the trading floor and with supervisors, and finally there was the broader social context of global financial regulations. When decision making at all these levels goes very wrong, mistakes are compounded and the final outcome can be fatal.

At the center of this storm of bad decisions was Leeson, who started his career by fixing the errors of others. In open-cry markets, where traders call out their orders to buy and sell, errors frequently occur. They are caught and corrected, usually within 24 hours, in the settlements department. Leeson had a knack for this type of dogged detail work and it helped him get his job at Barings Securities in 1989.

Within a year, Leeson was sent to the Barings' Jakarta branch to wade through the mountain of paperwork that lay idle in its settlements office. He helped Barings "to get rid of its 100 million pound hole" in its balance sheet.[2] His star at Barings was beginning to rise. Following his success in Jakarta, in 1992 Barings offered Leeson the position of running its new futures subsidiary in Singapore.[3]

It would be three years before Leeson's errors came to light and by then his own trading losses had accumulated to over $1 billion and took Barings down. Leeson pleaded guilty in December 1995 to having deceived Barings' auditors and having cheated SIMEX (Singapore International Monetary Exchange). He was sentenced to a six-and-a-half year term in a Singapore prison.

Lessons for Managers

Barings and Leeson made a number of strategic errors in decisions that contributed to the bank's collapse, including:

- *Being blinded by emotions.* Managers were overly enthusiastic about Leeson and so overlooked glaring problems. Not only did one of the oldest and most conservative merchant banks in England hire someone with no experience at trading, but it also hired someone who was being taken to court for outstanding debt.[4] Within days of arriving in Singapore, Barings received notice from the Securities and Futures Authority in London about two outstanding debts he owed (by one account, totaling over 2,000 pounds).[5] Leeson had not mentioned these debts on his application for a trader's license in London.

  Barings' management took a permissive, boys-will-be-boys attitude, and decided to look the other way. The lure of enormous profits in the emerging Southeast Asian markets was great, and Leeson was their golden boy. Leeson's supervisors clearly liked the job he was doing with settlements, a process none of them knew nearly as well as he did. Because they liked Leeson, they were reluctant to see his faults. The internal audit Barings conducted in 1994, which failed to expose Leeson's hidden errors on trading Nikkei 225 contracts (which by then had accumulated to more than 50 million pounds), was clouded by one of the auditors' admiration for Leeson.[6] Managers let emotions get in their way (greed, admiration for Leeson) so they made less effective decisions. The impact of emotions on decisions is discussed by Mary Frances Luce, John W. Payne, and James R. Bettman in Chapter 2.

- *Overreliance on intuition.* The Bank of England cited Barings' "managerial confusion" as contributing to an environment in which a dishonest employee could flourish. When Barings entered the futures business, it was essentially a one-man operation (Christopher Heath) that relied on an instinctive style of management. As business expanded rapidly, Heath and Barings failed to recognize that such an intuitive management style was no longer appropriate.[7] In Chapter 5, Stephen J. Hoch shows how both computer models and human intuition have strengths and weaknesses, so that it may often be more effective to combine the two for improving decision making rather than just using one or the other alone.

- *Emphasis on speed.* Barings executives also appeared to make decisions quickly, racing to take advantage of market opportunities and failing to institute a sufficiently rigorous system of controls. When Barings discovered problems with Leeson's record, the firm decided it was more important to get the Singapore office up and running than pay attention to such details. This Westernized, time-is-money, attitude contrasts with an Eastern view, which emphasizes patient reflection. Karen A. Jehn and Keith Weigelt explore these two contrasting views of decision making in Chapter 6. The expedient, time-is-money mode may not always lead to the very best choice, but there are times when speed is critical.

- *Failure to detect deception.* Barings' managers, like most people, overestimated their ability to detect deception. Essentially, Barings was "killed in an eyeblink by a problem they didn't even know they had."[8] Because Barings' managers didn't consider the possibility that Leeson could be cheating them, they didn't look for signs of deceit. Recognizing deception in negotiations is actually more difficult than people think, as Maurice E. Schweitzer discusses in Chapter 11.

- *Underestimating risks.* Leeson not only worked as the Jakarta branch's settlements clerk, but he also served as Barings' floor manager on the SIMEX—a breach of one of the basic rules of thumb in the securities industry.[9] Usually separate individuals hold these positions because they are supposed to serve as checks on one another: The trader's job is to make money and the settlement clerk's job is to fix errors that traders make. Leeson would prove to be very good at fixing (or at least hiding) his own errors. By making this decision, Barings' managers significantly increased their risks, but no one apparently understood how significantly. In the wake of the collapse of Barings, many other banks implemented much more stringent policies. Decision makers have great difficulty in evaluating low-probability, high-risk events before disaster strikes, so they tend to underprotect themselves beforehand and overprotect themselves afterward, as examined by Howard C. Kunreuther in Chapter 15.

- *Insufficient information technology for decision support.* Communications and information technology for decision support also broke down. Stephen Fay notes in his 1996 book, *The Collapse of Barings,* that as the securities division grew, "Resources were not committed to developing global computer systems which would enable management in London to know the firm's position anywhere in the world; nor was information technology applied to risk management."[10] Furthermore, the management at Barings failed to look at how technological advances, such as computer-assisted programs for risk management and electronically transferring money, could have prevented such long-term dishonesty. In Chapter 12, G. Richard Shell shows how technological advances have changed the way people negotiate and come to decisions, and how these new tools can both help and hurt the decision process.

- *Insufficient regulation.* As a result of Barings' collapse, the Bank of England, which oversees the banking industry in England, in 1997 began a "controversial reshaping of the way Britain's financial industry . . . is policed."[11] But these public protections faced private opposition. Critics have cautioned that the new laws could not only overwhelm regulators but also may cause certain investors to shift to other markets that are less stringently regulated. Further, increased fees for such regulation could discourage some investors. In Chapter 17, Mark V. Pauly looks at the many cases in which people make inconsistent decisions in public and private contexts.

Investigations by British, American, and Singapore institutions have raised questions about the management structure in place at Barings that contributed to the atmosphere that allowed a trader like Leeson to go haywire in the first place.[12] The Bank of England, while pointing to Leeson as the sole perpetrator of the fraud, also concluded that the astounding losses (around 700 million pounds or $1.2 billion U.S.) were incurred due to a "serious failure of controls and managerial confusion within Barings."[13] In other words, many people made many unwise decisions—as individuals, managers, negotiators, and, perhaps, as regulators—which had a compound impact leading to Barings' collapse.

The principal goal of this book is to help managers make better decisions at each of these levels. A deeper understanding of the process of decision making and strategies for making better decisions can give managers the tools and insights to improve their decisions. While this knowledge will not prevent all poor decisions (even well-formulated decisions can sometimes lead to negative outcomes), this deeper understanding of decision making can make the process more conscious, informed, and deliberate.

WHAT WE KNOW ABOUT DECISION MAKING

Humans are not well equipped to make the best decisions all or even most of the time. While decisions have been made from the moment of human consciousness, it has only been in recent times that we have systematically studied decision making and brain functioning, to gain new insights into how decisions are made.

Interest in the process of decision making is as old as human history. The dilemmas of choice in the face of an uncertain and complex world have long been the focus of religion, literature, and philosophy. From classic epic poems to modern philosophers, human choices have been the object of fascination, speculation, and education. But it was not until recent times that decision making and decision processes have been subject to systematic investigation. The emergence of the field of decision sciences draws insights from philosophy, economics, biology, psychology, and sociology.

In particular, business researchers have been very interested in the process of managerial decision making. As researchers explore ways to improve operations, develop human resources, manage risks, create strategy, plan marketing, and engage in diverse other management activities, decision making is at the heart of all these issues. The strength or weakness of managerial decisions is the linchpin of the business enterprise.

The Wharton School of the University of Pennsylvania has been a pioneer in this study and continues to address new challenges in a wide variety of applied areas such as consumer behavior, health care, and environmental and catastrophic risks, drawing on different disciplines ranging from marketing to operations management to policy analysis. This systematic work has offered new insights into decision making. While these insights have been published in academic circles, many of them have not made their way into the hands of managers. Bridging this gap is one of the reasons Wharton faculty in this area joined forces to write this book.

While there is still much that we don't know about decision making, more than three decades of systematic research on decisions has provided insights on a variety of issues. The approach to decision making we are taking can be viewed at three different levels—what should be done based on rational theories of choice (*normative models*), what is actually done by individuals and groups in practice (*descriptive behavior*), and how we can improve decision making based on our understanding about differences between normative models and descriptive behavior (*prescriptive recommendations*).

Normative analyses of choice have focused on how problems should be solved by making the assumption the decision maker has formulated a well-specified set of alternatives. In making choices, a rational consumer or manager is assumed to determine the utilities of different outcomes from each alternative. If the decision has uncertain consequences, these utilities are weighted by their probabilities and the individual determines the "expected utility" of each alternative. The alternative with the highest expected utility is then selected as the final choice. In other words, we weigh all the options carefully and choose the one with the highest payoff for us.

In reality, individuals often behave very differently from what this theory suggests. Another stream of behavioral research has studied what decision makers actually do. When there are uncertain outcomes many decision makers either do not take into account probabilities explicitly in their choices or use this information in rather strange ways when viewed from a normative perspective. For example, it is not uncommon for individuals to say, "This won't happen to me" and disregard a potentially disastrous event, even though they know in reality that it has a chance of occurring.

With respect to choices between alternatives, we may be able to change people's preferences just by asking the same question in a different way— the framing problem. People are more likely to choose certain insurance options (such as limited tort) if they are forced to opt-out rather than asked to opt-in. They therefore make very different decisions about the same set of options merely because of how the choices are presented. Similarly, people have a much harder time giving up something than acquiring it (loss aversion), even though it is the same object with the same value.

Human beings do not, in general, follow logical models of choice. Decisions are not made in frictionless environments. Just as classical physics offers insights into mechanics, normative models offer insights into the process of decision making. But these models are not the world. We thus need to carefully observe how people actually make decisions, when designing strategies for consumers and managers as illustrated in Parts I and II of this book.

When there are several parties involved in making a decision, the world becomes more complicated because we not only have to understand each person's decision process but also the interaction between individuals. Normative theories of choice simplify this process by assuming that everyone's behavior follows the rule "maximize expected utility." Since the expected utility of both sides is changing dynamically through multiple rounds of interactions, analyzing the payoffs of both sides and expected decisions can become rather complex.

Game theory is a normative approach for determining what strategies should be followed by a person who has to consider what others are likely to do. The alternatives are assumed to be well specified, as are the probabilities and outcomes. Now, the outcomes depend not only on what you are doing but also on what others are doing. Game theory places little emphasis on the process of determining what information to select for choosing between alternatives and how the different parties interact with each other. In many situations process does matter and has an impact on outcomes. For example, negotiators often get caught up in the heat of the moment, or respond to the cues of their partners rather than a detached assessment of the situation.

At the descriptive level, the emerging field of behavioral game theory is examining how different parties negotiate with each other and what they do in determining a mutually acceptable strategy. There has been considerable research showing that individuals do not behave in the way that the normative theory suggests they should.

Prescriptive solutions to multiparty problems require us to think about process as well as outcome. Are there ways to improve the negotiation process, knowing what we do about the behavior of individuals when confronted with a specific set of options? Can we present information to the different parties on the alternatives that they face so that there is a mutually acceptable strategy that improves both their positions from the status quo? These are questions that are now at the forefront of research in this area and are discussed in Part III of this book.

At the societal level, the normative theory of choice is benefit-cost analysis, which has a flavor similar to expected utility theory. Instead of determining the expected utility of an alternative for the individual, decision makers consider the costs and benefits of a particular option for society. The policy analyst evaluates public policies that impact consumers, managers, and citizens by determining their expected benefits and costs. He or she chooses the one that maximizes net expected benefits. Individuals who are affected by these specific public policies are assumed to be making decisions using normative models of choice such as maximizing their expected utility.

At a descriptive level, we already know from work on individual behavior that consumers and managers do not maximize their expected utility, so that the assumptions of benefit-cost analysis need to be challenged. By incorporating individuals' models of choice into an analysis of societal decision making, we will have a more accurate understanding of what is likely to emerge if we recommend a particular strategy. For example, when flood insurance was initially marketed in the late 1960s, the premium was subsidized approximately 90 percent by the federal government. If we assume that individuals maximize expected utility, then we would have predicted that residents in flood-prone areas would have purchased this insurance (for some 10 percent of its actual value). In reality few did, not because they expected disaster relief, but because they didn't make the tradeoffs suggested by normative theory. The factors that influenced their decision to buy insurance were knowing friends and neighbors who had purchased a policy and their past experience with the hazard. Hence, the policy to subsidize insurance premiums was based on a faulty model of choice and did not achieve the desired result. The chapters in Part IV of the book suggest a set of prescriptive recommendations for dealing with issues such as this one and other policy challenges.

DECISIONS AT MANY LEVELS

This book draws together insights from leading researchers on diverse aspects of decision making. The book is structured to look at decision making from several different vantage points. Part I explores the challenges of personal decisions. In Chapter 2, Mary Frances Luce, John W. Payne, and James R. Bettman examine the role emotions play in managerial decisions—for good or ill. Learning to recognize how emotions affect the daily business decisions we make—either by avoidance or delay—is the first step in constructively looking at some of the most difficult decisions any manager faces, such as laying off employees.

In studying decision making, we've come up with models that are elegant and effective but that very few decision makers actually follow. Are these decision makers foolish? In Chapter 3, Robert J. Meyer and J. Wesley Hutchinson explore how humans make surprisingly effective decisions even when using short cuts. They also identify situations in which these approaches are likely to lead to errors. To conclude Part I, Barbara E. Kahn and Andrea Morales discuss in Chapter 4 how the desire for variety can cloud decision-makers' judgments.

Part II focuses on the managerial decision-making process. There are a variety of analytic models that can be used, but how can they be combined with human intuition and other approaches to decision making? In Chapter 5, Stephen J. Hoch looks at ways to combine the strengths of humans in pattern matching with the power of computer-based models. Easterners and Westerners take very different approaches to decision making. In Chapter 6, Karen A. Jehn and Keith Weigelt examine the differences between the expedient Western approach and the more reflective Eastern strategy of decision making. Complexity is a significant challenge for decision makers, which Paul R. Kleindorfer explores in Chapter 7 using two examples: the electric utilities industrywide restructuring and how the insurance industry manages catastrophic risks from natural disasters in the face of much better scientific data and computer support than they have had available in the past. Finally, managers have to be able to manage their own frames, or they will be blinded by their own successes and the limits of their world views. In Chapter 8, Paul J.H. Schoemaker and J. Edward Russo look at the power of frames and offer ways for managers to make better choices.

Part III moves from a single manager to the next level of complexity—interactions among several managers in negotiations across multiple periods. Colin F. Camerer and Teck H. Ho use game theory in Chapter 9 to explore how people learn from experience by factoring in the payoffs from past decisions into the current choices, weighing options based on what the authors term "experience-weighted attraction." In Chapter 10, Steven Glick and Rachel Croson explore how reputations affect the way partners approach negotiations and how these reputations can best be used and shaped. Maurice E. Schweitzer in Chapter 11 looks at deceptions in negotiations, the different types of lies that are used and how difficult it is to detect them. Part III concludes with G. Richard Shell in Chapter 12, discussing the impact of new technology such as e-mail and the Internet on bargaining. He focuses on technology's strengths and weaknesses, and how decision support systems can be used to improve negotiations outcomes.

In Part IV, we move to the broadest perspective, by exploring societal decisions. In Chapter 13, John Hershey and David A. Asch show why decision makers do not always use medical tests based on analytic models, but sometimes use them to keep their options open or change their minds. People often claim to have "protected values" in making societal decisions, values, such as concern for the environment, that they claim they will not trade off at any price. In Chapter 14, Julie Irwin and Jonathan Baron explore how these immutable lines are often not as protected as they appear to be. In Chapter 15, Howard C. Kunreuther explores why people tend to underprepare for high-risk, low-probability events, such as not protecting themselves against the consequences of an earthquake or flood before the event and then overpreparing afterwards. In making broader decisions, we often look to others for guidance. In Chapter 16, Felix Oberholzer-Gee examines how this leads to lemming-like "information cascades" in which decision makers follow one another without carefully making independent assessments. Finally, in Chapter 17, Mark Pauly explores the inconsistencies between public and private decisions. For example, people call for stricter environmental policies but then refuse to pay for them in their own purchases.

UNPRECEDENTED CHALLENGES

With the increased speed and complexity of the business environment, the insights and frameworks provided by this book are more important than ever. Faster speed in business, as in automobiles, increases the chances that a small miscalculation can lead to a serious crash. Increased complexity in business makes it harder for human beings to retool their decision making and more "moving parts" mean more things can go wrong. Information technology is one of the driving forces in unleashing this Pandora's box of decision challenges on the world. But it also contains the hope that, used judiciously, computer models can help humans make better decisions.

This book offers current insights based on the latest research from authors who have looked at decision making from diverse perspectives. These include faculty in marketing, health care, operations and information systems, insurance and risk management, and public policy. We examine how people *should* make decisions according to the models, how they *actually* behave, and how they can *improve* their decision making.

Managers often are so caught up in making decisions that they rarely have the luxury of giving much thought to *how* they make them. Spending time thinking about the process of decision making can have significant payoffs, however, because it can help you improve the quality and effectiveness of your subsequent choices. Since making decisions is one of the central tasks of managers, improving your decision-making ability can make you a more effective manager. We invite you to join us in exploring diverse aspects of decision making—to think about the process. Knowing how to make better decisions does not assure that you will make excellent decisions, but greater awareness of the decision process will help you avoid the pitfalls and make better choices for yourself and your organization.

PART I

PERSONAL DECISION MAKING

As the cartoon suggests, decisions are rarely clear cut. Every decision presents a variety of choices, and, in practice, decisions are hardly ever made by dispassionate logic alone. Factors such as emotion and an inherent desire for variety play an important role in our decisions. Managers often rely on instinct rather than careful

15

deliberation. Part I explores a few of the personal factors that influence our decisions. We look at when you can use them to your advantage or need to avoid them to improve decision making.

In Chapter 2, Mary Frances Luce, John W. Payne, and James R. Bettman explore the impact of emotions on decisions when addressing challenging managerial decisions such as employee layoffs. Sometimes emotions can focus the mind, but other times they can lead to pointless wheel-spinning. In Chapter 3, Robert J. Meyer and J. Wesley Hutchinson examine how decision makers use mental short cuts to make complex, multiperiod decisions. Sometimes this intuition is surprisingly on target, but there are important exceptions. In Chapter 4, Barbara E. Kahn and Andreas Morales examine how the human desire for variety affects decision making. Sometimes variety can lead to innovation or customer excitement, but it can also lead to change for the sake of change.

CHAPTER 2

THE EMOTIONAL NATURE OF DECISION TRADE-OFFS

MARY FRANCES LUCE
The Wharton School

JOHN W. PAYNE
The Fuqua School of Business
Duke University

JAMES R. BETTMAN
The Fuqua School of Business
Duke University

Few management decisions are made without some emotional element. The trick is to understand the impact of emotions to make better decisions.

> On life's vast ocean diversely we sail,
> Reason the card, but passion is the gale.
> —*Alexander Pope,* Essay on Man

Decision makers are not completely logical machines that sift through various options and always churn out optimal decisions—although this is how many decision models view the situation. Decision makers are human, so emotions play a role in their choices. But what role? Compassion for employees, concern about future reputation, and other considerations may generate emotions that affect the way we make decisions. In this chapter, the authors, drawing upon their own research, look at the impact of emotions on the process and outcome of decisions. They show how decision makers often work harder, but not always smarter, in tackling emotionally-charged decisions. The authors discuss how decision makers try to avoid addressing the emotionally difficult aspects of decisions. Finally, the authors present suggestions on applied issues, such as how to use emotions strategically or how to limit the effects of emotion on decision making.

I magine a manager who is faced with the difficult decision of downsizing a department, letting go two of the 10 current employees. In some ways, this is a decision like any other: There are alternatives (the 10 employees), and each alternative can be defined along a series of attributes (e.g., tenure with the organization, job skill, age, family situation, current pay rate). In accordance with this view, we represent this decision in a standard multiattribute decision display, in Table 2.1.

Table 2.1 looks much like a summary table from *Consumer Reports* magazine, but the decision in this case is obviously much more challenging than purchasing a refrigerator. Why? Because there is emotion involved. The manager will probably *not* simply process the decision by weighting particular attributes, rank ordering the choices, and terminating the employees with the two lowest scores, even though normative models of decision making assume such a process. Although the motivation for a decision maker to do a good job may be extremely high in such an emotion-laden context, we argue that this motivation to do well will not result in the use of a more normative strategy by the decision maker. Thus, somewhat paradoxically, an individual may more often use a

Table 2.1
Downsizing Decision

	Tenure with Organization (Years)	Job Skill	Age	Family Situation	Pay Rate ($)
Craig	10	Average	37	Single	60,000
Steve	7	Average	38	Sole supporter of wife and 2 kids	52,000
Sandra	8	Poor	45	Single mother with 3 kids	49,000
Michael	2	Excellent	28	Single	55,000
Susan	9	Good	37	Married to working husband, no kids	57,000
Justin	3	Excellent	38	Married to working wife, 3 kids	41,000
Maria	6	Average	29	Sole supporter of husband and 1 kid	52,000
Jay	3	Excellent	42	Divorced, pays child support for 2 kids	55,000
Bob	2	Good	55	Married with 2 grown kids	38,000
Amy	1	Average	44	Married, no kids	37,000

normatively appropriate strategy when choosing a refrigerator than when making a crucial management decision. As the stakes of a decision increase, the desire to find the best normative solution may coexist with the desire to manage or minimize one's negative emotion.

Thus, the manager will probably factor in the consequences of coping with emotion, for example, how bad it feels to fire an employee with a large family to support. The coping will probably alter both the *process* by which the decision is made and the final *outcome* of that decision.

Research indicates that coping changes the process of a decision by causing decision makers to work harder, but not necessarily smarter. The manager in this case may spend a lot of time mulling over the choices. Although overall decision-making time is increased, emotion can cause an avoidance of the difficult, emotion-laden parts of the decision. For instance, almost any decision requires trade-offs; that is, any decision requires that the decision maker give up some considerations to maximize others. In the example in Table 2.1, a trade-off between organizational tenure and job skill is required in that the employees with the longest tenure (whom one would presumably like to keep) are not the employees with the highest skill levels (whom one would also presumably like to keep). Making the decision to downsize will require that these trade-offs be resolved (e.g., firing Sandra essentially involves trading-off her eight years with the organization to terminate her based on poor job skills).

In an emotion-laden situation, a manager may make such a trade-off implicitly, rather than explicitly. That is, a decision process may be used that does not consciously acknowledge (to the manager or to others) the trade-offs implied by the choice. To avoid explicit trade-offs, the manager may fall back on simplified, heuristic patterns of processing. For instance, the manager may make the decision solely in terms of job skill, never explicitly acknowledging that choosing on the basis of job skill involves trading-off tenure with the organization or the employee's family situation.

Emotional coping may also change the outcome of a decision.[1] For instance, consider again the downsizing decision in Table 2.1. A manager may be influenced by the emotional impact of the attribute relating to the employee's family situation. If a manager is sufficiently distressed by the prospect of harming an employee's family, the manager may choose the best level of this attribute by downsizing the employee that can most afford to be let go. Even if the choice that results is inconsistent with company or legal policy, it may be an attractive way to deal with the manager's negative emotions.

DECISION TRADE-OFFS

Every decision involves trade-offs. Decision making is essentially the process of accepting less of something to get more of something else. It is often assumed that decision makers explicitly weigh these trade-offs and calculate how much of one attribute they are willing to give up in order to gain a unit of another attribute. Explicit weighting and comparison of trade-offs is assumed, for instance, as part of the normative decision strategy of maximizing expected utility. Much research indicates that decision makers balance the potential accuracy of possible decision strategies against the cognitive effort required by these strategies and that decision makers will give up some decision accuracy if it is possible to save cognitive effort by doing so.[2] Thus, decision makers may avoid explicitly weighing different decision attributes against one another because doing so requires mentally-taxing mathematical calculations.[3] Our recent research indicates that decision makers are also concerned about something else: minimizing negative emotion.[4] Decision makers may, therefore, also avoid explicitly weighing or trading off different decision attributes because doing so requires emotionally costly consideration of what is being given up. Although explicit trade-offs between attributes are generally acknowledged as the gold standard for accurate decision processes,[5] these trade-offs may be avoided to save cognitive effort and/or to cope with negative emotion.

We believe that considerations regarding negative emotion actually become more prevalent in higher stakes decision situations. For instance, in the purchase of a refrigerator, the consumer might decide not to look at all the attributes or at all the models because of the cognitive effort involved. Instead, the consumer might focus on just side-by-sides, models from a single manufacturer, or otherwise simplify the process and reduce cognitive effort. In an emotion-laden decision, it is not just this cognitive effort that will be considered but also the emotional toll of the decision. Does the manager considering downsizing lay off Bob, who is a good worker but who has grown children, or Sandra, who is a single mother with less than stellar performance. It may be much harder emotionally to lay off Sandra, so the manager may be tempted to find a way to avoid this pain.[6]

The standard economic view of decision behavior assumes that all these trade-offs are the same and that decision makers have well-articulated preferences that they can weigh when making the decision. It assumes, for example, that a manager can compute the utility difference between firing an employee with two children to support and firing an employee with four children to support.[7] Although the utility-maximizing view acknowledges lack of information as a complicating factor in trade-offs, this view does not generally recognize that some trade-offs may be avoided because of these more emotional considerations.

Research indicates, however, that decision makers may either respond specifically to the emotional distress associated with particular trade-offs[8] or resist trading-off certain protected attributes, such as those regarding human life or the environment (see Baron and Irwin in Chapter 14). Most people would also be appalled by an explicit trade-off between love and money.[9]

We propose that decision makers respond to the level of what we call emotional trade-off difficulty. We define emotional trade-off difficulty at the level of subjective threat associated with a particular attribute pair under consideration, such as the trade-off between safety and monetary cost in choosing a car. Note that the difficulty of making trade-offs is associated with specific *pairs* of attributes. For example, consideration of trading off family situation against pay rate in the preceding decision to downsize is probably more emotionally laden than consideration of trading off job skills against pay rate.[10] The consideration of firing an employee with poor job skills but a family to support may be more threatening to some managers than is the consideration of firing an employee with better job skills but no children to support. For other managers, putting family considerations ahead of job skills may actually be more threatening. In general, giving up the family considerations attribute for the job skills attribute may be more, or less, threatening to a particular decision maker than would be giving up job skills for family considerations. This behavior is consistent with the well-known finding that people are often more willing to give up receipt of a payment to protect a value (willingness to accept) than they are willing to pay for it (willingness to pay).[11] This gap is greater for medical risks and environmental goods than for smaller items, such as candy bars and coffee mugs.[12] Although this difference is sometimes attributed to the limited information regarding large goods without clear markets, one additional reason for this gap could be the greater emotion involved in choosing a medical procedure in comparison to selecting a coffee mug. It may, therefore, be particularly threatening to consider giving up more of an emotion-laden attribute in return for more of a mundane attribute. Exactly which attributes are emotion-laden and by how much may differ across managers.

SOURCES OF EMOTION

The theorist Richard Lazarus argues that emotion results from two sets of cognitive appraisals.[13] The first set of cognitive appraisals involves the importance of a situation's outcome. Importance, or the primary stakes of a decision, is based on three sets of appraisals, or judgments. These are:

- *Goal relevance.* Does the encounter have any potential relevance for valued goals and, therefore, have any potential for emotion?
- *Goal congruence.* Is the encounter expected to involve positive or negative outcomes, based on the goals of the decision maker? Negative emotions can follow from actual nonattainment of goals (harm), but can also follow, more likely during decision making, from *potential* nonattainment (threat).

- *Goal content.* What goals are at stake and how will they influence the form of emotional experience? For example, will the lack of congruence lead to guilt or to shame?

The second set of cognitive appraisals that Lazarus associates with emotion is a secondary appraisal that assesses options and prospects for coping with the emotions involved: Can the decision maker improve the relevant situation? Are future outcomes expected to worsen? Is blame or credit for yourself, or another person, warranted?

Lazarus also discusses coping behaviors, and argues that emotion and coping are intimately intertwined, with emotion eliciting coping, which alters other, later emotions. According to Lazarus, coping behaviors can be either problem-focused or emotion-focused. Problem-focused coping involves attempts to solve the outside, tangible problem leading to the emotion. Emotion-focused coping, in contrast, involves attempts to directly alter experienced emotion without solving the problem, either by using avoidance or by changing the meaning of a situation. For instance, the manager in the downsizing situation may anticipate the emotional costs of her decision and avoid this negative emotion by arranging for her boss to make the decision. Both forms of coping are typically brought to bear on any stressful decision.[14]

Lazarus' theory of emotion is a general theory, and it is applicable to a wide variety of situations that include interpersonal interaction, workplace issues, health issues, etc. How can Lazarus' insights into emotions be applied to the study of decision making? We consider, next, how Lazarus' theory is applied to the specific domain of emotional trade-off difficulty in decision making. First, we use the theory to define how aspects of a decision will alter primary and secondary appraisals, which may result in emotional trade-off difficulty. Second, we consider how we use the theory to define how people will cope with the threats associated with emotional trade-off difficulty.

Causes of Emotional Trade-Off Difficulty

Decisions can be defined in terms of the identity of attributes that define potential options. For instance, the decision in Table 2.1 is defined by the attributes: tenure with organization, job skill, age, family situation, and pay rate. One must consider these attributes in order to make a choice. Decisions are further defined in terms of the values each potential option has for each attribute. For instance, in Table 2.1, Craig has a value of 10 years for the attribute tenure with the organization. Both the identities of decision attributes and their values influence emotional trade-off difficulty.

The identities of attributes determine which goals are threatened by a decision.[15] The job skills attribute in the opening example may relate to goals associated with performing departmental tasks or to professional success, whereas the family situation attribute may relate to goals of being a compassionate person. These very different goals may be associated with differing primary appraisals of a decision. To the degree that some goals are more important (e.g., if compassion happens to be more important than success in one's personal goal hierarchy), the decision maker should generate an appraisal of relatively higher stakes when these goals are threatened. Attribute identities should, therefore, influence potential for emotion in general and emotional trade-off difficulty specifically.

The relative values of choice alternatives also affect emotion. For example, choosing between firing one of two employees who are both crucial to one's department and have families to support (values consistent with the decision maker's goals along both attributes) is likely to be more difficult than choosing between two employees with very poor job skills and no families (values that conflict with the decision maker's goals along both attributes).

Finally, conflict among attribute values (the degree one attribute has to be sacrificed for another) has an influence on emotional trade-off difficulty. For example, it may be much harder to make the trade-offs in the case of a poor employee who has a large family to support or of an excellent employee who has no family than it would be in cases that have both attributes pointed toward the same choice. More must be given up to make the decision in the former case.

Primary Appraisal: Attribute Identities and Values. Attribute identities and values interact to determine emotional trade-off difficulty. We expect emotional trade-off difficulty to result from low values and/or from conflict between attribute values when these attributes are linked to important goals. In an experiment with MBA students, we presented decision makers with two choices, among five hypothetical jobs, to demonstrate this theory.[16] In an initial and separate session, we assessed the emotional potential of the attributes for each decision maker; for example, by asking a decision maker about relative reluctance to accept lower job security versus lower levels of other attributes. We used this session to identify the attributes for each decision maker that were associated with links to important goals, in order to identify attributes that we thought would be associated with primary appraisals indicating high stakes or high importance.

Then, we constructed choices among jobs for each decision maker. Each job was specified by four attributes. The identity of two of the four attributes was manipulated on an individual basis for the decisions each subject completed. Instead of simply using more versus less emotion-laden attributes, we sought to disentangle the specific notion of decision threat/emotion from the more general notion of attribute importance. For instance, the attribute job security is likely to be more emotional and more important than is the attribute quality of office furniture in choosing a job. For example, many of our subjects thought that job security and yearly salary were both very important, but security was often associated with more emotion than salary was. Thus, we manipulated the identity of attributes such that subjects made two decisions with equally important attributes, but for one decision, the attributes were more emotional. For example, if subjects rated the attributes of yearly salary and of job security as equally important but job security as more emotional, the subjects might find little emotion in making trade-offs that involve alternatives defined by yearly salary but might find more emotion in making trade-offs that involve alternatives defined by job security.

We also manipulated levels of decision conflict, or the degree that jobs were good on one attribute (very secure) but were bad on others (bad location). Both high-conflict and high-emotion attribute identity, and particularly their combination, resulted in more self-reported negative emotion, as expected. More emotional attributes were generally associated with more negative emotion, but this effect was stronger in the higher (versus the lower) conflict group.

Secondary Appraisals: Avoidance Helps Reduce Emotional Difficulty.
Because of coping strategies, emotional trade-off difficulty may be different from the level of emotion *actually* experienced during a choice. As previously stated, emotional trade-off difficulty is defined as a *subjective threat* associated with an *explicit trade-off* between two attributes within the context of a particular choice. One factor that might influence whether this subjective threat results in experienced emotion is how the decision maker imagines coping with the decision or actually copes with it. This idea that coping behavior can influence emotion is consistent with Lazarus' inclusion of secondary appraisal in his definition of how emotion is elicited.

Options for avoiding or otherwise coping with the emotional difficulty of the decision tend to mitigate feelings of negative emotions due to the acceptance of poor values on attributes linked to valued goals. We examined this use of coping in a study of automobile purchase decisions defined in terms of more or less emotion-laden attributes (i.e., manipulating attribute trade-off difficulty).[17] We offered participants a number of different options for avoiding or for coping with the decision. A control group was faced with a simple choice among the available alternatives for a car, and others were given opportunities to sidestep the decision. For example, one group was given the opportunity to maintain the status quo by choosing a previously chosen alternative. It was expected that this would satisfy emotion-focused coping goals because it allowed the decision maker to choose based on the status quo label, which was independent of specific attribute trade-offs. A second group was given the option to prolong the search instead of committing to one of the currently available choice options. Again, such a choice can be made without explicitly considering the relative merits of the various alternatives and it avoids difficult trade-offs.

Immediately after the process, subjects were asked to report their expectations regarding the emotionality of the decision task if repeating this same decision in the real world. The control group, which was not given avoidance options, showed a significant increase in rated negative emotion. Emotion ratings, however, in both (noncontrol) avoidance option groups were insensitive to the attribute identity manipulation. By avoiding the trading-off of specific attributes, subjects reduced the emotional difficulty of the decision.

CONSEQUENCES OF EMOTIONAL TRADE-OFF DIFFICULTY: WORKING HARDER, BUT NOT NECESSARILY SMARTER

One important question is how decision makers cope with emotional trade-off difficulty. Consistent with the notion of problem- and emotion-focused coping, decision makers may generate multiple coping behaviors. We believe that the desire to engage in both problem- and emotion-focused coping will influence decision processing.

To understand how emotions affect decision processing, we explore how decision makers look for information.[18] In computer laboratory experiments, we look at whether subjects examine one attribute across all options or whether they examine multiple attributes for a single alternative. For example, does a car shopper look at engine size across all available models (attribute-based processing) or attempt to make trade-offs between color, power, trunk space, and so on, for a single model (alternative-based processing)? The latter approach generally involves more explicit trade-offs; that is, considering the attributes power and trunk space together suggests that the decision maker is trading-off between these attributes. We also look at how much information each subject considers; obviously, decision strategies that consider more information are more effortful.

In low-emotion decisions, decision processing that involves more effort also typically involves more alternative-based processing.[19] Decision makers appear to choose either low-effort, attribute-based strategies (heuristic strategies that do not involve trade-offs) or higher-effort, alternative-based strategies (more normative strategies, which involve trade-offs). For example, in our research, we found that decision makers who considered choices with low-emotion attribute identities responded to increased conflict in attribute values by using more effort and more alternative-based processing strategies. These decision makers apparently worked harder and smarter.[20]

Our prediction for increased decision processing in negatively emotion-laden environments runs counter to this research in less emotion-laden contexts.[21] First, consistent with work in low-emotion settings, we found that for more emotionally-laden decisions, decision makers spend more time and consider more information in making their decisions. They tend to put more effort into processing the decision. They try to do a good job at making this important decision.[22] We hypothesize that the decision makers want to engage in problem-focused coping. This problem-focused coping is consistent with the goal of maximizing decision accuracy. In this sense, they are working harder. These problem-focused coping behaviors are actually focused on making a better decision and do reflect the ability of people to focus under pressure.

But decision makers in environments of high emotion don't just work harder. They also *change* their decision-making patterns in ways that are not fully explained by focusing on addressing the problem at hand. These emotion-focused coping efforts, particularly avoidance, can have a significant impact on how decision makers approach emotional decisions and the choices they make. The major form of emotion-focused coping during decision making involves attempts to avoid particularly distressing explicit trade-offs between attributes.[23] In particular, decision makers avoid explicit trade-offs in emotional decisions. Instead, they make implicit trade-offs or find ways to circumvent these trade-offs completely. By avoiding and by sidestepping explicit trade-offs, these emotion-focused coping efforts can lead decision makers to work harder, but not necessarily smarter. We found that in more threatening decision environments, decision makers tended to use more attribute-based patterns of processing—effectively avoiding the more direct trade-offs, even while they expended more effort.

Thus the problem-focused and emotion-focused coping behaviors impact decision processes and outcomes differently. Whereas problem-focused coping behaviors are likely to mirror accuracy maximization behaviors, emotion-focused coping behaviors are expected to involve avoidance of particularly emotion-laden or of threatening process operations.

In summary, it appears that subjects work harder, yet not smarter, in more emotion-laden conditions. Research subjects appear to think about the decision longer, yet also use patterns of processing typically associated with more simple, heuristic decision rules. So, how can you avoid the pitfalls of emotionally charged decisions? Ways to manage effectively in decision making follow.

MANAGE EMOTIONS TO MAKE BETTER CORPORATE DECISIONS

In general, decision makers construct their choice strategies by maximizing accuracy, minimizing decision effort, and minimizing negative emotions.[24] In the decision presented at the start of the chapter, accuracy maximization means making sure the correct employee termination decision is made, and effort minimization focuses on making the employee termination decision as efficiently as possible. But looking at these two issues means an important part of the decision is overlooked. The manager is also concerned with minimizing the painful emotional impact of firing employees.

This last consideration creates a twist on how we typically view decision making. Given that emotions *will* be factored into the decision somehow, managers need to pay attention to *how* emotional difficulty will affect the processes and outcomes of their decisions. How can managers and organizations use an understanding of the emotional difficulty impact to make better decisions? First, it is important to recognize that emotions may influence management decisions. Second, there may be times when one wants to structure decision processes for themselves and their organizations in a way that removes emotion as much as possible, or in a way that shields the decision maker from experiencing emotion. Finally, there may be other times when one wants to circumvent decision makers' coping behaviors, encouraging the active and explicit consideration of emotional trade-offs.

Understand How Emotions Influence Decisions

The first step to using our approach to emotion-laden decisions is simply to recognize that emotions have an impact on decisions. Neglecting these considerations may be costly. Consider, for example, the organizational impact of Al Dunlap's downsizing decisions on Scott Paper or Sunbeam Products. Although the short-term gain was profit maximization, greater harm was created by the negative public and staff perceptions of such massive layoffs. An organization that eradicates emotion from every decision may ultimately pay an even stiffer price by eroding employee loyalty and public perception. There may be a real danger in treating organizational decisions, involving real employees, the way you treat decisions about purchasing an appliance.

To help the decision-making process, one crucial goal is to clearly specify the objective function and to include such seemingly collateral issues as minimizing the anger and the blame elicited in affected parties. For instance, see John Hershey and David A. Asch in Chapter 13 on the goal of ruling out uncertainty in an emotion-laden genetic testing context.

Even incorporating notions of one's own and other's anticipated emotional reactions into models of decision behavior does not incorporate notions of in-process negative emotion, or emotion that is generated, or even avoided, during the decision process. One important implication of our work is that decision makers want to obtain pleasure and to avoid pain while making a decision (i.e., focus on the process) rather than only wanting to maximize the anticipated utility of, or even the anticipated emotion associated with, decision outcomes.

Although emotion is ignored or actively avoided in utility-maximizing approaches to decisions, there may be a place for emotions in decisions. As a specific example, individuals often make decisions that they feel will minimize future regret.[25] This goal of minimizing future regret, which seems to have no place in decisions, may be more reasonable than it first appears. Regret (or its positive cousin, satisfaction) is generated by comparing the outcome of your final choice to your knowledge (or expectation) regarding the outcomes that other alternatives would have generated. For instance, an individual winning $1,000 in a lottery may experience extreme regret if she had considered a lottery number that would have paid $100,000 and rejected it in favor of the number paying only $1,000. Thus, her reaction to the final outcome (winning $1,000) may be swamped by regret generated by consideration of other possible outcomes (winning $100,000). This is in contrast to most normative theories of choice, which assume that the benefits of a chosen alternative are independent of the other choices. Recent studies found evidence that the utility for a particular item is, in part, dependent on the set from which that item is chosen.[26]

Avoidance of anticipated blame or regret may be reasonable decision making goals.[27] In some cases, choices consistent with the avoidance of regret and blame produce fairly good results.[28] And given that decision makers are not good at predicting their own preferences,[29] it may sometimes make sense to choose based on anticipated emotional consequences. These anticipated emotions might, paradoxically, be easier to predict than anticipated utilities are. For example, it might be difficult to predict your satisfaction, over time, with the enjoyment of driving a high-performance automobile but easier to predict your envy or regret from choosing a lower performance model than a neighbor has.

One area where the decision maker's emotions are often recognized is in advertising. Marketers have long-recognized the uses of emotions in shaping customer decisions. There are times when a company wants to use the emotional aspect of a decision to encourage the customer to gloss over objective details, such as price. Michelin does this in its tire ads, which prominently feature babies, and the ads subtly indicate that Michelin's tires are related to the attribute of protecting your family. Mercedes Benz often does this in ads that implicitly indicate that a Mercedes automobile is the right choice because the purchase of this brand indicates the trading-off of greater expense in return for the more emotional consideration of greater safety. Although this approach may not lead to the optimal decision for the decision maker, it may lead to the optimal decision for the company selling the product. If the goal is to lead the decision maker to a specific decision, the use of emotion to influence the decision process can also be used to move the decision making in a certain direction.

Finally, decisions elicit emotions in the individual decision maker and also across the organization. For example, the manager who makes the downsizing decision may be concerned with making a choice that fulfills company objectives, but the manager may also be interested in having other employees and managers perceive that a good choice was made. The manager will live with the negative emotions in the workers who are left behind; this concern will likely influence the outcome of the manager's choice. In fact, decision makers sometimes consciously want to subvert decision accuracy in order to be seen in a good light.

Although it is necessary to recognize that emotion affects decisions, it might sometimes be desirable to help (or require) decision makers to overcome their comfortable patterns of coping with decision conflict and threat. For instance, in the case of a corporation, stockholders probably want managers to make decisions that maximize profit rather than make decisions that minimize the negative emotion managers feel. Thus, the profit motive is expected to replace an individual manager's minimization of negative emotion. Stockholders may want managers to make layoff decisions by maximizing the final outcomes to the firm. That is, stockholders may want to ensure that managers do not trade-off such interests as company profits to minimize their own emotional reactions to a choice. Or a health insurance company, although aware that most consumers do not like to consider the choice between bottom line cost and their own health, may want to outline the economic realities of modern medical costs as a way of illustrating the value of the coverage customers are receiving.

We next discuss two very different tactics for reducing the impact of emotion on decisions. First, one might want to shield decision makers from emotion. In essence, this involves using proactive coping strategies to keep potentially larger effects on decision processing from resulting once emotion is experienced. Conversely, it might sometimes be necessary to force decision makers to experience negative emotion if it is necessary to get them to work through the difficult trade-offs.

Protect Decision Makers from Feeling Emotion

If they can see how their emotions affect their strategic decisions, managers can also learn to identify which strategies are effective and which are dysfunctional. Emotions can become dysfunctional when they persist indefinitely or when they are situationally inappropriate. In these cases, you want to help yourself or others (for example, employees or customers) make decisions so that feeling this emotion is minimized.

There are several approaches that help minimize the emotional difficulty the decision poses to the decision maker. We now discuss three approaches.

Use Avoidance Constructively.   The primary emotion-focused coping behavior identified in our work is avoidance of distressing trade-offs. This is inconsistent with the normative model. This behavior, however, may actually have hidden, long-run benefits; that is, avoidance of particularly threatening decision aspects may alter appraisals (resulting in a decision situation to be appraised as involving less negative emotion) and encourage active, problem-focused coping. Avoidance of particularly difficult aspects of a decision may be necessary to keep the decision maker from disengaging from the decision altogether.

In addition to the avoidance of emotional trade-offs, by changing the process of decision making, it may be possible to engage in avoidance by presenting particular choices in some situations, as we discussed with the options presented in the car purchase decision. We call such choices avoidant options, and specifically define an avoidant option as a choice recommended by some objective reason or label independent of value-based trade-offs. For instance, for the car decision, we offered subjects a status quo model. This allowed decision makers to respond to that label while they avoided making explicit trade-offs among the specific attributes. Selection of these options may satisfy emotion-focused coping motivations to avoid distressing choices. Decisions can be made without engaging in difficult explicit trade-offs.

In emotionally difficult decisions, decision makers use avoidant options if they are available. Making these avoidant options available allows decision makers to sidestep the more difficult emotional issues while not avoiding the decision itself.

Consider Attributes Sequentially rather than Simultaneously.   Another way to avoid the negative emotions of a decision is to remove the explicit trade-offs from the decision. That is, make trade-offs implicitly rather than explicitly. If the manager who faces the downsizing decision is particularly threatened by the possibility of explicitly trading-off an employee's job skill in favor of less appropriate considerations regarding age and family status, the manager may find protection by considering only employees who are new to the organization (and hence, relatively young and less likely to have family obligations). The manager would then let go only employees with the lowest level of job skill in this subset. Thus, such a phased decision strategy, which screens on one or more attributes (e.g., screens out all employees with long tenure) makes difficult decision trade-offs implicitly rather than explicitly. Decision strategies that consider attributes sequentially rather than simultaneously often make trade-offs implicit.

Using this method, the decision maker never explicitly confronts the additional characteristics of the alternatives screened out of consideration. For example, the relative job skill of employees with a great deal of longevity is never considered, even if some of them have low levels of job skill.

Reframe the Decision to Reduce Emotion.   One way to reduce the emotion experienced by the decision maker, and therefore, to reduce emotion's effects, is to reframe decision trade-offs so that attributes are emotionally equivalent to one another. This approach helps neutralize emotion-focused coping considerations. For example, to avoid the more emotionally-charged trade-offs of health against dollars in medical decisions, we could present decision makers with a trade-off of one health state against another.[30] Health itself, rather than money, becomes the currency of interest. The decision maker no longer faces the problematic situation of trading-off a sacred attribute, such as health, against a more profane attribute, such as money.[31] Customers may have a hard time trading safety for price when buying a car, for instance, because the risk of an accident is so emotionally-charged. Because explicitly weighing risk versus money presents such an emotionally-charged environment, it may be better to present customers with a trade-off between two risks instead—for example, the risk of getting into a car accident versus being hurt if an accident does occur.[32] Because both risks yield unpleasant outcomes, the decision maker knows ahead of time that the lesser of two evils is being chosen. If you are trying to help an individual make the best overall decision, this sort of frame lets the individual think more constructively about the relevant safety risks.

The manager making the downsizing decision at the opening of the chapter will be more able to trade-off individual employee's family situations if reminded that actions with implications for the firm's performance (e.g., keeping an employee with relatively low levels of job skill) may eventually, through lowered profitability, have implications for other employees' abilities to support their families. If the company does not remain economically viable, no one will have a job. Because families will be hurt either way, it removes most of the emotional pressure from the decision.

Force Decision Makers to Confront Emotion.   Even if removing emotion helps to optimize a decision in the short run, it may still lead to a suboptimal outcome in the long run. For instance, an individual who avoids thinking about risks (e.g., from flooding) may pay an extremely high long-term price if the risk is not mitigated (e.g., purchasing insurance; see Howard Kunreuther in Chapter 15). More generally, the goal of minimizing emotional costs during a decision is often at odds with the goal of minimizing emotional costs in the long run. It is sometimes better to face these emotionally difficult decisions head-on and to make explicit decisions about them. If these emotional factors are not considered explicitly, they are likely to have an implicit impact. This will be much more unpredictable and often damaging. For example, if an organization wants to demonstrate a commitment to employees' families, then it should make that value explicit. This step adds clarity to the decision process, but it is at the potential cost of greater emotion.

In cases where organizations want managers to face emotional issues head-on, they must structure decisions and decision processes in a way that makes avoidance more difficult. They need to ensure that the emotional issues are an explicit part of the decision process. In a downsizing decision, for example, organizational leaders might create a framework to examine these decisions that incorporates emotionally charged attributes, such as family obligations. This approach ensures that these issues will not be swept under the rug, as would be the tendency if these attributes remained implicit.

CONCLUSION

Organizations can explicitly address emotions or remove them from the decision process, depending on the context of the decision. What managers should *not* do is ignore the impact of emotions on decisions. If we do not think about the impact of emotions, they will still affect decision processes and outcomes. But their effect will be beneath the surface—often in ways that undermine effective decision making. By considering emotions *explicitly* in decision making, managers can increase their ability to manage these effects.

CHAPTER 3

BUMBLING GENIUSES: THE POWER OF EVERYDAY REASONING IN MULTISTAGE DECISION MAKING

ROBERT J. MEYER
The Wharton School

J. WESLEY HUTCHINSON
The Wharton School

Humans are notoriously poor at looking into the future, yet despite our myopia, we often manage to see our way to good outcomes.

The art of prophecy is very difficult, especially about the future.
                                                   —Mark Twain

Humans are notoriously poor at looking into the future. This myopia seems to put us at a great disadvantage to powerful, forward-thinking decision models that can carefully weigh dynamic, multistage decisions. Yet, like the bumbling cartoon character Mr. Magoo, despite our severe myopia we somehow manage to make our way to surprisingly good outcomes. The authors look at how managers use shortcuts or rely upon intuition to address dynamic decisions that must be made in multiple stages. They also examine why intuition and simple heuristics are surprisingly on target in many cases. Finally, they look at important exceptions, when everyday reasoning takes us down the wrong path, and what can be done to avoid those pitfalls.

Consider the following problem:

Your company is beginning to sell goods in a foreign market, and you are faced with the problem of choosing a distributor. The first choice is a long-term contract with a firm with whom you have done business in the past, and whose distribution system reaches 50 percent of all potential customers. At the last moment, however, a colleague suggests that you consider signing a one-year contract with another distributor. Although a year ago their coverage reached only 25 percent of customers, they claim they invested heavily in distribution resources and now expect to be able to reach 75 percent of customers.

Which distributor would you choose? The answer here may not be obvious. On one hand, while the new firm has a higher upside potential (75 percent versus 50 percent coverage), if their claims are overblown you could be left with as little as 25 percent coverage in your first year of operations. On the other hand, the only way you'll know whether the new firm has improved is to try it. If its coverage turns out to be superior, then you can enjoy higher coverage, not only this year, but also multiple years into the future. If the coverage is worse, you've lost in the short run, but you can always switch back to the more familiar distributor next year.

As managers, we routinely face decisions that involve similar trade-offs between the short run and long run consequences of current actions—

dilemmas that decision theorists term *dynamic decision problems*. Whether it is a mundane crisis over whether to try out an unfamiliar route to work on a busy morning or a career-defining decision whether to accept a position at a start-up business, problems that require anticipation of future consequences are among the most ubiquitous in managerial decision making. They also are among the most difficult to solve, and therein lies our interest: In no other area of behavioral decision theory is there a greater gap between how a class of decisions *should* be made and the rules of thumb that describe how they actually *are* made.

In this chapter we explore this disparity and reach some rather surprising conclusions about its implications. Perhaps the foremost conclusion is that although our cognitive abilities are poorly equipped to solve complex dynamic-optimization problems, our intuitive guesses about optimal solutions turn out to be, in some instances, surprisingly good. In essence, knowledge of the mathematics of dynamic optimality does not appear to be a prerequisite for individuals to act *as if* they have this knowledge when they make decisions. But there is an important catch to this result: Although this ability to act optimally holds *at times,* it does not universally hold, and therein lies a danger. As decision makers we are prone to be overconfident in our occasional successes and overgeneralize the degree to which good intuitive solutions to some dynamic problems also offer good solutions to other problems. As such, when intuitive solutions go astray, the errors are often sizable, and their negative consequences are potentially long term.

We will explore, in detail, these limits to managers' abilities to solve dynamic decision problems. We start by offering a brief tutorial on how such problems *should* be solved, from a decision theorist's perspective. One of the lessons we hope to convey is that optimal-decision methods, as important as they are for economic theory, are too complex to offer much practical advice for how managers, constrained by time and degrees in business rather than math, might actually hope to solve such problems on their own. The structure of optimal decisions reveals how everyday decisions can go wrong. After examining how managers should be acting, we then explore how they *actually* solve such problems and look at the quality of these intuitive heuristics. We conclude with an attempt to offer advice on what is probably the most difficult problem of all—knowing when to trust our intuition and when to cede the stage to the formal mathematical tools available from decision analysts and in decision-support software.

THE WAY RESEARCHERS SOLVE MULTISTAGE PROBLEMS

Let us return to our opening problem: Which is the best distributor? As with many decision-making problems, there is no one right answer. There is, however, a right way to *structure* the problem so that we each define our own best answer. The optimal process solution works like this: We would start by agreeing that our goal in this case is to choose a course of action that maximizes the long run profitability of the firm. Whichever distributor we choose, we need to consider not only sales levels for this year but also consider how these results might affect future choices and profits.

Before we can proceed with such planning, we need to set some ground rules. Specifically, we need the following simplifying assumptions.

1. *Accumulation of knowledge.* Our knowledge about distributors will evolve over time and depends on the choices we make. To keep things simple, we assume that the true level of coverage offered by the new distributor could be discovered, with certainty, through a one-year trial, and this trial will reveal exactly one of two levels of coverage: 25 percent (as it was last year) or 75 percent (as projected). In addition, we'll assume that whatever the coverage is for both distributors, it will not change over time.

2. *Decision policies.* How we will choose a distributor in each year based on this knowledge—what we will henceforth call our *decision policies.* The two choices here are to give a long-term contract to the familiar distributor (Policy 1) or give a one-year contract to the new distributor now, and base next year's decision on observed coverage (Policy 2). For example, if the new distributor delivers only 25 percent coverage in Year 1, we would switch to the familiar distributor in Year 2. If the new distributor produces 75 percent coverage, we would renew their contract.

Once these assumptions are in place, choosing between Policies 1 and 2 now becomes a matter of computing the expected long-term profits each would generate. Assume that we know that the market potential is V and that $V = V_1 + V_2$, where V_1 is potential profit in the first year and V_2 is the net present value of potential profit in all subsequent years. Since we know that the familiar firm will allow us to realize 50 percent of this potential in each year, the expected value of Policy 1 [$E(P_1)$] is:

$$E(P_1) = .5 \times (V_1 + V_2) \tag{1}$$

By this same logic the expected value of Policy 2 (hiring the new distributor) is:

$$E(P_2) = p \times .75 \times (V_1 + V_2) + (1 - p) \\ \times (.25 \times V_1 + .5 \times V_2) \tag{2}$$

where p is the probability with which we believe the new firm will provide 75 percent distribution (and $1 - p$, the reverse, is the probability of the other outcome). Note that in the second part of the expression, if the firm realizes 25 percent coverage in Year 1, we shift to the familiar supplier, as reflected by the .5 multiple for Year 2 and beyond.

Suppose we believe that $p = .5$; that is, the new firm is just as likely to be inferior to the familiar one as it is to be superior. Which firm should we choose? If we make our decision by comparing only the immediate (Year 1) profits likely to be produced by each firm, we would either be indifferent between the two (because in this case $E(P_1) = E(P_2) = .5 \times V_1$) or, if we are averse to risk, be inclined to go with the familiar distributor, as the sure thing. This short-term choice, however, would be a mistake. While in the *current year,* the two may offer similar expected profits, the *long run* expected profits—those implied by equations (1) and (2)—are higher with the choice of the new distributor now, because $E(P_2) = .5 \times V_1 + .625 \times V_2$. In essence, by choosing the new firm now we are engaging in a 50-50 lottery where, if we win, we can realize 75 percent distribution rates for as long as we are in the market, and if we lose, we are only slightly worse off than we would have been had we signed a long-term contract with the familiar firm.

Although the example we offered here is simple, it illustrates a form of logic that is used to solve a wide variety of far more complex problems in dynamic decision making. Once the values and probabilities are known, the answer is relatively straightforward. The general approach is called *dynamic programming,* a process for solving multistage decision problems that is widely credited to the mathematician Richard Bellman, who worked on the solutions to such problems while at RAND Corporation in the 1950s.[1] Dynamic programming exploits the idea that even though a decision problem may involve a large number of stages—for example, covering the period a firm expects to be in a market—one need not enumerate and take expectancies of all possible contingent future realizations to arrive at an optimal decision policy. Bellman showed that one can derive the solution to a complex, multiperiod decision problem by solving it as if it were a series of independent two-stage problems, where the answer to each later stage dictates the solution to each successive earlier stage. This is called *backward induction,* and it reveals the value of looking forward to the endgame when you consider your opening moves. Although the mathematics of dynamic programming are well beyond the scope of this chapter, the two-year example above and the principle of stringing together these two-stage problems, indicates the general process.

Dynamic programming is a powerful tool, but not all multistage decision problems can be solved in this way. The probability of given states at given times must be determinable, the total value must be equal to the discounted sum of all the values at each point in time, and future values must be discounted at a constant rate. Because total utility or value is not always so linear and additive, this approach is not always appropriate. For example, we would not suggest using Bellman's equation to determine when one should get married or have children. Nevertheless, for most business problems these assumptions *are* reasonable, and indeed normative; after all, long-term profits *are defined* as the sum of yearly profits, and most accounting systems employ constant discounting.

WHAT MANAGERS ACTUALLY DO

As beautiful as these equations may be, it goes without saying that few people actually solve dynamic decision problems in the manner described above. Managers would choose the distributor based on some more simplified approach of weighing the two options. In his writings, Richard

Bellman never suggested that dynamic programming is a model for how managers actually solve multistage decision problems. Rather, dynamic programming was advanced as an effective decision support tool, a way that decision theorists (with the aid of computers) might help managers make *better* decisions.[2]

But how much help do managers really need? Although we may not literally employ the mathematics of dynamic programming when making decisions, we use heuristics that mimic its central properties. We have been urged to consider the future in the present from the time we were first encouraged by our parents to tie our shoes as children, to avoid smoking as teenagers, and to plan for retirement as adults. Yet, the fact that this advice must be given so frequently suggests that it may not always be heeded—implying that our heuristic solutions to problems may not always be as good as we might wish them to be.

Precisely measuring how good (or bad) we are at making dynamic decisions, however, turns out to be more difficult than one might presume. The reason is that dynamic decision theory does not provide an absolute benchmark for what optimal behavior should be in all situations. Rather, it only offers a *method for defining optimal behavior* conditional on the set of assumptions one chooses to make about how the world operates. And therein lies a dilemma: Behavior that seems to deviate from the optimality may not reflect faulty reasoning, but it may reflect the outcome of optimal reasoning applied to a different (and possibly faulty) set of assumptions. For example, if a manager decides to sign a long-term contract with the familiar distributor, it may simply be because the manager believes the odds the new firm will have higher coverage are significantly less than 50:50.

In light of this ambiguity, attempts to measure the quality of intuitive dynamic decision making tend to take two tacks. The first explores whether we have the basic cognitive abilities to solve problems in an optimal manner, given whatever set of beliefs about the world we might hold. For example, how far into the future can we plan when we make an effort to do so? The second tack attempts to comment more directly on the quality of intuitive decisions by comparing actual behavior to normative benchmarks in settings where optimal behavior can be uniquely defined—most commonly, in controlled laboratory settings.

HOW WELL-EQUIPPED ARE WE TO SOLVE DYNAMIC DECISION PROBLEMS?

Optimal dynamic programming solutions are based on two foundational assumptions about problem solving that, if violated, would likely lead to the poor performance of any intuitive solution:

1. *Complete forward planning.* When maximizing total utility over a horizon, decision makers are assumed to look ahead to all future periods and anticipate all possible choices and outcomes.
2. *Optimal learning.* Decision makers are assumed to fully utilize past information to update both current beliefs and future predictions.

Assumption 1, of course, is the essence of dynamic problem solving; one seeks to choose a course of action that maximizes utility in the long haul not just in the present. Assumption 2 is a bit more subtle but no less critical. It states that an optimal decision requires that the decision maker be as effective in learning from the past as in planning for the future, and this skill can be counted on when making future plans. Formally, this usually translates to an assumption that decision makers update their beliefs about the world (e.g., beliefs about probabilities) by employing Bayes' rule.

Myopia: Limits to Forward Planning

How well are decision makers able to incorporate beliefs about the future when making decisions in the present? Sadly, as any dieter who has ever succumbed to a tempting dessert in a moment of weakness can attest, forward planning is not something we are particularly well-equipped to do. If we isolate a single critical fault in human abilities to act as efficient decision makers, it is that we do not think ahead. We are prone to be temporally myopic and often, severely so. Indeed, studies find that people generally can plan no further than just one step beyond the current decision.

For example, a sample of MBA students was asked to choose an airline for a series of business trips: based on the following information:[3]

> You need to make a series of 20 business trips to a distant city, and it is critical that you always arrive on time. There are two airlines you can choose

from: Airline A is a familiar carrier that has an on time departure rate of 75 percent, and Airline B is a new carrier with an unknown departure rate. Analysts estimate, however, that Airline B's rate will likely turn out to be a constant percentage between 50 to 100 percent. Each time you arrive on time you receive a cash reward R, and each time you are late you are charged a penalty C.

Subjects then took each of the 20 hypothetical trips (on a computer), and after each trip they were informed whether the carrier they chose was on time or late. Note that the problem bears similarities to the distribution problem we started with, but the difference in this case is that the true value of the unfamiliar option is not revealed by a single trial choice. Each choice of the unfamiliar airline provides only one more bit of evidence about its true value. Here, the optimal policy is to start choosing the unfamiliar carrier and note whether it is on time or delayed. Keep choosing the new carrier until the number of late flights reaches a switching point. Then, switch to Airline A for all remaining trips.

The challenge is in determining the switching point. To find this point, the dynamic programming approach would work backward from the twentieth trip. To take that trip in this case, the switching point would clearly be a failure frequency of 25 percent. Otherwise, it would make sense to go with the familiar Airline A from the outset. By continuing to work backward to the first round, this yields a set of failure frequencies that are increasingly lower. This means decision makers should take a more lenient attitude toward Airline B earlier in the process.

But actual decision makers are much less patient. While some 64 percent tried B on the first trip, an optimal move based on the model, they stopped too soon. In many cases a single negative experience with Airline B sent them fleeing into the arms of the familiar and predictable Airline A. This would be the right decision for a series of two or three trips but not for twenty. Decision makers seem to use optimal approaches—but only look one period into the future.

Other studies similarly confirm the inability of decision makers to look ahead more than one stage in negotiations.[4] Managers also often undervalue opportunity costs when making investment decisions,[5] undervalue the information value of price variation when setting prices in unfamiliar markets,[6] and intuitive scheduling seems better characterized by moment-to-moment opportunism than by long-term holistic planning.[7] Moreover, when myopia arises, it can often be severely dysfunctional.[8]

But what about chess grand masters and other experts who seem to display Herculean abilities to anticipate consequences in specific tasks? What underlies these abilities, we argue, is not overt forward calculation. Although grandmasters often look 8 to 10 moves ahead, most moderately skilled players only look ahead one or two moves. For humans (and in contrast to the best chess-playing computer programs), knowledge is more important than is extensive searches into the future. The solution process is more one of astute pattern matching and recall (for example, established protocols for board positions) than it is brute force computation (see Chapter 5). Hence, by saying that decision makers have limited ability to forward plan, we are explicitly referring to tasks where correct solutions cannot simply be retrieved from memory but actually have to be calculated on the spot.

The Reasons for Myopia: Cognitive Limitations and Concreteness Bias

What drives our tendency toward shortsightedness? The most obvious culprits, of course, are cognitive limitations. As much as we might see the value in computing the implications of a decision over a 20 period horizon, our mental capacity is just not designed to perform such a task. But capacity constraints alone is insufficient to explain all instances of myopia. Although we might blame our brains for being unable to outplay Big Blue in a chess match, no such excuse exists for shortsightedness in other domains, such as one's inability to stay on a diet or a firm's failure to anticipate technological innovation.

In such contexts, a compounding culprit is at work—a concreteness bias. When processing information, we are inherently prone to give more weight to that which is more concrete and vivid at the expense of that which is more intangible and ambiguous.[9] Hence, managers often find it difficult to spend money to refit factories simply because it requires them to experience a very vivid and certain pain (the cash outlay) in exchange for a less vivid and more ambiguous gain (enhanced future profits). Likewise, dieters recognize that their only hope of avoiding the temptation of chocolate cake is to keep it out of the house.

A final factor that contributes to an undervaluing of long run conse-quences is that individuals tend to be poor intuitive arithmeticians when it comes to aggregating temporal sequences of outcomes. For example, when deciding whether to accept a job offer versus going on three more inter-views, one is essentially comparing the merits of the current offer with the expected merits of the *best* of the three unseen positions. When aggregat-ing information, decision makers tend to be overly conservative by virtue of being subject to what Kahneman and Tversky [10]called an *anchoring bias*. Even in instances where present consequences are no more vivid than fu-ture ones, we might still expect to see individuals make decisions that sug-gest myopia. The reason, however, is the opposite of that which usually is offered to explain the undervaluing of opportunity costs: it is not that the present is being *over*valued, but rather that payoffs that come from aggre-gating over the future are *under*valued. In recent studies conducted at the Wharton Behavioral Laboratory, we have found that most people, even those with statistical training, underestimate the value of future options (i.e., opportunities to choose the best of several options that are uncertain at the time of valuation, but known at the time of choice). We expect that this will prove to be a major source of decision biases because evaluating future options is a critical component of optimal decision methods.

Limits to Observing in the Present and Learning from the Past

Optimal dynamic decision analysis is built on a presumption that individ-uals are no less astute at drawing proper statistical inferences from current events and learning from the past as they are planning for the future. This essentially translates to two related assumptions:

1. *Decision makers draw unbiased insights about the current state of the world from available data.* On the surface, this assumption seems innocuous. It simply says, for example, that if in a given year half of the customers you ask report having an account with a certain dis-tributor, you will draw the inference that they have a 50 percent coverage rate—not some other number. Not only is this a property that any normative analysis should have, but it is also hard to imag-ine anyone—particularly managers with money on the line—not

conforming to it. But it turns out that it is less true than one might think (and hope) is the case; we are, as it turns out, frequently poor observational statisticians.[11] The central problem is that observational data rarely come to us in summarized form, as we illustrated above, and we are not naturally gifted at doing arithmetic in our head.[12] Not surprisingly, inferential errors become even more pervasive when the statistical calculation is more complex.[13]

2. *Previous beliefs about the world are updated in light of new data in an unbiased manner, following Bayes' rule.* Evidence about our ability to update past beliefs by observing new data—that is, engage in statistical learning—is not much more encouraging. On one hand, individuals obviously *do* learn from data and update in the direction predicted by Bayes' rule. Trivial examples of this abound; although we may have positive prior beliefs about the quality of a restaurant, a case of food poisoning would likely revise our opinion downward. Although we may not have Bayes' rule in mind when we are doing this, it is what Bayes' rule predicts we should be doing. Yet, whether individuals update beliefs in a *statistically optimal* manner is quite another question, and it is here where we seem to stumble.[14] Although a review of work that has documented learning and updating biases is beyond the scope of this chapter,[15] suffice it to say that the overwhelming weight of evidence rejects Bayes' as a precise descriptive account of how people revise beliefs based on data. The most common finding is that revisions tend to be insufficient—an effect[16] termed the *conservatism bias*.[17] Specifically, given a set of prior beliefs about the world (for example, a belief that I am untalented at tennis), we tend to revise the beliefs in the direction of new sample data, but the revision is consistently insufficient, or overly conservative. The bias, for example, has been used to explain the perpetuation of social stereotypes and the inability of older firms to respond with sufficient quickness to changing technologies.[18]

When we are actively learning (seeking out information), we tend to filter information to confirm our opinion. Such biased sampling is perhaps even more acute when hypotheses are tested by recalling events from memory. One often hears, for example, older Americans who grew up in the northeast voice the recollection that winters during their childhoods were snowier than they are today. Although this belief has little statistical basis (e.g., the 1950s were exceptionally dry years while the 1970s were exceptionally snowy), this biased recollection is understandable. A snowstorm is likely to be a far more salient—and positive—experience to a child than it is to an adult, and of course, a six-inch snowfall is more substantial when viewed from the height of a child.

THE PERFORMANCE OF HEURISTICS: WHEN MULTIPLE WRONGS MAKE A RIGHT

The previous discussion would seem to give us little basis for optimism that we might emerge as serviceable dynamic decision makers. The simple fact is that none of the ingredients seem to be in place: We have limited abilities to anticipate the future, we are poor at learning from the past, and even our perceptions of the present are distorted. Moreover, we are not very well-calibrated about our levels of knowledge and ability, so we tend to be overconfident.[19] Taken like this, not only does it seem that we could benefit from Bellman's ideas about optimality but also that the benefit would be great.

But this conclusion invites a curious, contradictory, observation: If we are, indeed, so bad at intuitive dynamic decision making, why aren't the damaging effects of errors more readily apparent? Both Microsoft's Bill Gates and GE's Jack Welch, after all, seem to have managed, and we guess that their knowledge of dynamic programming is limited. Moreover, as suggested at the outset, we face and resolve dynamic decision problems of considerable mathematical complexity on a daily basis without knowing them as such, and we are often quite happy with the outcomes.

For example, consider the intuitive solutions to Gilbert and Mosteller's[20] marriage problem:

> Beginning at age 19 you date one candidate a year, and at the end of that year make a decision whether to marry the candidate or reject him (or her), with there being no ability for later recall. This process can continue until age 50, when, if you have yet to get married, you wed the last eligible candidate. Candidate qualities in each year are independent random draws

from a distribution, and there is no chance that a candidate might reject your marriage proposal. You seek a dating strategy that maximizes the probability that you marry the highest-ranked candidate (i.e., as if you could date all of them and then go back in time to marry your favorite).

Most subjects do fairly well at addressing problems such as this, even without formal models. What explains the good task performance? We suggest it can be credited to three principles that, when taken together, have led to similar demonstrations of performance in a wide variety of dynamic decision tasks:

- *Optimal answers are often obvious.* If you are not mathematically inclined, we guess that you would simply draw on life experience to come up with an answer . . . and that, it turns out, would serve you well. For example, in real life, it obviously makes no sense to marry the first one or two people you meet (given the objective here) since you would want to see more of the distribution. But you also don't want to bypass a good option if it comes along, so you don't want to spend too much time window-shopping. So the rule has to be something like, "Look at a few (say N) of the candidates to get a sense of the distribution (without intending to marry them), and then marry the first new candidate that is better than any of those you have seen before." What should N be? On one hand, you know it has to be more than one or two (by the above logic), but 15—half the potential search pool—is probably too many. So you might strike a compromise and guess seven or eight. If you do this, you'd be virtually correct; the optimal policy is to date without intending to marry until you are 27, then marry for the candidate you encounter who ranks higher than any you have seen so far.
- *Task environments are forgiving of mistakes.* The second principle that contributes to intuitive optimality is that many decision environments are quite forgiving of mistakes, in the sense that they admit a wide range of erroneous behaviors as optimal or nearly optimal responses. In the marriage problem, for example, whereas 27 may be the optimal age to begin seriously looking for a spouse, a suitor who begins the process at age 24 or waits until 30 will face only slightly

lower odds of marrying the true best spouse in the distribution than one who follows the optimal rule. Also, in many situations a firm does not need the perfect plan, just a plan that is better than those of the competition.

- *One can learn by trial and error.* The final principle that contributes to apparent intuitive optimality is perhaps the most important, and certainly the most universal. Even when naive guesses about solutions to dynamic decision problems are seriously in error, these errors often diminish or disappear if decision makers are simply allowed to engage in a bit of what psychologists call *reinforcement learning:* be more likely to repeat actions that generate good results and less likely to repeat acts that produce bad ones.

To more precisely illustrate the power of heuristics,[21] consider an experiment in which subjects were asked to set prices for a new product, under two different levels of demand. The subjects, MBA students, played the game over 20 periods and received feedback on each round. In Figure 3.1 we plot the actual prices set by subjects, under two different demand regimes, and compare them to the prices that would be set if they were making decisions optimally. The actual decisions (solid line) eventually converge with optimal pricing (dotted line). Figure 3.1 suggests that subjects had some intuitive appreciation of setting the initial price at a high level. Although learning was a bit slow, they appeared to learn which demand regime they were operating in by the third or fourth trial, by the eighth trial they were reasonably close, and by the seventeenth trial they were setting prices that were almost identical to those that Bellman would have prescribed. Considering the complexity of the normative solution, intuitive performance is remarkably good.

Now, it should be clear that there was no evidence that the deficiencies in problem solving mentioned above were any less acute among the subjects being studied here. For example, while subjects appeared to show some foresight by initially setting a high price, they seemed to learn little from this experiment. Subsequent prices were far more conservative (set closer to the $150 price median) than would have been predicted had they been applying Bayes' rule to update their beliefs about demand probabilities. Likewise, while subjects' *first price* appears to display some foresight, later

Figure 3.1
Actual and Optimal Prices for the Demand-Uncertainty Problem

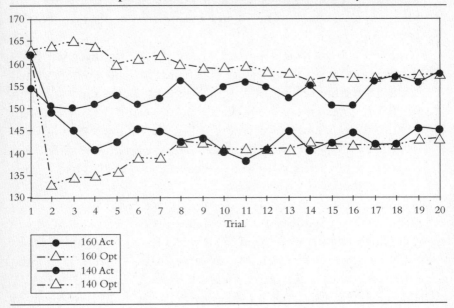

prices show no hint of an active interest in experimenting. Yet, in the end, subjects managed to overcome their cognitive limitations.

This is not to suggest, of course, that trial and error is a particularly *desirable* approach to the achievement of dynamic optimality. In the above pricing problem, for example, the several trials that preceded the discovery by subjects of the true optima would have represented substantial foregone profits for a firm. Moreover, the method does not yield generalized skills in problem solving that could be used to help solve other dynamic decision tasks. The fundamental message however, remains the same: As impaired as we are as intuitive statisticians, such skills are simply not always *needed* in a world that allows us second chances.

THE DARK SIDE OF HEURISTICS: WHEN TRIAL AND ERROR DOESN'T HELP

It would be nice if we could end our chapter here. If we did, our message would be remarkably upbeat: Although the tools that we use to make decisions may be flawed, in the end we usually make the right decisions, albeit by a process that occasionally subjects us to mistakes. The benefits of optimal dynamic decision theory thus lie at the margin. The theory helps us make decisions when humans are not there to make them and when the problems are unique and give little opportunity for learning. Optimal decision models can speed up the process of discovering right answers, and for the more academically inclined, inform us *why* the optimal behaviors that we exhibit are so.

Unfortunately, we can't end here, because the evidence on intuitive optimality turns out to be somewhat less rosy. Although it will *often* be the case that naive behavior will approximate optimal benchmarks, the previous results were based on two assumptions:

1. We are given unambiguous feedback about the quality of the decision we make, and
2. We are more likely to repeat behaviors that produce higher rewards.

Under these conditions, even the most naive of us will stumble our way toward optimality. But these two assumptions are less innocuous than they seem. There will be cases where the optimal answer is hard to guess and where enormous sums are won or lost depending on how close one is to a point optimum (for example, underpricing by 5¢ on a $1 item has huge opportunity costs when millions of units are sold). And, most critically, there are cases where trial-and-error learning fails to lead us to coincidental optimality.

Ambiguity and Learning

A big problem with these assumptions is that the *dominant mode* of feedback in the real world, it might be argued, is more likely to be *ambiguous* rather than unambiguous. This fact, in turn, can stand as a major barrier to any attempt to learn. Take the case of the large investments most firms recently made in upgrading software to preclude Y2K meltdowns. What did firms learn from this about how to respond to future software threats? This is not at all clear. The problem is that, for most firms, it is impossible to know what to make of the fact that nothing happened. The nonconsequence could be taken as proof of the wisdom of wise forward planning just as easily as it could be proof that the computer industry overstates threats.

To provide a more complete illustration of the consequences of such ambiguous feedback, we recently designed a computer simulation whose purpose is to explore how individuals make multiperiod decisions about investing in instruments that would protect a possession from damage due to an earthquake (a low probability catastrophic event). In the computer simulation, subjects face a succession of 40 periods in which they could purchase protection or experience an earthquake.

The problem was that subjects did not know the efficacy of the protection they purchased. If they avoided damage in a particular period, they could not tell for sure whether their protection saved them or the weaknesses of the earthquake saved them (they varied in both magnitude and distance to the epicenter). Subjects also faced ambiguity about their goal. They had to decide whether to invest in protection or long-term profitability.

The optimal investment policy in this case is straightforward. Given the long time horizon, subjects should consider experimenting with levels of protection early in the simulation, which should allow them—combined with the effects from observing the experiences of other players—to quickly determine whether investing in protection indeed serves to lower earthquake damage. Given this knowledge, the optimal policy becomes straightforward: In cases where it is effective, subjects should purchase the largest allowable amount (as measured by a protection level score of 0 to 100); if it is ineffective, they should buy nothing.

Although the optimal policy may indeed be straightforward, getting there from the subjects' perspective is another matter. The central difficulty is that the connection between trial-to-trial decisions and the optimization objective is both highly indirect and ambiguous. Subjects would not see any immediate return at all on their investment when there was no earthquake, and when there was an earthquake (akin to the calendar turning to the year 2000 for the Y2K problem), there was inherent uncertainty about how to interpret the meaning of observed associations between protection levels and damage. If damage was small, for example, one could attribute it to the wisdom of earthquake protection or, just as easily, the weakness of the earthquake itself.

In Figure 3.2 we plot the average level of purchased protection for each trial of the simulation—spanning the ownership of eight homes—for each of the two effectiveness conditions.

The figure reveals a disturbing pattern. Not only does subjects' behavior provide little evidence of optimal learning over time (which would be evidenced by a drift toward the protection extremes, 0 and 100), but for most trials, subjects seem to reach conclusions that are the *opposite* of the normative prediction. Subjects invest most heavily when protection is *least* effective. At best, by the end of the trial we see no difference in investment levels, but we speculate that this may reflect an endgame effect for those who would otherwise invest more (the low effectiveness subjects). In this case, reinforcement learning, rather than leading subjects to an optimal decision, may actually be leading them *away* from one.

An analysis of trial-by-trial antecedents of investment decisions provides an explanation for this result. Subjects, as it turned out, based their decisions about how much to invest on the most salient feedback cue that was available to them: the amount of damage they suffered in either their previous home or in the previous time period. The greater the damage, the more they would invest. While superficially sensible, this clearly makes sense *only* if the protection actually works—something that is impossible to judge from any one point of observation. Reinforcement learning was,

Figure 3.2
**Optimal versus Actual Protection Investment Levels over Time,
Earthquake Simulation**

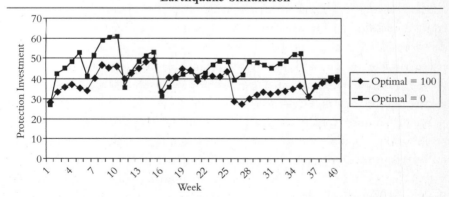

indeed, occurring, but the wrong behavior was being reinforced: When subjects saw that a given level of protection did not prevent them from suffering earthquake damages, instead of concluding that the investment was ineffective, they concluded just the opposite—that they were not investing enough.[22] In contrast, when subjects were placed in environments where the protective investment *was* effective, this very fact suppressed additional investments, because it removed the central motivator—damage.[23]

Although this example is perhaps an extreme one, the literature contains numerous other examples of failures to learn in the face of noisy or ambiguous feedback. Perhaps the best-known of this work is that conducted by Sterman and colleagues,[24] who examined the optimality of decision making in multiplayer business channel delivery problems. Known popularly as the beer game, players are faced with a problem in which they form a chain of suppliers who are trying to meet a stochastic source of demand. In the game, time lags occur when the initial producer sets production levels, orders are placed by wholesalers and retailers, and goods are actually purchased by consumers. Although players begin the game with setting reasonably efficient production and order levels, the channel system collapses when an unexpected shift in demand occurs. Given a sudden unanticipated upward shift in demand, sellers are suddenly unable to meet demand and find themselves back ordering so that they can meet both old and new orders. Producers then increase production to meet this surge in orders but find themselves overstocked after the demand from back orders relaxes. What results is an oscillating cycle of over- and underproduction and ordering from which subjects are unable to extricate themselves. The reason is similar to that in the earthquake experiment. Since the long-term consequences of actions are difficult to compute, subjects end up making decisions based on the most salient sources of feedback available: current and last-period order levels. By doing this, they are, in effect, reinforcing the wrong behavior and making it impossible for an optimal production and ordering equilibrium to emerge.

As a final note, we should stress that as disturbing as such evidence may be about our learning abilities, it reveals the failings of only one mechanism for learning, that of simple reinforcement. In practice, individuals and firms have other options and make use of them. For example, the question of the cost-effectiveness of Y2K investments need not be a matter of pure speculation; for any given firm one could gather concrete evidence on the degree the ordering of software erred when dealing with pre-1900 and late 1990s birth dates, and compute the cost-effectiveness of manual versus automated fixes for such problems. But with this observation, we are simply coming full circle to the point we used to launch this chapter: While there *are* optimal solutions to most dynamic decision problems, they will not always be the solutions our intuitions instinctively lead us to.

CONCLUSIONS: SURVIVING WITHOUT DYNAMIC PROGRAMMERS

The study of dynamic decision problems is littered with contradictions and paradoxes. The mathematics that underlie the optimal solution to even the most simplistic multistage decision tasks are not easy and are likely beyond the ability (or certainly the patience) of most real decision makers. Moreover, when we take the microscope and analyze our ability to perform the type of statistical inference tasks that are essential to these solutions, we fail, often miserably. Yet, when one compares the quality of intuitive solutions of dynamic decision problems to normative benchmarks, the correspondence turns out to be surprisingly high in some cases, particularly given task experience.

In addition, there is little tertiary evidence of widespread failures of intuition; we routinely face and resolve dynamic decision tasks, often with great apparent success. And therein, we feel, lies an important danger: Given this track record, the temptation is to conclude that our intuitions will be sufficient for *all* dynamic decision problems—but we would be severely mistaken. Eventually, we will all face decisions where the stakes are high and our intuitions are misleading.

Avoiding the Failure of Intuitive Decisions

This gives rise to a critical, final question: Is it possible to know, before the fact, what the quality of an intuitive solution to a dynamic decision problem will be and how to improve it? To answer this, it is useful to first summarize what we know about why intuitive solutions fail in the first place.

When we intuitively solve dynamic decision problems, we do so by using simplifying heuristics. Although these heuristics can take a wide variety of forms, we suggest that most adhere to the following template, which we call *adjusted pattern matching:* We study the key features of the problem and re-call a similar problem for which a known (correct) answer exists. Then we adjust this previous case to accommodate differences in the current task by using available information. Although perhaps sensible, this heuristic process will often be prone to miscalculation. For departures from optimality to be *costly* and *sustained,* however, two other conditions need to be present: (1) The problem itself must be unforgiving, severely penalizing departures from optimality, and (2) trial and error must fail because feedback is am-biguous or because the opportunities to learn are few.

These principles, therefore, suggest that to answer the global question Will I be making a mistake? managers should in turn ask themselves the fol-lowing four questions:

1. *Am I being myopic?* As we stressed at the beginning of the chapter, most decision makers do not look more than one step ahead, and they do not appreciate the value of future options. Although we also stressed the fact that formal methods of backward induction are too complex for practical application, it is relatively easy to avoid being blindsided by simply considering the future implications of current decisions. The most common example of insufficient foresight is probably the neglect of competitive response. This leads to price wars and overinvestment in innovations that are easily duplicated. A less obvious form of myopia occurs when managers ignore the informa-tion value of current decisions. When the short-run financial payoffs are slim or uncertain, it is particularly important to ask, Will we learn something, by taking this action, which will help us make better de-cisions in the future? Or conversely, Will we limit our future options by taking this action now? Considerations of the future provide an excellent tiebreaker.

2. *How appropriate is the starting analogy I am using to solve a problem?* There is nothing wrong with solving a new problem by starting with the solution to a familiar problem. In fact, the ability to do this well, by developing a large memory bank of examples that can be matched,

defines expertise in human judges.[25] As discussed in Chapter 5, this human ability to match patterns is one of our greatest strengths, but the drive is so strong that we tend to find patterns that are not there. If one draws the incorrect analogy, the actions that follow are almost certain to be inappropriate. For example, IBM's failure to be a dominant player in the desktop PC market came, in part, by presuming that the same business model that led to its success in mainframes could be extended to PCs. IBM overestimated their value as a brand name in the market and the strategic and technical capabilities of smaller upstart competitors, such as Compaq and Dell.

When making analogies, we tend to look for similarities and overlook differences in the patterns. Managers need to pay more attention to these differences by:

—Having critical awareness of the analogy (or set of analogies) one is drawing upon when solving a problem.

—Formally noting the pattern's points of *difference* from a current problem, not just its similarities.

—Being prepared to make significant adjustments to the previous solution when the similarity between a current problem and the base analogy is low.

3. *What are the penalties for making an error?* The fact that one has made an incorrect calculation—even a severe one—does not imply that there will be negative consequences. Indeed, one frequently used explanation for why we commonly use simplifying heuristics to make complex decisions is that we can get away with it.[26] But this will not always hold, and the formal study of how rewards (or penalties) might vary across a range of possible answers is an essential step in a prospective analysis of a decision problem. If the penalties are great for erring in a certain direction, decision makers would be well advised to err on the side of caution. This is, in fact, what intuitive decision makers often do.

4. *What am I learning from the feedback I am receiving?* As careful as we might be in paying attention to feedback, odds are we will make mistakes when trying to come up with intuitive solutions to complex dynamic decision problems. In this sense, a case could be made that what matters more in a given setting is not whether our initial attempts at

solving a problem are prone to error, because they will be, it is what we *learn* from these mistakes. As we noted earlier, it will not necessarily be the case that all learning paths will lead to optimality, and one needs to be just as careful in exploring the long-term implications of one's *reaction strategy* as in formulating an initial answer to a new problem. We need to be on guard against knee-jerk reactions. Switching policies every time an outcome is negative will almost certainly never lead to overall optimality. In the long run, one's behavior will, at most, be a blending of policies with use of suboptimal rules interspersed with the use of optimal ones. Although the advice Stick to long-term strategies is well-known in the context of stock market investing, often forgotten is that it applies equally well to *any* decision problem whose outcome is subject to occasional fits of chance. As a related issue, we must be formally mindful of the inferences we draw from feedback, and the fact that individual experiences are often less informative than we might think.

We must plan to learn. Don't forget that the decisions one makes now can be strategically used to help make better decisions in the future. If there is one pervasive bias that consistently surfaces in analysis of intuitive dynamic decision making, it is that people do not fully appreciate the future information value of the choices they make. If there is uncertainty about which one of two states of nature characterizes our environment (e.g., whether customers are willing to pay a high price for our products or not), the strategy should be to learn over multiple periods. Initially setting prices at an extremely high level may seem like an excessively risky action, but the risk is only short term. One needs to anticipate that we will learn from this experience, and *anticipation* of learning should be an integral part of our decision policy.

Let's return to the example of the problem we posed at the beginning of the chapter: *Would* managers sign a contract with the new vendor? The evidence we reviewed about how people solve dynamic decision problems says that, in all likelihood, they would not. Odds are that managers of the firm, whose performance is judged by stockholders on an annual basis, will find themselves unable to take the long-term view required to justify choosing the new firm. But the managers might be loath to sign a long-term contract with the familiar firm because it is not certain that it is the best deal. Their instincts are to seek a short-term resolution, putting off the difficulty of long-term thinking until next year.

The good news about multistage decision making is that in many cases everyday reasoning provides nearly optimal decisions. The bad news is that when later stages depend on what is learned in earlier stages, everyday reasoning fails because we seldom consider those later stages in the beginning. By understanding this important distinction, managers can efficiently and effectively use heuristics when appropriate and use more systematic and laborious analysis when appropriate. Human intuition can be quite powerful but works best when it is balanced with judicious use of models. Myopic individuals may be able to see the big picture but would be foolish not to wear corrective lenses when they drive. Just as this balance between humans and models helps compensate for myopia in multistage decisions, it also can provide a check on the human tendency to see patterns that are not there, as discussed in Chapter 5.

CHAPTER 4

CHOOSING VARIETY

BARBARA E. KAHN
The Wharton School

ANDREA MORALES
The Wharton School

While you might prefer to spend your entire vacation on the beach, you might add in less enjoyable activities simply for variety. This desire for change for the sake of change may not be a problem on vacation, but could cause trouble when it comes to management decisions.

To sing the same tune, as the saying is, is in everything cloying and offen-
sive; but (people) are generally pleased with variety.

—Plutarch A.D 46–120.

People like variety and will sometimes make what appear to be suboptimal
choices to maximize their variety. In this chapter, the authors consider why
decision makers seek variety and how they maximize variety in their choices
over time. They also look at ways that managers can shape the choice-set of-
fered to customers and employees. Finally, they consider ways managers can
maximize variety, while minimizing costs of offering options, by creating the
highest levels of perceived variety without actually enlarging the assortment
of offerings.

It's been known for centuries that peo-
ple enjoy variety. Assortments or menus that offer variety generally are
preferred. And people frequently prefer change in their consumption patterns over time. When managers make decisions, they do not weigh options
in isolation but look at these options in comparison to either past selections or other available choices. The desire for variety thus has an influence
on how the decisions are perceived and the choices that are made. How
does the desire for variety affect decision making? In this chapter, we draw
upon behavioral research in marketing to explore how variety influences
choices, for better or for worse.

Variety offers two distinct advantages to decision makers. If decision
makers are making many choices over time, then variety or depth in the
choice-set will enable exploration and choice of different options over time.
If the decision maker is making a single choice, then variety or breadth in
the assortment will enable one to find the desirable customized option
among those offered.

Opting for variety and choosing something different from what was
chosen in the past can provide a new outlook or a fresh approach to an old
problem. Variety can also enhance routine activities. For example, some
organizations regularly rotate jobs to give employees a fresh perspective on
their work. The company 3M encourages variety seeking and new ways of
thinking by allowing employees to spend 10 percent of their time working
on their original ideas. This approach is designed to stimulate innovation

by providing an incentive for employees to break out of the routine ways of doing things. One also might think of General Motor's successful Saturn initiative as a break from routine ways of doing business. It is telling that Saturn's slogan emphasizes that it is not just a different car but a different kind of company. These companies recognize that variety can be a source of creative ideas and excitement in an organization.

On the other hand, the human desire for variety does not always have positive consequences for organizations. Variety can add cost and complexity to decision making and slow down the process as managers or customers sift through endless arrays of options. Offering more variety imposes a cost in being able to deliver the options and in choosing from among them. If there is too much variety, decision makers can become frustrated or confused.

Another problem is that decision makers may make suboptimal choices simply for the sake of variety. While this may be personally fulfilling and make the work more interesting, it does not necessarily lead to better business decisions. We all have experienced this pursuit of variety in the more benign context of personal decisions. For example, a tourist planning a vacation may decide to schedule many different activities, even if the person's preferred activity is relaxing at the beach. Since a vacation that consists only of sitting at the beach provides a less interesting memory than one that includes museum visits and deep-sea fishing, the tourist might choose activities that may not provide the most enjoyable experiences at the time but will create the best overall retrospective photo album. (The photo album is, of course, part of the overall utility of the vacation, because the experience of maximizing variety, itself provides a benefit. This is not always the case with business decisions.) Similarly, although market research has shown that the most popular flavor of *Lifesavers* is cherry, the biggest seller is, traditionally, the five-flavor roll, not the cherry only roll. Once again people opt to include suboptimal individual choices, such as pineapple Lifesavers, to maximize overall variety.

In hedonic decisions, where the goal is to derive pleasure from the consumption, choosing less-preferred items such as pineapple candies or intriguing sounding vacation activities may not be a bad thing if the choice makes the overall experience more enjoyable. Applying the same reasoning to a business decision, however, could be destructive and lead to a tendency to change for the sake of change. This approach can result in such counter-productive patterns as rotating suppliers, consultants, or employees (just to try something different), or choosing the management theory of the month.

In the first part of this chapter, we begin with a discussion of a traditional model in which decision makers seek variety in their choices over time. In this model, decision makers maximize their overall utility on each choice occasion. They don't always choose their traditional favorites for each choice occasion because they have needs to allay boredom, create a portfolio of options, or obtain flexibility for the future, but they do choose the alternative for each choice occasion that offers the most overall value. We then consider a new model of decision making that allows the decision maker to maximize utility over the sequence of choices rather than on each choice occasion. Using this model of behavior, we can describe variety-seeking behaviors that do not provide maximum utility on each choice occasion. In fact, when they maximize utility over the sequence, decision makers may even choose options, on specific occasions, that themselves offer very little utility but somehow contribute to the utility of the sequence.

In the second part of the chapter, we discuss how managers can use an understanding of variety-seeking behavior to shape the choice-sets presented to customers or employees. Choice-sets can be constructed in ways that increase perceived variety while not actually changing the real variety of the set. In addition, the method of presenting the choice options can also affect the decision makers' satisfaction.

REASONS FOR CHOOSING VARIETY

Variety seeking in purchase behavior has been defined as the tendency of individuals to seek diversity in their choices of services or goods over time. Why do people seek variety? Several normative explanations for this type of behavior have been proposed in marketing and psychology literature.[1] Among the primary explanations for variety-seeking behavior are to: allay boredom, create a portfolio of options, and enhance flexibility for the future.

Allaying Boredom

Probably the oldest explanation for why individuals seek variety is that they become bored or satiated with their current selections and desire something new. Psychological evidence has shown that individuals' reactions to a stimulus can be characterized by a single-peak preference function.[2] In other words, once an optimal level of that stimulus is reached, then satiation sets in and the person looks for something different on the next choice occasion. For example, one might crave caviar, but if it is offered in unlimited amounts, one would satiate when an optimal level is reached and would choose something else on the next occasion.

In other situations, people who are not totally satiated may still look for something new or different to try, for the thrill of it. Some researchers have proposed that individuals have an intrinsic drive for stimulation or exploration[3] or have a curiosity to learn about new things.[4] This drive often leads to a desire to purchase exciting and novel options. Consumers may seek variety among familiar items in a product class or may switch to new, untried items just for the pleasure inherent in experiencing a new stimulus and not because they are satiated. There are obviously individual differences regarding this need for stimulation, and consumers with higher needs for stimulation will engage in more variety seeking.

Creating a Portfolio of Options

Another explanation for variety-seeking behavior is based on the idea that people may not believe they can get everything they need in one option, and therefore, it is preferable to consume a portfolio of options. Consumable options rarely have optimal values on all attributes,[5] and one strategy to maximize utility would be to choose a mix of products, each having its own distinct advantage.[6] For example, if you eat the same foods every day you're not getting a well-balanced diet. Exercise experts counsel you to cross-train or rotate activities and not engage in just one type of exercise. Lastly, instead of hiring only accounting majors from the same university, managers generally hire employees of different backgrounds in order to diversify their workforce.

Enhancing Flexibility for the Future

Another reason people choose to consume a portfolio of options is to hedge against future uncertainty.[7] In this case, a portfolio is chosen, not because of the utility for the diversity per se, but because it is not certain what choices the decision maker will face in the future.[8] People's preferences often change across time and consumption occasions. If a consumer shops only once a week, then the purchase is made in anticipation of the actual consumption occasion. Choosing a variety of options will help ensure that the desired option is available at that future time. Similarly, one frequently chooses the restaurant before the choice of the meal, so it would make sense to choose a place that provides ample variety and maximizes the probability that the dish you crave is offered.[9] In the same way, hiring people with different strengths and areas of expertise increases the chance that a company will have the ability to successfully meet any future problems or challenges. This flexibility can reduce costs by allowing the organization to seize new market opportunities quickly.

It has been suggested that this drive for variety is a natural, survival instinct. By trying a variety of options, individuals learn to adapt to the changing environment, and they ultimately grow and improve. Clearly, being able to adjust to the evolving marketplace is key for today's managers. Those who can adapt and follow the twists and turns in the market will survive, while those who continue to cling to the knowledge of the past will be left behind. This flexibility is more important today than ever, in the context of rapid changes driven by information technology (particularly the Internet), globalization, and other forces.

MAXIMIZING VARIETY OVER A SEQUENCE OF CHOICES

The previous explanations suggest that people seek variety to maximize their utility or pleasure for each choice occasion. But people do not frequently make each of their decisions in isolation. Instead, they may see a given choice as part of a sequence of choices over time. Sometimes decision makers will make suboptimal choices along the way to optimize the variety of this entire sequence of choices. This maximization of utility or pleasure over a stream of choices is known as global maximization[10] and is in contrast to focusing on single choices, which is labeled local maximization.[11] Why do people seek this global maximization instead of concentrating on each decision as it occurs? Among the explanations that have been suggested for this behavior are: forecasting satiation, saving the best for last, and maximizing the retrospective memory.

Forecasting Satiation

Because decision makers know from past experiences that if they consume too much of a good thing they lose their taste for it, they may vary their consumption patterns by including options to protect their tastes for their favorite. The weekend appears more enjoyable than the workweek because of the change of pace the weekend offers; however, a constant weekend may quickly become boring. Similarly, managers can offer variety to employees through job rotation or by diversifying responsibilities. In this way, employees will not tire of the jobs they enjoy the most, and they may, in fact, appreciate their jobs more when compared to their less preferred positions.

Saving the Best for Last

People like to end on a high note. For example, some people eat the cake first and then the icing so that the favorite part can be savored at the end. Similarly, some people schedule their least favorite activities early in the day to obtain a positive contrast effect with those activities they do enjoy. It is like the explanation offered in the joke: Why are you hitting your head against the wall? Because it feels so good when I stop. With this behavior, people may choose a variety of options, especially options that are not the most enjoyable, so they can maximize the pleasure of consuming options they do like. The consumption of a favorite item may *benefit* from being preceded by something distasteful because the utility for the favorite item will be enhanced by the contrast with the less desired item. Thus, variety seeking may be a strategy to purposefully include distasteful (or at least neutral) alternatives in order to enhance the pleasure of favorite items. In addition, when people are consuming items for enjoyment, they may try to pattern their consumption in such a way as to continually increase utility over time.[12] People are more averse to negative changes than they are elated by positive changes.[13] A stock that steadily trends upward by 100 points each month, for example, may be viewed more favorably than one that jumps by 300 points one month and then declines by 100 points in the next.

Such sequences, where the consumption utility increases over time, are thought of as a series of gains; sequences where the consumption utility decreases over time are thought of as a series of losses. Not only do people prefer gains over losses, but there is some evidence that losses are considered more negative than equivalent gains are considered positive. This asymmetry between gains and losses is known as loss aversion and is one explanation why, for example, retailers are inclined to offer their customers off-peak discounts rather than on peak surcharges (even when the effects are equivalent). Frequently, when people are planning how to consume diverse items over time, they'll choose to save their favorite for last. Similarly, in presenting results to employees or shareholders, it may be advisable to build up to the good news.

Maximization of Retrospective Memory

As we saw in the case of our vacationer, sometimes variety leads to a better retrospective *memory* of the pleasure or pain associated with events, which is quite different from the actual real-time pleasure or pain.[14] Given this difference, people may choose a pattern of consumption that maximizes the memory of the events rather than the actual utility in real time.

For example, researchers have found that memory for painful experiences can be characterized by a peak and end rule where the memory of the event is shaped by what happens at the end and at the most intense moment—not by the duration of the painful event. Someone might, therefore, choose to endure longer experiences with pain that end on a happy note than shorter experiences that end on a painful note. People will sometimes choose to consume a highly varied sequence of options (including some options that are not particularly enjoyable but are included for variety)—not to maximize the real-time experience of enjoyment but to maximize the memory of the overall sequence.[15]

One possible way for managers to build on the idea of maximizing retrospective utility is by allowing employees to have more flexibility in their work hours and vacation time. Although employees may not have a better real-time work experience when they arrive at 6 A.M. instead of 8 A.M., in looking back over their work week, they are likely to remember leaving work at 3 P.M. every day (rather than 5 P.M. or 6 P.M.) with great fondness. In the same way, offering flexibility in vacation time may allow employees to work longer periods of time without a day off in order to have longer periods of vacation time. Again, the peak and end rule suggests that employees are more likely to remember the extended vacation time rather than the long period of work preceding the vacation, and to evaluate the overall experience more highly.

MANAGING VARIETY

Given the positive and negative implications of variety, managers need to carefully think about how they manage variety in their own decisions and how they present choices to others. When the manager wants to offer greater variety to decision makers (whether employees or customers), the challenge is to create apparent variety without sending costs through the roof. In other cases, managers may want to limit perceived variety and avoid overwhelming decision makers with too many choices.

Increasing Perceived Variety while Managing Costs

Offering a vast array of options is one way to ensure that decision makers are given a high level of variety. This is very rarely practical, because the organization must present these options, and even more challenging, deliver them. Given these costs, if managers are interested in increasing perceived variety, they need to do so in a way that also manages costs. This can be done by focusing on the right dimensions of variety, tailoring the choice to the setting, and using a variety of strategies to increase *perceived* variety without actually expanding the total choice-set.

Focus on the Right Dimensions of Variety. Not all variety is created equal. Although offering a line of cars in a large variety of colors would be appealing to consumers, providing them with a large assortment of warranty options would be less likely to produce as favorable a response. It may actually frustrate or confuse a consumer.

Which dimensions benefit most from variety? Some new research [16] has sought to answer the question: What kinds of attributes are decision makers most likely to seek variety on? If we focus on satiation or stimulation, one answer is to look toward the attributes that are related to the senses (e.g., flavor, color, sound, etc.). These attributes are the ones that are most likely to cause satiation, and they are also most likely to be the ones in which people seek variety. Empirical studies have shown people do not like listening to the same song over and over and that they are more likely to seek variety with flavors rather than with brands. Offering variety along the dimensions that matter, while keeping other dimensions fixed, can increase perceived variety while managing costs.

Choose the Right Setting for the Decision.   The context for the decision also will affect the level of variety desired.[17] For example, the beverage one may choose at 9 A.M. is different from the one consumed at 6 P.M., and this suggests preferences change with circumstances and that the resulting behavior resembles variety seeking. Usage situations could differ owing to the season, leisure versus business activities, presence of others, or presence or absence of other consumable products. At the household level, purchase histories may resemble variety-seeking behavior due to the aggregation of individual household members' purchases.[18]

Social context also seems to affect variety-seeking behavior. It has been proposed that individuals may perceive it as a social norm to consume a variety of items[19] when consuming food. Laboratory experiments, based on the decision strategies people use when choosing from gourmet food, snacks, or candy, show that when given the opportunity to choose a plate of items for future consumption, people choose more variety when the choice is made in public than when the choice is made in private. These subjects expected to be evaluated more favorably and thought to be more interesting when their choice-sets had a variety of items. These effects were higher for those people most concerned with adhering to norms (the high-monitors) and reinforced the idea of a social norm that guides this behavior.

Social context has also been shown to influence the variety of a group's selection. Experiments conducted in which choices were made in a group setting (even when individuals were choosing items for their own consumption) found that the resulting choice-sets tended to have a more diverse set of options than would be found if the individuals were alone and choosing for themselves.[20] In addition, the decision makers were less satisfied with their selections made in the group setting than they were with their selections made in private. It appears that in a group context, decision makers often sacrifice the choice of their most-preferred item to satisfy other goals, such as information acquisition and identity. Thus, individuals within a group context often balance or trade off their individual-only goals of personal taste satisfaction against the individual-group goals for the sake of group-level variety. When the organization wants more creativity and greater variety in decisions, posing the questions in a group setting may encourage this result. This can clearly be seen in the value of group work in activities such as brainstorming, where fresh ideas are desired. On the other hand, if the goal is not creativity but closure, or if you want to limit the variety in the choices, posing questions in a private setting may be preferable.

Other factors in the setting for the decision may also influence the desire for variety. The psychology literature[21] shows that moods can affect the way people process information and their ultimate behavior. Building on this theory,[22] researchers found that if participants were placed in an experimental situation where positive mood was induced (through the unexpected gift of a bag of colorful candies with a bright red ribbon tied around it), there was an increased desire for variety as compared to participants in a control situation. Based on other measures collected at the time of the experiment, researchers concluded that the positive mood encouraged the participants to elaborate more when processing the attributes of the offered alternatives. This elaboration, coupled with tendency toward more optimistic anticipation of the consumption, resulted in more variety-seeking behavior.

Another series of experiments[23] found that pumping scents into the environment could affect variety-seeking behavior. In these experiments, participants who were choosing among chocolate candies were more likely to choose more variety when the environment was scented with a chocolate fragrance than when the environment was scented with a flowery fragrance. These results, that a congruent ambient odor generated more variety seeking, while an incongruent ambient odor generated less variety seeking, were replicated across other product categories.

Generalizing from these laboratory results, the creation of a fun-filled, festival-like environment may encourage decision makers to choose more novel items, or items different from the normal pursuits. However, other experiments[24] suggest that if there is too much stimulation, decision makers may try to simplify their behavior and thus choose less variety, or exhibit less creativity and openness to new ideas.

Managers must also be careful about the global context of decisions. Although the effects of social context on variety seeking are quite strong, current research has only been conducted in the United States. Presumably, social context would not have the same effect in all countries, due to distinct differences in Western and Eastern cultures. Researchers have shown that Asians tend to exhibit higher levels of uniformity in choice in comparison to their Western counterparts, and this results from a strong emphasis on the value of conformity in Eastern cultures.[25]

Manage the Perception of Variety.   One of the most significant limits on variety is the cost of providing it. As the number of options offered to customers or other decision makers increases, so does the cost of manufacturing, warehousing, or shelving these different options. More variety can also increase administration costs. If an organization offers more health care options to its employees, for example, it would generally increase the costs of administering the plan. A significant challenge for managers is how to convey a feeling of great variety without increasing costs too much. When it began including blue M&Ms, Mars was able to increase the variety of its standard product by the change of only one attribute (color) rather than design a new flavor, package, or candy size or increase the number of individual candies per bag.

The true sense of variety goes beyond simply the number of items offered. The perception of variety is based on *how* these items are offered. By increasing perceptions of variety, it is possible to get the benefits of offering more variety, without incurring the costs. How can you increase the perception of variety? Three factors have been shown to influence people's perceptions of variety in assortments:

- *The Presence of a Favorite Option.* In many cases, perceptions of variety can be increased by the presence of a person's favorite or most preferred item in the choice-set.[26] In this way, instead of determining an assortment's level of variety based on the entire choice-set, people use the availability of their favorite product as a cue for the overall variety of the assortment. As long as their favorite product is available, they assume that the assortment offers high variety.

- *Organization of the Assortment.* How choices are displayed also affects perceptions of variety. More specifically, perceptions of variety differ and depend on whether the choice-set is presented in an organized or random way. Recent studies have shown that when people engage in analytic processing, organized displays appear to offer more variety. When people engage in more holistic processing, however, random displays are seen as providing more variety.[27] In these studies, organized assortments refer to displays with more similar objects positioned closer to one another. Thus, the simple position of products in an assortment can influence perceptions of variety.
- *Duplication.* On the other hand, the avoidance of redundancy in some parts of the assortment can increase perceived variety. Studies show that the presence of the same item repeated in the assortment—when the two examples are not positioned close to one another—can result in lower levels of perceived variety.[28] For example, on a restaurant menu, if something is highlighted as a special, but also appears on the regular listing, the perceptions of variety can be lowered. On the other hand, if the duplication does not appear to be contrived, such as increased contiguous shelf facings of an item on a grocery shelf that makes the space allocated to the category larger, then the duplication can sometimes increase perceptions of variety.

Avoid Overwhelming the Decision Maker

In addition to offering variety while managing costs, another factor in managing variety is to avoid overwhelming the decision maker. Too many choices can be overwhelming for employees or customers, so shaping the choice-set to provide sufficient levels of variety, without driving the decision maker to distraction, is a key concern. When decision makers are only making a single selection from an assortment, it is critical that they can find easily the option that best meets their needs. Where a company is offering a large number of choices, it must find a way to present these choices in manageable subsets for the decision makers.

For example, Choice Seating Gallery is a customized sofa shop that allows consumers to design their own sofas by choosing from 500 different styles of sofa, 3,000 different types of fabrics, and 350 different leather grades and colors. The enormous number of potential options—150,000 different fabric sofas and 17,500 leather sofas—can be quite confusing, and even overwhelming, especially for a customer unfamiliar with the product class.

To prevent people from being overwhelmed with complex choice-sets, it is useful to help them navigate through the complexity so they can appreciate the benefits of the high variety. In a series of experiments,[29] researchers found that decision makers are likely to be more satisfied and perceive less complexity in a choice-set when they are asked to formulate their preferences for attribute levels of the options (Do you want leather or fabric?). This approach is less overwhelming than are the more difficult tasks, such as formulating trade-offs in importance among attributes (Which is more important to you, the type of fabric or the shape of the sofa back?), but this approach is more involved than asking the decision maker to just be aware of the attributes without formulating active preferences. Further, helping consumers learn their preferences through an attribute-based information format, as opposed to an alternative-based format, also increases satisfaction and learning when complexity in a choice-set is high. When managers present decisions with many complex options, it is important to present them in a way that does not overwhelm the decision maker.

CONCLUSIONS AND IMPLICATIONS

Variety truly is the spice-of-life, but like any spice it must be used in moderation. The desire for variety influences how decisions are made, for better or worse. Variety can lead to higher satisfaction or it can be overwhelming. It can lead to the development of creative options or the pointless search for change, for the sake of change.

Given the natural human desire for variety, managers need to look carefully for signs of destructive variety seeking in their own decisions and those of their employees. When does variety really have benefits for the organization to change and when are changes being made just for the sake of change? For each decision, it is important to look for indications of variety-seeking behavior at work, particularly in decisions that reflect a series of shifts in direction, suppliers, employees, or other vectors. Although some of these minor changes (such as brewing new flavored coffees) will be harmless and may contribute to the sense of excitement about the workplace, more substantial decisions should be more carefully screened to make sure the change is beneficial rather than counterproductive.

Among the questions to ask are the following:

- What is the optimal decision? Is the proposed choice the best, or is it being made just for a change of pace?
- If the choice is just for the sake of change, does the decision serve a purpose in the organization (make employees feel better about their jobs; keep options open with a wide range of suppliers)? Are there other ways to achieve these goals without making the change?
- What are the costs of this variety? Are the benefits worth the costs?
- Can decisions be presented to others in a way that increases the perceived variety without either significantly increasing costs or overwhelming the decision maker?

This set of questions offers a simple filter for identifying when variety seeking is effective and when it might be counterproductive.

By understanding this human tendency for variety seeking, managers can better manage it and use it. In some cases, the desire for variety should be heightened, while in others the desire for variety is best mitigated. By understanding the motivations behind decision makers' choices of variety and the factors that influence the perception of variety, you can limit the negative effects of the natural desire for variety and can use it to encourage creativity and increase flexibility in your organization.

PART II

MANAGERIAL
DECISION MAKING

Even when you are not literally facing a spring-loaded decision, as our hapless manager is above, managers have many traps to avoid when making decisions. How can you make better management decisions? Part II explores a variety of tools and perspectives that can help improve decision making in fast-changing environments.

In Chapter 5, Stephen J. Hoch examines how models (particularly computer models) can complement human intuition. Humans and computers, together, can make better decisions than either can alone. In Chapter 6, Karen A. Jehn and Keith Weigelt compare Eastern (reflective) and Western (expedient) approaches to handling decisions and discuss how Western managers might benefit from the addition of more reflective approaches to their decision–making toolbox. In Chapter 7, Paul R. Kleindorfer offers insights on making decisions and on the increasingly complex and risky environments; he uses the electric utilities industry and the coverage of catastrophic risks as examples. In Chapter 8, Paul J.H. Schoemaker and J. Edward Russo examine how the way you frame a problem can often change the outcome of a decision. They offer advice on taking control of your frames to make better decisions.

CHAPTER 5

COMBINING MODELS WITH INTUITION TO IMPROVE DECISIONS

STEPHEN J. HOCH
The Wharton School

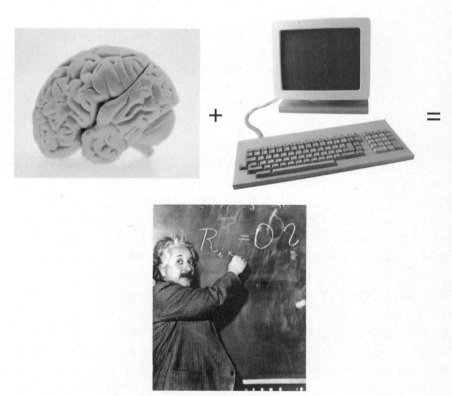

Because of their complementary strengths and weaknesses, humans and machines are more powerful together than either one alone.

One machine can do the work of fifty ordinary men. No machine can do the work of one extraordinary man.

—Elbert Hubbard

The real danger is not that computers will begin to think like men, but that men will begin to think like computers.

—Sydney J. Harris

Like chessmaster Garry Kasparov and computer Deep Blue, humans and machines are often seen as locked in an epic battle for superiority of decision making. On the one hand, human intuition is brilliant in recognizing patterns—so good, in fact, that it finds patterns that are not even there. On the other hand, machine-based models sometimes have trouble seeing the forest from the trees. Because the strengths and weaknesses of humans and models are complementary, a combination of the two works better than either one does on its own. In this chapter, the author draws upon original research, which shows improvement of results from combining the precision of models with the creativity of human intuition. The author also examines specific strategies for combining models and human intuition effectively.

It is clear throughout this book that as information processors, human beings often do not live up to the standards implied by the economic view of people as rational utility-maximizers. But it does not follow, as some advocates of decision modeling and information systems might suggest, that humans should be jettisoned overboard like the poor crew members dumped over the side by their mechanical crewmate, HAL, in *2001: Space Odyssey.* Nor does it necessarily follow that we should pull the plug on the computer-based models, despite their own well-recognized flaws. Both humans and models have strengths and weaknesses, and a more careful examination shows that in many ways, the strengths of models help shore up the weaknesses of humans, and vice versa. Experts and models, if combined appropriately, can be complementary. In this chapter, with the focus on the challenge of expert forecasting, the strengths and weaknesses of humans and models are examined as are ways to combine the two.

THE CHALLENGE OF THE INFORMATION AGE

Rapid advances in information technology have changed decision making. New technology has drastically reduced the costs of collecting, storing, and analyzing massive amounts of data and information. And if Moore's law continues to hold, the importance of information technology to decision making, in all walks of life, will continue to grow. Computers cannot be ignored in decision making. Decision makers who rely on seat-of-the-pants intuition ignore vast universes of information. But the central challenge in designing information-driven decision support systems (DSS) is how to divide up responsibilities between computers and humans. There are three basic strategies:

1. *Minimize the human element.* This involves automating the decision process to the point where human intervention is kept to a minimum, with the intention of dramatically reducing cost and human error. Most successful examples of highly automated decision-making systems revolve around simple and repetitive tasks where scale economies are possible. Examples include yield management systems, credit scoring models, data cleaning, and inventory reorder systems. Many diagnostic tasks, ranging from car repair to medical tests, are completely automated, although, as with automatic pilot systems, the pilot still plays an important override role. The same is true of yield management systems in which analysts may adjust airfares, depending on local knowledge.

2. *Use information technology as a power tool.* Here, the technology is used to extend the strengths of the decision maker, but the process for making decisions is largely unchanged. For example, the decision maker may be given a graphical interface to display data in a variety of ways, quickly and seamlessly, which makes it easier to see patterns and come to conclusions. This approach uses technology in much the same way a carpenter uses a pneumatic nailer to replace a standard hammer. The same work is done in much the same way, but more quickly and effectively. The process is not changed, as it would be if the carpenter switched from using nails to a superadhesive.

3. *Use information technology to cover up or complement the decision maker's weaknesses.* Instead of designing decision support to exaggerate the strengths of decision makers, we use systems to compensate for some of the inherent flaws in human information processing and thinking. This approach, advocated in this chapter, changes the decision-making process so that human decision makers and computer models act as partners to arrive at a better decision.

To illustrate this principle of complementarity, one important type of decision-making activity—expert forecasting— is examined. The strengths and weaknesses of expert judgment and how database models can improve predictive accuracy will be considered. Then, how even relatively simple combinations of experts and models can improve forecast accuracy will be explored.

STRONG SUITS CAN BECOME ACHILLES' HEELS

The basic premise here is that people's (and models') greatest strengths can also quickly turn into their Achilles' heels. Numerous examples come to mind. Consider sports. A right-handed power-hitter will have difficulty hitting to the opposite field in order to bring home a runner from second base. A great blitzing defense is vulnerable to the delayed draw play up the middle at the end of the game. Similarly, virtues can become deadly sins if they are taken to extremes. It has long been recognized that each of the seven deadly sins can be viewed as a virtue gone out of control. Vanity and hubris arise out of unchecked pride. Anger, properly controlled, leads to focus and commitment. An easygoing, relaxed demeanor is good for one's health, though it can degenerate into sloth. Enjoying life to the fullest can result in gluttony, strong desires can become envy, love sometimes gets confused with lust, and there may be a thin line between thrift and greed. And because this is so, it makes sense to design decision-support systems that allow decision makers to play to their strengths without overplaying them.

Similarly, too good a memory can be a problem. On the one hand, we value memory and seek to improve it. An entire cottage industry flourishes by selling audiotapes on how to sharpen memory, and an industry flourishes in external memory devices, such as DayTimers and PalmPilots, that can take the place of our faulty memories (assuming that we don't forget where we place them). On the other hand, too much memory can be a weakness. Imagine that we never forget anything: Our heads would get so filled up with unorganized and worthless detail, that thinking efficiency surely would decrease. In fact, certain psychiatric disorders are associated with highly developed eidetic (photographic) memory, in a sense, confusing the forest with the trees.

Although humans are not well-suited to the memorization of minute detail, they have great strength in finding and remembering *meaning*. But this strength can become a weakness. Years of psychological experiments show that people are very efficient in fitting incoming information into existing knowledge. (Why reinvent the wheel every time?) Jerome Bruner called it going beyond the information given, as people make inferences, fill in details, and add meaning. Generally, this results in better memory and faster decision making—a strength. The inevitable weakness here is that humans tend to see patterns and fill out pictures that may not be there. This trait results in false embellishments and distortions, and makes it difficult to distinguish real from imagined experiences. One example of the negative side of this human trait is the controversy surrounding the legitimacy of the therapist's role in helping people retrieve repressed memories of traumatic childhood events.

The strengths of models, however, such as their rigorous consistency and reliance on historical data, can also become weaknesses. In dynamic, rapidly changing decision environments, models built upon historical data may become obsolete before they can be implemented. Models are sometimes impractical because it may be too costly to build a forecasting system for many situations that are unscalable. Sometimes, incomplete data or lack of good theory impedes efforts to build an adequate model. These are some of the reasons why, in many decision-making domains, it is impossible to completely automate the forecasting process and eliminate the need for expert intervention. The expert almost always brings something worthwhile to the party. A more practical goal is to use information technology to aid, rather than replace, the expert.

Both models and experts have strengths that can become weaknesses if left unchecked. Because these strengths and weaknesses are in many ways complementary, the combination of humans and models can help decision makers avoid making poor decisions because of the excesses of both.

PATTERN MATCHING BY HUMANS AND MODELS

One example of how human experts and computer models complement each other is handwriting recognition. The human visual system has long provided a tough standard for computers to beat. To reduce labor costs, check processing companies have spent millions of dollars in research and development to automate the process of recognizing the handwritten numbers written in the box on the right (the identity of the bank and account holder is identified through the bar code at the bottom). The software has some built-in intelligence (a credit card operation knows the minimum payment and total balance due) and amazing speed. However, 20 to 30 percent of checks still require human intervention. At present, there is enough variability and imprecision in handwriting for people to interpret better than computers can. A similar situation exists with speech recognition. Although speech-recognition devices are quite accurate when the domain is constrained (such as with the digits 0 to 9), accents, cadence, and mumbling create major difficulties, which is why we still have expensive human operators at the other end of the line (if you have the patience to wait long enough).

This strength in pattern matching, demonstrated in handwriting and voice recognition, is characterized as one of the fundamental building-blocks of human cognition. For example, a primary determinant of expertise appears to be a person's deep reservoir of domain-specific knowledge, which allows experts to quickly match the pattern of the current situation to one of many archetypal situations stored in their memory. How extensively experts rely on this process is illustrated by how the performance of experts quickly falls to that of novices when the format of a problem is unfamiliar. For example, chessmasters are remarkably adept at reconstructing arrangements of chess pieces from actual games but are no better than novices with randomly arranged pieces. Chessmasters can draw upon their deep knowledge of the logic of the game, which constrains the likely location of pieces. This example highlights the difference between literal memory (like that of a computer) and memory for meaning, which is aided by prior knowledge of a domain.

Rigorous, computer-based models excel in situations in which complexity and information are more important than big-picture creative leaps. For example, computers do a great job of fingerprint identification, a domain where detail generally overcomes imprecision and humans have a hard time keeping up.

The rigor of models can also limit the overactive pattern-matching capability of human experts. Despite the well-documented success of the human perception system in detecting patterns, humans also tend to see patterns that are not, in fact, present. For example, research shows that people have difficulty distinguishing random from nonrandom patterns. When people are asked to construct random patterns (e.g., sequences of 0s and 1s), they use too many alternating (010101) sequences and underestimate the probability of runs (000111).[1] People also see local patterns (in short segments of the numbers) that are not there. For example, it is widely believed that athletes (and, maybe, stock pickers) can develop a hot-hand: At times everything they do works and at other times they cannot buy a basket. Extensive research, however, shows that most of the runs of successes (and failures) do not deviate significantly from chance.[2] Instead, people impute a systematic pattern onto the noise and impose a more-ordered view of the world than is justified by the data at hand. In statistical modeling, this is called over fitting the data. This results in a great fitting model of the past but one that generally does not predict very well moving forward.

Human experts also tend to overcategorize when they make judgments under uncertainty. People often make categorization judgments (e.g., How likely is it that object A belongs to category B?) according to how well the current situation matches the stereotype of a category stored in memory. When making judgments of this type, people should pay attention to general tendencies in the environment (called *base-rate* information) and to features of the current situation (called *case-specific* information). People, however, overemphasize case-specific information (i.e., the pattern) at the expense of base-rate information, which they often ignore completely. This tendency is partly at the root of the controversy over racial profiling done by law enforcement officials. Similar results characterize the voluminous literature on the formation and maintenance of social stereotypes.

This neglect of base-rate information may result from the human propensity for pattern matching and also from the well-known mechanism for anchoring and adjustment. Decision makers may use a pattern-matching process to classify the case-specific information into a known category. The category then serves as a judgment anchor around which the decision maker can make adjustments, depending on the similarity to the case at hand. Since adjustments away from an anchor are often insufficient, this would give greater weight to the case-specific information than to the base-rate information when the judgment is determined. The base rate and expertise examples illustrate the pervasive role of pattern matching in intuitive judgment.

Models tend to take a more rigorous approach to the historical data. Although models may not be as adept at recognizing patterns, they are more reliable at identifying where patterns *do not* exist. In many cases, they can make sense of an avalanche of data, which would overwhelm a human expert, and separate the random noise from the underlying reality of the situation more effectively than humans can.

COMPLEMENTARY STRENGTHS AND WEAKNESSES

As we see with pattern matching, there are many areas in which human experts and models are complements. Experts excel where models fail, and vice versa. Consider some of the most important ways that the two serve as complements.

Where Experts Fail and Models Excel

- Experts are subject to biases of perception and evaluation; models are unbiased though subject to specification error.
- Experts suffer from overconfidence and may be influenced by organizational politics that encourage strategic responses; models take base rates into account and are immune to social pressures for consensus.
- Experts get tired, bored, and emotional; models do not. Models can process and summarize massive databases. With modern statistical

techniques, models can identify useful empirical regularities in massive databases that are not observable to the human eye.
- Experts do not consistently integrate the evidence from one occasion to the next; models optimally weight the evidence.

Where Models Fail and Experts Excel

- Models know only what the expert tells the model builder; experts know what questions to ask and can identify new variables that should be included in the model. Whereas experts can diagnose and predict, most models can only predict. But many artificial-intelligence models, such as in the medical arena, are specifically designed to diagnose the cause of a problem.
- Experts are proficient at attribute-valuation and provide subjective evaluations of variables that are difficult to measure objectively. Models can only operate on the data provided.
- Models are consistent, but as a consequence are also rigid; experts are inconsistent but can be (too) flexible in adapting to changing conditions.
- Experts have highly organized, domain-specific knowledge. They may have superior pattern-matching skills and may be able to recognize, and then interpret, abnormal cases containing what Paul Meehl calls broken leg cues—cues that are very diagnostic but are so rare that they are difficult to anticipate and, therefore, to include in a model.[3] Models label unusual cases as outliers and work to reduce their influence.

As decision inputs, experts and models are both substitutes and complements. They are substitutes because both types of predictions take into account much of the same decision-relevant information; they also are substitutes because models derive from the experts' knowledge. At the same time, models and experts are complements, because where one decision input is weak, the other is stronger and vice versa. Previous research has usually framed the problem as expert versus model, a substitute perspective, rather than as expert/model, a complement perspective.

BENEFITS OF COMBINING MODELS AND INTUITION

Thirty years of research in psychology, economics, and statistics has shown that combined forecasts always outperform single forecasts. The reasoning behind this is as follows: Accurate forecasts by many experts tend to be highly correlated; after all they are trying to predict the same thing and are doing it very well. At the same time, however, forecast errors from these expert predictions tend to be less-correlated, except when the forecasting procedures are close to identical. Therefore, if the forecasting errors are independent of each other (random errors), they tend to cancel each other out.

The ideal situation is when forecasts have negatively correlated errors. For example, imagine two forecasters, Fred and Barney, who tend to look at the world in a similar fashion. When Fred misses on the high side, however, Barney tends to miss on the low side, and vice versa. Combining the predictions of Fred and Barney can only lead to an improved forecast. Although their forecasts are substitutes for each other, they also are complements. There have been many fancy statistical arguments about the exact combining rule to optimize combined forecasts. Virtually every systematic comparison of combining rules has shown that the exact combining rule does not really matter. In fact, a simple average works as well as, or better than, more complicated combining schemes.

Because the underlying forecasting mechanism is very different for a human than it is for a mechanical model, forecast errors are likely to be uncorrelated. Thus, a forecast developed through a combination of humans and models is likely to outperform either single forecast. The basic idea behind the combination of models and experts is to institute an appropriate division of labor. Specifically, it makes sense to let the model optimally weight the quantitative evidence contained in the database. At the same time, the experts can provide added value by exploiting their ability to spot: (a) unusual cues, (b) changing conditions, and (c) omitted evidence not amenable to inclusion in a database.

Take, for example, the classic missing data problem in model estimation. Imagine you do not have data on all the attributes for all of the cases. A model cannot be estimated on an incomplete data matrix. Either the analyst has to impute values for the missing data or eliminate cases without a complete history. Discarding observations that are missing values is equivalent to throwing away information. And although statisticians have come up with sophisticated means for filling in missing values, experts have few problems handling the incomplete data cubes that are ubiquitous in most practical forecasting situations.

The benefits of combining models and experts can be seen in a study I conducted on the forecasting decisions for six different firms.[4] Three companies (firms A, B, and C) were forecasting sales of fashion apparel through direct mail catalogs. The other three companies (firms D, E, and F) were predicting coupon redemptions for consumer-packaged goods (dry grocery items and health and beauty aids). In each case, the companies had assembled databases. As part of professionally commissioned consulting projects, our objective was to build database models that would improve forecast accuracy and potentially reduce managerial effort and costs.

Each of the fashion apparel firms sold products through direct mail catalogs. Buyers were responsible for estimating demand for an item at the stocking keeping unit (SKU) level. Predicting fashion is extremely difficult—fashions are constantly changing and buying decisions need to be made anywhere from three to six months in advance of the catalog drop, to ensure adequate inventory. There were two types of variables available for each item: (a) characteristics of the item and the manner in which it was merchandised in the catalog, and (b) consumer reaction to the item, obtained from a survey.

Product characteristics and merchandising were identified through discussions with buyers and included: percentage of the page devoted to the item, location in the catalog, department (e.g., overcoats), price and percent markup, and other variables such as the number of colors and sizes. Consumer reaction was gauged from a sample of target consumers who browsed through a catalog mock-up and answered a number of attitude questions (Is the item a good value?). Consumers also could purchase any of the items at a 10 percent discount. After all the decision variables had been set (e.g., price, location), the responsible buyer also made sales forecasts for each item, as would be done in the normal course of business.

In companies that used coupons, brand managers routinely made predictions about redemption rates for price-off coupons on frequently purchased consumer-packaged goods. Accurate forecasts were important in anticipating the total cost of the coupon promotion facing each brand and in helping to decide on the appropriateness of different promotional activities, depending on tactical goals (e.g., trial versus repeat purchase). The database included the following information about each coupon offer: coupon face value, percent discount, brand, duration of the offer, category penetration rate, and media type (newspaper insert, direct mail, in-pack, on-pack). Managers again made forecasts at the time of coupon drop, after all decision variables had been set.

The statistical models we used were of the practical kitchen-sink variety and were not driven by strong theory. Instead, the models were designed to extract as much information from the data as possible. The models were estimated using standard regression software; all models were cross-validated on holdout samples to avoid overfitting of the data. As shown in Table 5.1, the measures of predictive accuracy[5] were higher for the combination of model and expert than they were for either the model or the expert alone.

Taken singly, model and expert are reasonably accurate; each forecast method, on average, is able to explain over half of the variance in either sales or redemption rates. Sometimes the model fits better, sometimes the expert fits better. What is more interesting is the improvement obtained by using a combination of model and expert. The fourth column, labeled Model + Expert, represents a combination of the two inputs where the

Table 5.1
Comparison of Model, Expert, and Model-Expert
Combinations in Accuracy of Forecast

Company	Model Performance	Expert Performance	Model + Expert	50% Model + 50% Expert
A	.47	.30	.53	.55
B	.63	.67	.74	.75
C	.48	.57	.62	.64
D	.56	.52	.66	.65
E	.71	.74	.83	.87
F	.39	.39	.50	.52
Average	.54	.53	.65	.66

relative weights were determined empirically, based on the relative accuracy of the model and expert in predicting the estimation sample. Although these relative weights are optimal when used to predict the estimation sample, they are not necessarily optimal for the forecasting sample because relative accuracy may not stay constant over forecasting periods.

Across all six companies, the combined forecasts increase accuracy by over 20 percent, compared to the model, and 22 percent compared to the experts. In addition, the Model + Expert combination provides a 15 percent improvement in accuracy over the single best forecast (model or expert). The fifth column reports results using a simple, unweighted average. The 50-50 combination works just as well, suggesting that the exact weights do not matter as much; this has been found in previous research on combining forecasts. This improvement occurs even when the model is much more accurate than the experts (Company A) and vice versa (Company C) are.

What if the model is poorly chosen? To test the robustness of the findings, we conducted simulations to investigate whether Model + Expert combinations work even when they rely on less-sophisticated models with poorer fits. Specifically, models were degraded by systematically omitting variables, resulting in what statisticians refer to as mis-specified models (in this case mis-specified on purpose). Models containing half of the original variables obviously fit much worse than the full-blown models (average $R^2 = .34$ compared to .54 for the full models). Still, when combined with the experts' forecasts, the combination increased accuracy by 9 percent over the single best input. Even degraded models containing only one-fifth of the variables (average $R^2 = .18$) improved accuracy by over 3 percent when combined with expert judgments. Thus, even incomplete, simplistic models yielded improved results when combined with expert forecasts.

STRATEGIES FOR COMBINING MODELS AND INTUITION

Given that models and experts work better together than either alone, the next challenge is how best to combine the two. Do different combinations of experts and models work better? We saw that the weighting of models and experts did not erode the results. We also saw that the models and experts complemented one another, even when the model was poorly chosen.

But beyond the simple combination of predictions, what is the best division of labor between models and experts in practice?

As we have seen, humans and models are complementary. Experts displayed substantial intuition. They knew more than they could describe to the model builders, since by definition, intuition cannot be described. Experts displayed enough consistency so as not to overwhelm their intuition with noisy or erratic predictions. Experts also were able to recognize patterns not incorporated into the models. They also may have been able to recognize rare and unusual case-specific cues with high diagnostic value, something that statistical models are not adept at handling. Models can contribute a measure of consistency and stability to the prediction process and can place a damper on any extreme predictions made by the experts, in a way that is similar to a governor placed on the accelerator of a habitual speeder.

Experts and models need to be combined in a way that takes advantage of their complementarity. Most decision-making activity can be viewed as consisting of three interrelated stages: (1) identify the relevant attributes (e.g., total debt to assets), (2) value the level of each attribute (e.g., 2.7 to 1 ratio), and (3) integrate the individual attributes into an overall evaluation (i.e., figure out the importance of debt to assets relative to other attributes, such as revenue trend or cash flow). As shown in Table 5.2, research on the psychology of decision making repeatedly shows that experts are very good at the first two stages but are no match for even simplistic models when it comes to the third stage. Although models can have no flashes of creative insight, they also do not experience the occasional flame-out of inconsistency that can plague even the most expert of experts.

There are several different approaches to take when combining database models with intuition. The primary ones are: (a) simple, mechanical combination of models and experts, (b) expert adjustment of model predictions,

Table 5.2
Stages of Decision Making

Decision Activity	Superior Approach
Identify relevant attributes	Intuition
Value the level of each attribute	Intuition
Integrate individual attributes	Models

and (c) pattern-matching decision support tools. In each case, one of the primary goals is to exploit the experts' skill at pattern recognition without letting them overfit the data and see patterns that just are not there.

Using Decision Support Systems to Improve Judgmental Forecasting

Humans naturally rely on an anchoring and adjustment strategy when making intuitive predictions. They select a starting value and then adjust from this value to take into account additional information. This type of judgment process is ubiquitous. For example, in anticipating my wife's reaction to a new car, I may think about my own reaction and adjust from there, based upon how our tastes diverge. When predicting next year's sales, I am likely to start with last year's and make adjustments that are dependent on new information.

Anchoring and adjustment is a reasonable strategy, easy to implement, and can lead to fairly accurate predictions. Research shows, however, a systematic bias when using this strategy to make predictions. Specifically, people consistently anchor too heavily and, therefore, make insufficient adjustments; the anchor gets too much weight, the adjustments too little weight. This is not that big a problem if people choose the right anchor. For example, consider an investment decision where you have two forms of information: long-run historic returns for firms in the particular business sector, and specific information about the firm at hand. In this case, I would argue that anchoring and adjustment will work a lot better if the investor anchors on the historic returns and then insufficiently adjusts for the case-specific information rather than do what people typically do, which is anchor on the specific pattern of the firm and then insufficiently adjust for trends in the industry. Engaging in the latter strategy is likely to result in an intuitive overfitting of the data—seeing stronger, more compelling patterns than actually are there.

A decision support system (DSS) can improve the anchor choice and ultimately, the quality of the forecast. For example, consider a merchandising manager for a retailer who each week selects items to put on sale (and must make a sales forecast to have adequate inventory). The manager has a database with historical information about the sales performance of previous promotions, as shown in Table 5.3. With a DSS like this, the manager does

Table 5.3
Promotion Planner DSS

Brand	Date	Price	Feature Ad	Display	Sales Forecast
MM OJ 12 oz.	8/6	1.29	¼	Coffin	?

Historical Sales

Brand	Date	Price	Feature Ad	Display	Actual Sales
FG OJ 16 oz.	7/30	1.39	No	None	55,231
DFF OJ 12 oz.	7/23	1.29	¼	Coffin	44,888
Trop OJ 12 oz.	7/9	1.29	⅜	Coffin	22,854
MM OJ 12 oz.	7/2	0.99	⅛	Upright	98,345
CH OJ 12 oz.	6/25	1.29	¼	Coffin	35,666
DFF OJ 12 oz.	6/18	1.29	No	None	18,999
MM OJ 12 oz.	6/4	0.99	¼	Upright	73,235
Trop OJ 16 oz.	5/28	1.49	No	None	66,447
CH OJ 12 oz.	5/21	1.29	¼	Coffin	51,232
MM OJ 12 oz.	5/14	1.25	No	Upright	33,946
CH OJ 12 oz.	5/7	1.29	¼	Coffin	49,111

not have to rely on memory and can search for previous cases that are close matches to the promotion at hand (i.e., MM OJ 12 oz) and then make fine-tuned adjustments to reflect the imperfect match. In other words, the expert first pattern matches to find similar cases, anchors on that case(s), and then adjusts for differences and the inherent uncertainty in such a situation.

MODELS ARE MORE VALUABLE IN UNPREDICTABLE ENVIRONMENTS

The predictability of the environment also affects the effectiveness of human pattern matching and the combination of humans and models. The efficacy of a pattern-matching prediction strategy depends on two things: (1) How well does the historical case match the new one? Mismatches can occur because of a paucity of previous cases (a data limitation problem) or error in pattern matching (an expertise problem), and (2) How inherently predictable is the decision environment? That is, how much signal value is there in a previous case compared to the amount of random noise in the system? For example, the stock market is inherently more unpredictable than the weather. Figure 5.1 plots the theoretical relationship between environmental predictability and predictive accuracy (percent of variance explained) of a flawless pattern-matching strategy, that is, one that finds an exact matching case with no error. (i.e., the 45-degree line).

In predictable environments, human pattern matching works great, by virtue of history repeating itself. In unpredictable environments, however, it falls apart. In noisy decision environments, pure pattern matching results in predictions that are too extreme (high or low) instead of regressing toward the mean, which is normatively appropriate. Evidence suggests that people are not particularly attuned to environmental predictability and do not adjust their pattern-matching strategy and confidence level appropriately.

Models are particularly useful in more unpredictable environments. This was demonstrated by a study in which subjects were trained in the role of a loan officer and then asked to predict credit ratings under different conditions.[6] Subjects received one of four different types of decision support: (1) a control group with no decision support system, (2) a database containing historical data with realized outcomes similar to that shown in Table 5.3, (3) a forecast from a statistical model that uses three out of the four cues and explains two-thirds of the predictable variance in the outcome variable, and (4) the database plus the statistical model. An

Figure 5.1
Variance and Environmental Predictability

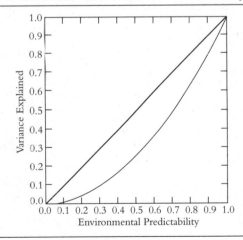

Environmental Predictability

additional key manipulation was whether the people in the study faced a predictable (80 percent signal, 20 percent noise) or unpredictable (20 percent signal, 80 percent noise) environment.

In general, subjects who were given both a database and model perform best, as summarized in Figure 5.2. (The vertical axis represents the average predictive accuracy, R^2 = percent of variance explained, of each of the groups after controlling for the underlying predictability of the two decision environments).[7] Subjects using the database and model achieve a more

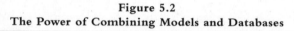

Figure 5.2
The Power of Combining Models and Databases

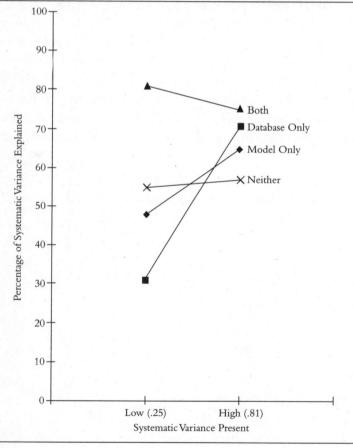

than 40 percent improvement in accuracy, compared to the control group, that had neither database or model. The model provides a measure of consistency and stability to forecasts while the database allows for more efficient pattern matching by human experts.

The decision support system clearly sharpens people's pattern-matching skills, but in unpredictable environments, sole reliance on the DSS leads to an unexpected negative impact on forecasting performance. Ironically, people would have been more accurate with no DSS at all. Why? By reducing the costs for people to pattern match, the system made it too easy for experts to find patterns that were not there. People anchored too heavily on the pattern and could not adjust for the inherent uncertainty of the environment.

Pattern matching works well in predictable environments. In less-predictable environments, this strength in human pattern-matching skills can be overused, and some decision support systems may only exacerbate the problem. Because people do not automatically adjust to the predictability of a given decision situation, decision support systems must be designed to prevent the expert from overfitting data that by its very nature, cannot be very well fit.

DATA MINING AND OTHER DEVELOPMENTS

Improvements in information technology are placing more powerful forecasting tools and more extensive information at the disposal of decision makers. For example, data-mining technology exploits high-powered computing technology to recognize recurrent patterns. One of the advantages of data miners over human pattern matching is that they offer large economies of scale, and they are thus able to process large amounts of data in short periods of time and with very low variable costs (once the software code is written and the disk storage is in place). But data mining may be susceptible to the same problems of overfitting data as human experts are. A financial-services data mining expert said, "Turning a mining tool loose in a large data set might produce more than 2,000 findings, all but 20 of them obvious, irrelevant, or flawed. . . . One tool told us income is higher for people who have big balances."[8] Because of this limitation, performance can drop precipitously when moving to a new data set. Can we reign in the data-miner's ability to pattern match as we did with the experts?

Recent work by Lee Cooper and Giovanni Giuffrida[9] illustrates a strategy for harnessing the power of data-mining, while keeping it in check, that combines it with conventional statistical models. Cooper and Giuffrida studied the challenge individual store managers have when they forecast the number of cases of products needed to meet weekly demand. This required estimation of weekly sales, of thousands of different grocery items, when the item is promoted with reduced price, in-store display, and advertising. Cooper and Giuffrida started with a proprietary, commercially available model. The model, which could be described as a standard sales-response regression model that contains close to 70 variables, performs quite well. It forecasts the exact number of cases sold, 49 percent of the time, and is within plus or minus one case 82 percent of the time.

What is unique about the Cooper and Giuffrida approach is the role they set up for the data miner. Instead of unleashing the data-mining algorithm on the raw data, they mine the residuals from the model. Residuals, very simply, are the errors that the model makes, or differences between the model's forecast and the actual sales for each item. Used in this clean-up role, the data miner is able to reduce forecast errors by an additional 9 percent, which is quite remarkable given the fine performance of the original sales-response model.

Cooper and Giuffrida create an interesting division of labor. First, they let the statistical model do the bulk of the heavy lifting. The model is consistent and methodical, but not particularly adaptive, and can only pick up the most basic and robust patterns. Cooper and Giuffrida then let the data miner loose on everything that is left over. The data miner's constrained role reduces the likelihood that it will identify idiosyncratic or ephemeral patterns that cannot be reliably reproduced in other settings. By focusing the data miner on the residuals reduces the risk that, like its human pattern-matching brethren, it will go beyond the information given.

CONCLUSIONS

Most decisions have three stages: (1) variable identification, (2) variable valuation, and (3) information integration into an overall evaluation.

Experts are good at the first two stages but are plagued by inconsistency in stage three. By outsourcing stage three to a mechanical model, the quality of decisions can be enhanced. By carefully combining human experts, statistical models, and new data-mining tools, we can improve the quality of forecasts and other decisions. Each approach has strengths that can become weaknesses if left unchecked. Recognition of these limits is part of the cure. Decision support systems should be designed to not only help experts exploit their strengths but also to compensate for their inherent information processing limitations.

As technology advances, the relative advantages and relationships between humans and models may shift. In May 1997, IBM's Deep Blue was ultimately triumphant in its ongoing battle with human chess masters—after more than half a century of contests between human chess masters and machines. While the details for the combination of models and experts may change, the principle of using the two as complements, to balance one another's strengths and weaknesses, will continue to be a powerful organizing strategy for using models and machines to make better decisions.

CHAPTER 6

REFLECTIVE VERSUS EXPEDIENT DECISION MAKING: VIEWS FROM EAST AND WEST

KAREN A. JEHN
The Wharton School

KEITH WEIGELT
The Wharton School

The fast-food, time-is-money culture of Western decision making may have something to learn from the more patient reflection of the East.

Remember that time is money.
—Benjamin Franklin

When the time is not yet ripe to act, and you are waiting on the fringes of
the situation, you will not go wrong if you remain steady and avoid giving
in to impulse.

—Lao Tzu, The Book of Changes

While Western decision making emphasizes expedience—based on the be-
lief that "time is money"—Eastern traditions emphasize the principle of
patient reflection. The authors explore how these differing perspectives af-
fect decision making and how they can be used to make better decisions.
Faster decisions have a higher probability of suboptimality, but patient de-
cision making may be inappropriate in a crisis. The authors explore the dif-
ferences in these approaches and examine when one works better than the
other and how to combine them.

In 1994, to increase customer use of a
telephone credit card NYNEX managers ran a sweepstakes. Because managers at NYNEX believed that customers may have forgotten their personal identification number (PIN), they included each customer's PIN in
a mass mailing. A simple foldover card was used to announce the sweepstakes, with the customer's PIN printed on this card. Many customers were
outraged because thieves now had the necessary information to charge
phone calls and other services to the accounts of others. When asked about
the situation, a NYNEX manager replied, "In hindsight, maybe we should
have done it differently. If we had it to do over again, we'd give it more
thought."[1] This was a case of sending in haste and repenting at leisure.

Western decision makers are often in a rush to make quick decisions.
They want to outpace competitors to be the first to market or meet their
quarterly earnings targets. As with NYNEX, this emphasis on speed can
sometimes lead to negative results. In contrast, a patient decision maker is
reflective and considers both short- and long-term payoffs.

In this chapter, we contrast the views of expedient decision makers versus patient decision makers, explore the strengths and weaknesses of each
approach, and examine how synthesizing these views provides an advantage
to top managers and other strategic decision makers.

TIME AND DECISIONS

Organization theorists and strategists often neglect time in their research, given the difficulties associated with this type of research.[2] Cross-cultural researchers as well have focused on static dimensions of cultural differences such as individualism-collectivism, face maintenance, and power distance while ignoring more dynamic concepts, such as time.[3]

Time perception is a main differentiating factor across cultures. Although time variables were largely ignored by decision theorists, recent studies show the significant impact they have on decision-making behavior.[4] Time perception affects both the decision-making process and the resultant decision. It naturally follows then that members of cultures with different time perceptions may differ in their decision-making processes and outcomes.

These differences are apparent in cross-cultural ventures. A study of American and Chinese managers found that American managers focus on making quick, immediate decisions and hold this decision-making technique in high esteem.[5] Chinese managers value a more patient, reflective form of decision making, especially when faced with an intraorganizational conflict situation. They commonly use techniques of stalling and extending the timeframe to build relationships as a way of managing critical issues.

A major failing of American managers in global companies and bicultural joint ventures is a lack of reflective decision-making techniques and a short-term outlook. A study of 115 Beijing joint venture offices, found a lack of focus on long-term issues was critical to the failures of effective operations.[6] Xerox reports a study of 552 joint ventures in which over half of the ventures fail, that patience was integral in those that succeeded.[7] In Singapore, researchers found that across multiple organizations patience and Confucian values were key success characteristics that were largely ignored by Western managers.[8] A study in Vietnam notes that patience and understanding in work styles and problem solving are crucial to the success of U.S.-Vietnamese business arrangements.[9]

DIFFERENT WORLD VIEWS

Patience and expediency are two very different approaches to decision making. At the risk of oversimplification, we characterize the former as Eastern and the latter as Western. While we use these terms as a kind of shorthand

Table 6.1
Approaches to Decision Making

Eastern Reflective Approach	Western Expedient Approach
Reflective	Expedient
Long-term (balanced vision)	Short-term (myopic)
Calm mind	Emotional

for these different perspectives, neither side of the world has a monopoly on one or the other approach. Rather than cultural generalizations, these are two distinct approaches to decision making. The Western view of decision making considers speed a virtue. Benjamin Franklin's advice to a young tradesman that "time is money," the frequent admonitions that "time is of the essence," or the rush to be "first to market," or gain a "first-move advantage," all reflect this perspective. On the other hand, Eastern philosophers view patient reflection as a virtue in decision making.

The two approaches differ along a number of dimensions (Table 6.1). The Eastern approach is reflective, taking time to consider carefully, while the Western approach focuses on deciding and acting quickly. Because the Eastern approach stresses reflective thinking, it is more focused on the long-term relative to Western thinking. The Eastern approach focuses on acting from a calm mind, while the West, moving quickly, often acts more from emotion. The Western decision process is systematic and linear while the Eastern decision process may make greater holistic leaps in nonlinear ways.

THE WESTERN APPROACH TO TIME: EXPEDIENT DECISION MAKING

For over a decade, the popular press and practitioner-oriented journals in the United States and Britain have sung the praises of patience and correct timing in both profit and nonprofit business.[10] Strategy theorists also have listed patience as a virtue[11] while marketing researchers have examined the benefit of waiting.[12] In addition, quality control and financial consultants suggest patience as a key to successful investing and operating.[13]

Many managers, however, are not taking the advice. In fact, expedient decision making appears to be highly valued by Western managers.[14] Western managers prize high-speed decision making[15] often based on an inability to handle delays constructively.[16] This Western tendency toward delay aversion, or impulsivity, was discussed years ago by personality psychologists[17] and more recently in work on hyperbolic time-discounting functions.[18] Western social cognition theorists suggest that individuals' need for closure is a motivator of impatience.[19] In addition, a low tolerance for ambiguity will lead managers to quickly assess their environment with a possibly irrational desire to take immediate action.

Strengths and Weaknesses of the Western Approach

The greatest strength of the expedient approach is that it gets the job done. This approach avoids the delays and indecision that can lead to missed opportunities. It counteracts the inertia often found in large organizations. This approach is extremely effective in dealing with crisis situations such as emergencies. The emotion and adrenaline rush of rapid decisions can focus the mind (although it can just as easily lead to hasty and ill-formed decisions). In an Internet era of increasingly rapid cycle times, narrower windows of opportunity, and winner-take-all markets, there is an argument for moving more and more rapidly. In some markets, at least, one must arrive first or not at all.

Haste Makes Waste

At the same time, however, expedient decision making has inherent weaknesses. It is not beneficial to arrive first with the wrong product, as Apple Computer learned painfully with the launch of its Newton PDA. The expedient approach has a variety of weaknesses, including:

- *Haste.* An emphasis toward expedience tends to lead to hastily made and ill-formed decisions. Think of John Sculley's decision to leave Apple for Spectrum Information. Four months later, he quit Spectrum embroiled in a scandal involving fraud. After the smoke cleared, he admitted he had not really taken the time to research the company or its officers. Fast decisions have a higher probability of suboptimality—they lack a long-term perspective and assessments of resources, decision paths, and consequences are generally inferior.

- *Myopia.* The immediate focus of expedient decision making also can lead to the related problem of myopia, which is a barrier to effective decision making. The managers at NYNEX certainly appeared myopic in focusing so much on short-term marketing concerns that they were not able to see the implications for customer privacy and security. Their plan to include PINs in the mass mailings probably did increase the use of the phone credit cards, but they did not consider the longer term consequences of thieves getting hold of the numbers and then charging services to unsuspecting customers. Another example is the decision by executives at NBC to broadcast the 1992 Olympic Games on pay-per-view channels. They did marketing studies and found that under 3 percent of their sample would definitely pay for the right to see events. They wanted to make their figures look better so they combined the 3 percent with those that said maybe they would pay to watch events and came up with more respectable numbers. Unfortunately, most respondents who said "maybe" opted out and did not purchase the service. NBC lost millions on the venture.

- *Excessive emotion.* As discussed by Luce, Payne, and Bettman in Chapter 2, emotions can sometimes focus the mind but also can lead to unproductive coping strategies such as avoidance. The focus on expedience in the West increases stress; even if emotions help some decision makers to focus, better results do not necessarily follow. In Western psychology, stress is viewed as having an inverted-J curve suggesting benefits of focus and direction to a limited amount of arousal (i.e., emotion or affect). In work with Division I basketball players on decision-making skills, we noticed that when players got emotional (usually angry) their focus did improve. However, when we looked at the statistics, overall performance did not improve. So while emotions may have helped them get more focused, it also distracted them from the task at hand.

EASTERN APPROACH TO TIME: REFLECTIVE DECISION MAKING

Eastern philosophy values reflection.[20] It considers gestalt or a holistic view. Reflection is a value that is representative in Eastern cultures and noted in

Eastern philosophies such as Taoism or Buddhism.[21] Four ancient works, Sun Tzu's *The Art of War,* Miyamoto Musashi's *The Book of the Five Rings,* Lo Kuan-chung's *The Three Kingdoms,* and Gao Yuan's *The Thirty-six Stratagems,* are cited as works used by businesspeople in Japan, Korea, Hong Kong, and Taiwan.[22] One major shortcoming of Western executives in their dealings with Asian executives is that they do not understand the strategic use of patience.

The philosophy of Japan's Samurai ethic, Bushido, also provides advice for business.[23] Bushido stresses patience, frugality, and constant self-improvement. It requires the individual to reflect and act on the whole situation, rather than to analyze individual components. An example of this holistic philosophy in the workplace is Just-in-Time (JIT) business practices such as inventory management in which companies look beyond their own plants to manage the whole system.[24]

The Eastern approach or patient decision making is calmer, more detached and holistic, nonlinear, with a long-term focus. Blount and Janicik define patient behavior as "the act of calmly adapting one's intrinsic temporal preferences and/or expectations to unwanted delays presented by the external, social environment."[25] It is a calm approach to time-pressured issues incorporating reflection and relaxed demeanor. This reflective approach requires that intuition becomes an equal partner with logic. Hence, it requires decision makers to use what has been termed *whole brain thinking.* Physically, most individuals have a dominant hand they use in physical tasks. It is not that they cannot use the other hand, they simply never practice with it. Mentally, most follow the same pattern—they rely on a dominant side of the brain. It is difficult for one to be reflective if only one side of the brain is used since intuition requires more spatial thinking relative to logic.

Strengths and Weaknesses of Patient Decision Making

To the ancient Chinese, reflection was closely linked to knowledge. Because the Chinese believe all things are interdependent, knowledge was the ability to trace out the connections between things. Once this was accomplished, the decision maker would know what actions to take today to reap the benefits of the future. This idea was summarized in a saying, "To know after seeing is not worthy of being called knowing."[26]

Reflection is a two-part process: You must first visualize all possible future states, and then choose actions that will enable the decision maker to attain the desired outcome. The process is difficult (and time consuming) because it requires the ability to visualize the big picture (all possible outcomes) and understand the underlying casual model (choose actions today that will enable one to reach the desired outcome in the future).

If done correctly, a reflective decision maker then has no doubts about the decision outcome. She knows what actions to take given the situation and acts accordingly. There is no doubt or waver. As Sun Tzu writes in his military classic, *The Art of War*,[27] "The victorious army only enters battle after having first won the victory, while the defeated army only seeks victory after having first entered the fray."

Nonreflective decision makers are strategically disadvantaged because they can be surprised. A surprised decision maker is one who has not considered the situation now faced. For if he did consider it, he would know what to do, and would not be surprised. Facing the unexpected puts one at a strategic disadvantage since now he must "think on the fly" and decide what actions to take. Reflective decision making is nearly impossible in such a situation.

Balanced Vision

Backward induction also helps decision makers be more patient because it counters the tendency to be myopic. By definition, myopic decision makers have high discount rates (e.g., would prefer $10 today rather than $30 in a month). Backward induction counters this tendency because it forces decision makers to extend their outlook.

Myopia is caused by many factors; we focus on two: (1) emotions and (2) crisis situations. Emotions come in many different forms and degrees: anger, joy, fear, panic. Emotions are often felt in the workplace and interfere with cognitive decision making and focus.[28] Both positive emotions (joy, elation, surprise) and negative emotions (fear, sadness) cause decision makers to lose focus on the work task at hand. In addition, if the emotion is negative, employees will tend to shift their focus from work to relieving the negative emotion. Thus we associate myopia with emotion-laden decisions. People want to resolve the problem/make the decision as soon as possible to relieve themselves of the discomfort they feel from the effect. This can lead to hasty, suboptimal decisions.

Crisis situations also cause myopia. When the decision maker feels pressure to resolve a crisis situation, he will make a decision focusing on the short-term problem. This focus on the immediate crisis situation often precludes decision makers from considering alternatives and long-term repercussions. For example, in work at NASA mission control we found that flight directors managing control crews in crisis situations often make ineffective, dictatorial decisions based on past experience with dissimilar events.[29]

A decision maker who is both reflective and nonmyopic never puts himself in a crisis situation. Using their reflective thinking, they plan for the difficult while the difficult is still easy. Being nonmyopic they use their everyday normal mind and remain calm. In his book, *The Book of Five Rings,* Miyamoto Musashi states this principle in relation to sword fighting (certainly a crisis situation for most of us):

> In the science of martial arts, the state of mind should remain the same as normal. In ordinary circumstances as well as when practicing martial arts, let there be no change at all—with the mind open and direct, neither tense nor lax, centering the mind so that there is no imbalance, calmly relax your mind . . .[30]

Being reflective also helps the decision maker in the following areas:

- *Avoiding overconfidence.* Patient decision makers are more likely than expedient decision makers to look for disconfirming evidence. This makes them more likely to identify both strengths and weaknesses of a position accurately. The inability to see weaknesses leads to an overconfidence bias in decisions. The more time and attention that is given to studying a given issue, the more likely it will be that initial overconfidence will be deflated in the process. Also, reflective thinkers are more likely to seek out weaknesses in their strategies.
- *Weighing long-term payoffs.* Patient decision makers are more likely to think through all possible contingencies and devote resources to strategies that have higher payoffs in the long term. For example,

successful Asian managers tend to look to the future and build long-term relationships.[31] They are willing to sacrifice short-term results for higher long-term payoffs. Also, patient decision makers are able to understand and anticipate the longer term implications of actions. For example, Warren Buffett has earned himself an unique place in the business world through his patience and ability to anticipate outcomes in the long term.

- *Detachment.* Being able to detach yourself from emotions in making decisions is a characteristic of the patient decision maker. Emotions tend to make decision makers more myopic, they focus almost wholly on the short term. Think of the last time you became angry or you sought revenge. When angry we sometimes realize the actions we are about to take are detrimental in the long term, but we are so emotionally upset, we can only focus on the present. Sun Tzu, in *The Art of War* discusses weaknesses in generals that can be exploited. These weaknesses are emotional in nature (e.g., anger, love, honor, fear). Many of us, for example, have sent e-mails we later regretted sending because we did not wait for our emotions to subside. The Chinese have a saying that words that have left the mouth cannot be returned. An emotional mind cannot be calm, hence actions we take when emotional result in suboptimal performance.

Also, some research does attach positive aspects to emotions and decision making. Research on interpersonal interaction and decision making shows that people use emotions to signal importance, commitment to an idea, and certainty around the viewpoint they espouse.[32] In addition, the contagion of positive emotions increases effort and cooperation among decision makers.[33]

Like all things, reflective decision making does have its weaknesses. Perhaps the greatest weaknesses of reflective decision making is that it takes time. In an Internet age this is often unacceptable. It also can lead to paralysis by analysis. Flight directors and managers in high-reliability organizations with fast-changing environments must react quickly to identify and resolve potentially disastrous events. The speed to resolution is critical and thus NASA is working to implement patient, reflective decision making in a timely manner by using multiple system interfaces, redundancy of systems, and forethought.

GLOBAL PERSPECTIVE: COMBINING THE BEST OF EAST AND WEST

How can you combine expedient and patient decision making? For managers, having these two options available offers another way of solving problems—a more effective approach. The key challenge for American managers is to overcome cultural biases and integrate the two approaches relative to the problem.

We encourage reflective, patient decision making in key organizational decision makers, though we recognize that environmental conditions dictate quick, yet strategic decisions. One example of this trend is our emerging, global, networked economy. As is true for most factors, patience in decision making has both advantages and disadvantages. Using the recommendations that follow, we believe that patient, reflective decision making, if practiced diligently and carefully, can be done quickly.

Can reflective decision making be taught? Yes, we believe managers can learn to do this. To begin to take a more reflective approach:

- *Look for disconfirming evidence.* Most individuals do not look for disconfirming information, or if they do, they discount it (see our example of NBC and the Olympic Games). It is difficult for most of us to admit our weaknesses. Several authors offer advice on overcoming this reluctance.[34] This advice includes getting second and third opinions or holding individuals accountable for their decisions.
- *Install multiple systems.* When managers feel time pressure they tend to act impulsively and often with error. At NASA, they attempt reflective decision making in time-pressured situations by having multiple monitoring systems of critical components of the system.[35] Organizational managers can do the same by having multiple systems and decision makers (such as other managers, line workers, vice presidents) in tune to critical pressure points in the environment and within the organization.
- *Direct energy and focus.* To create a calm mind and overcome the negative aspects of emotions involved in decision making, we recommend that managers constantly monitor their own behavior to redirect energy and focus. In our work with basketball players, the most difficult task they face is maintaining the normal state of mind.

We find the same is true with students. Many do poorly on tests simply because they become emotional (usually fear or anxiety). Maintaining a normal state of mind requires constant practice. As Musashi states in *The Book of Five Rings,* "This is something that requires thorough examination, with a thousand days of practice for training and ten thousand days of practice for refinement." (p. 32)

Thanks to the Internet, instant contact with worldwide colleagues is now as easy as a few keystrokes. As cross-cultural interaction becomes easier, perhaps cross-cultural solutions to strategic and everyday business challenges can also become easier. The potential for this type of combination of East and West is suggested by a set of haiku error messages that have been proposed to replace the frustratingly vague error messages from Microsoft. They would transform the cryptic and expedient messages of a Western corporation into the more patient reflections of the East, such as:

Stay the patient course.
Of little worth is your ire.
The network is down.

If these messages do not inspire true patience in the frustrated user, they may at least help to soften the wait with humor.

CHAPTER 7

DECISION MAKING IN COMPLEX ENVIRONMENTS: NEW TOOLS FOR A NEW AGE

PAUL R. KLEINDORFER
The Wharton School

A man surveys the damage of a Buddhist temple after the Kobe earthquake in January 1995. Not only insurers were shaken up by this disaster, but also the whole process of decision making for insuring catastrophic events.

Be prepared!
                    —*Motto of the Boy Scouts of America*

Good decision making has often been described as following an orderly and logical process from framing a problem, assembling alternatives, evaluating them, and choosing the best one to implement. The turbulent environment of the e-Economy has made this model of choice infeasible. Compressed decision time and complexity are swamping the orderly flow of information and authority, characteristic of traditional decision making. Managers are turning to new approaches, emphasizing options thinking and managerial flexibility. Using examples from the restructuring of the electric utilities industry and the insurance industry in its new approaches to catastrophic risks,[1] the author explores some of the challenges of making decisions in environments of high speed and complexity. The "silicon lining" to this storm cloud is that information technology, which has contributed greatly to this complexity, can be used to mitigate it. The author explores new approaches such as data mining and large-scale simulation models that companies and markets are developing to help navigate the complex, data-rich environments of the new economy.

The United States and Europe have undertaken a radical restructuring of the electric power sector, reflecting the worldwide trend to replace regulation in all network industries with competition. The changes have been facilitated by new technologies in generation, power systems control, demand-side management, and information systems. They also have been propelled by new actors (brokers, financial intermediaries, and risk managers) and by huge sources of new real-time accessible data on energy prices, on the weather, and on scores of other elements that affect the demand and supply of electric power. As a consequence, the old supply-driven electric power industry is giving way to a more vital, customer-oriented, demand-driven industry.

With the change, however, come great uncertainties as to what regulators, customers, and competitors will do. While these are hardly different than the challenges confronting many other industries, they represent a sea change for incumbent firms and prospective entrants to the electricity market.

For an existing utility, the complexities are gripping. They represent critical choices about the organizational structure to be adopted, technology bets to place, new forms of risk management and trading to be mastered, and a host of other strategic options not previously faced and for which no blueprint exists. How can senior management of such a utility evaluate and choose among these very different, competing opportunities and strategies?

SEISMIC SHIFTS

Similarly, the insurance industry faces complex challenges in addressing catastrophic risks. The significant increases in the risk of natural disasters in the United States have strained private insurance markets and created troublesome problems for disaster-prone areas. The threat of mega-catastrophes resulting from intense hurricanes or earthquakes striking major population centers has dramatically altered the insurance environment. Estimates of probable maximum losses (PML) to insurers from a mega-catastrophe in the United States range from $50 to $115 billion depending on the location and intensity of the event, with even more frightening numbers for several other countries presaged by losses in excess of $100 billion in the Kobe earthquake in 1995 (only a small fraction of which were actually covered by insurance at the time). Using current approaches, many insurers would become insolvent or financially impaired if a mega-catastrophe occurred, with rippling effects throughout insurance markets and the economy. How can insurers better address these complex challenges?

Consider the strategies of an insurer writing business in a catastrophe-prone area. Such an insurer must consider:

1. The structure and geographic concentration of its risk portfolios
2. Contract design of its policies, including bundling of perils and cross-marketing of insurance products
3. The purchase of reinsurance and use of capital market instruments to hedge catastrophe risk
4. The pricing of its catastrophic-risk insurance.

Of special interest is how these strategies are affected by the trade-off between the efficiencies gained from geographic concentration and the higher risk of a catastrophic loss due to concentrated exposures.

In a market with strong competition, multiple sources of new capital to finance its operations, and unpredictable state regulation of insurers, how should the senior management team at such an insurance company evaluate the consequences of different portfolios? How should they gauge their exposure to catastrophic losses? What marketing and financial strategies can they use for reducing the chances of a large loss while still building a profitable business? How should they assess the interactions of the catastrophe line with other (typically more profitable) lines of business that could be compromised if financial distress is caused by the catastrophe insurance line?

DECISIONS UNDER COMPLEXITY

These examples illustrate some of the fundamental challenges presented by decision complexity. In electric power, this complexity is being driven by changes in the regulatory and market structure of the industry. In insurance, the previous structure came to be viewed as unsustainable in the 1990s following Hurricane Andrew and the Northridge and Kobe earthquakes.

In both cases, new developments in modeling and information technology were fundamental contributors to the change. For example, in catastrophe insurance, new developments in risk assessment modeling and information technology allowed insurers and reinsurers for the first time to assess in great detail the likely profit and loss consequences of their portfolio of insured properties. In electricity supply, detailed economic and power flow models helped to legitimate the existence and magnitude of benefits that might result from introducing market forces into a very conservative industry.

These examples are by no means isolated. The environment of business has become a maze of information and Internet-driven change. This change is intertwined with the globalization of economic activity, the attendant growth in the size of companies and markets, the increasing importance of knowledge-intensive processes in business activities, and the natural evolution of systemic stress on organizations facing increased competition resulting from these forces.[2] One result of these changes is a significant increase in the complexity of business decision making. How do managers make decisions in this new environment?

NEW APPROACHES TO DECISIONS

Let us consider electric power trading as an example that illustrates the consequences of this increased complexity on decision making in business organizations. Trading has been a central feature of electric power supply for decades. Buying bulk power from a neighboring utility and arranging for its transmission to a local utility's franchise area has been a major source of capacity saving and interregional power system reliability. In the good old days of yore, such trading was known as bulk power contracting, and the resulting contracts often covered a period of years. Decisions regarding these contracts also followed the standard model of decision making:[3] Key decision makers carefully assessed their status and their needs for additional bulk power; alternative sources of power were listed and evaluated as to cost, reliability and timing, often using sophisticated optimization models; a decision was made and implemented.

Contrast this orderly, traditional decision process with the current situation in bulk power trading. In the new world, ushered in first in natural gas and then spilling over quickly into electric power, the trading arm of the local utility has typically been spun off as a separate profit-making subsidiary, only one of whose customers is the local distribution utility. Traders now make hundreds of trades a week, balancing supply and demand constraints in the short run and helping the market to coordinate costs, prices and physical demands and supplies.

In this world, decision making about a particular contract does not take months and it doesn't follow a uniform or consistent process. The information on the value drivers of contracts must be available and ready for use by traders minute by minute. In the new model, the focus has shifted from making an optimal decision for an isolated contract to providing an infrastructure that will support an on-going set of decisions on bulk-power contracting as a business. The new contracts don't have durations of years, but of days or even hours.

Fueled by the profitability of successful market participants such as ENRON, the new model has transformed bulk power trading across the globe. It has done so because modern information technology has allowed the development of an information and decision infrastructure that provides for a much closer coordination of supply, demand, and customer value than was previously possible. The efficiency gains have been significant.[4]

A Flexible, Two-Stage Process

This example illustrates the essence of the new decision-making paradigms emerging in complex environments. In the new approaches, decision making is viewed as a rolling two-stage process: The first stage focuses on enhancing knowledge of the environment, response flexibility, and the value of future options. The second stage is concerned with cashing in on those options that are in the money. The essential characteristic of the new approach is the interconnectivity of the different forms of available data and access to this data on a just-in-time basis by decision makers. This interconnectivity is built upon new tools (such as data mining, neural networks, artificial agents, and genetic algorithms, discussed further later) to make sense of the huge amount of data available to support decision making.[5]

While some adherents of the standard theory of multi-period decision making would claim that these new approaches, emphasizing information, interconnectivity, and flexibility, are old hat as far as normative theory is concerned, the nature of managerial decision making in practice is nonetheless of a fundamentally different character now than even a decade ago. In environments that are sufficiently complex or undergoing rapid change, refining decision models is less important than being able to assure oneself that tomorrow will bring a full plate of interesting choices, and that these can be evaluated at the moment of choice in a prudent manner.

TOOLS FOR NAVIGATING IN COMPLEX ENVIRONMENTS

As the power trading example suggests, there are a variety of new tools and approaches for managers to use to master environmental complexity. A few of the challenges presented by complexity and the tools that can be used to address them are discussed next.

Navigating Data-Rich Environments

The flood of data resulting from advances in IT and e-business has transformed managers and policy makers into researchers, whether they like it or not. Managers are using tools such as data mining and data warehousing to harness this avalanche of data in their business decisions. Divining trends from weak signals in huge databases and making sense of them to understand consumer behavior, internal costs, and supplier performance have come center stage in the past decade. If the information is there and there is something of value in it, you must understand it before your rivals do.[6]

In the insurance industry, companies increasingly are using data mining and data warehousing to understand characteristics that make loyal customers. For example, in automobile insurance, this approach has led to important new ways of detecting and mitigating fraudulent claims. Inspectors comb through claims data to identify commonalities relating to plaintiffs, plaintiff attorneys, types of accidents and injuries claimed, treatment types, and expenses, and so forth. Any patterns in this data can be used to begin the process of focused detective work. Using traditional statistical techniques to undertake this task would be more difficult. The sheer volume and complexity of the data creates challenges in getting it into a standard format for analysis, determining the right variables to model, and testing for interactions across variables. The new data mining techniques, combined with various artificial agent approaches, have proven valuable allies to insurers in their fight against fraud.

Doing Something about the Weather.   Similarly, a key uncertainty in the electric power industry is the weather, which above all else affects the demand for power and the costs of supplying it. Companies that can better anticipate these demands and costs will have an advantage, but this is an extraordinarily complex challenge. Distribution companies, traders, and financial intermediaries have developed sophisticated means to track weather to help predict demand and supply conditions. Managers might use a pattern-matching algorithm based on neural nets or genetic algorithms[7] to identify a set of days and weather conditions from the past five years that look similar to the weather pattern expected a week to a day in advance. By studying the demands of different customer segments on one or more of these "similar days" and adjusting for changing price effects, a very accurate picture emerges as to who will be demanding energy during which periods. This, in turn, indicates what supply-side contracts need to be set up to meet this demand profitably. These tools allow decision makers not only to anticipate the weather, but also to do something about it in planning their supply portfolio.[8]

These new models allow for quite a bit of flexibility. Responsible managers can include judgmental factors, for example, as adjustment factors.[9] Adjustment factors can be new data on local economic conditions, a plant closing, or just mere hunches—anything the manager believes might affect the smoothed history-based prediction of demand to fit the conditions likely to actually occur. Traditional demand-forecasting models have no way of screening and incorporating the huge volume of data on historical levels of demands and weather conditions, let alone providing understandable and validated results. That is the power of the new data analysis techniques.

Navigating Systemic Complexity

Data is not the only factor driving complexity. Further complexity is created by interactions across multiple system boundaries surrounding a particular decision context. There are nested, or systems consequences, to decisions. In former times, these system interactions were simply ignored, but as businesses (and decisions) have come to depend more upon networks, these interactions can no longer be ignored.[10] Increasingly, managers are attempting to capture these interactions through computer models. These models build on three important pillars: data, the model itself, and some means of optimizing or evaluating alternative decisions in the context of the model.

For all three pillars, the sheer growth in computing power and the ability to connect and execute locally validated models and data worldwide via the Internet have increased the sophistication of such modeling efforts. A popular example is Enterprise Resource Planning (ERP) and associated optimization software for supply chain management. Such models provide an integrated computer representation of a company's sales, production, logistics, equipment uptime and maintenance, and associated financial and accounting information. This integrated representation can be used to track sales orders, to make and optimize production and delivery commitments, and generally to be the backbone infrastructure for operations of a company. These are truly monumental modeling efforts that dwarf in their scope anything previously seen in the management of enterprises.[11]

Suppose an insurer or reinsurer wants to assess its expected profitability from its catastrophe line of business, or the probability that losses in its catastrophe line in any given year would exceed its allocated financial resources. Traditionally, managers would use actuarial science to answer these questions. However, even though this approach gave reasonable answers to pricing questions for individual properties and groups of similar properties, it often missed systemwide effects of catastrophe risks since these are the results of complex and correlated interactions.

Large-Scale Simulation Models.   In the 1990s, insurers developed newer and more refined approaches based on large-scale simulation models. Consider the case of earthquake modeling.[12] For a given region subject to seismic risk (for example, California), the magnitude and location of possible earthquakes in the region would first be specified. This might give rise to a list of, say, 10,000 representative events that could occur in a given year. The consequences of each event can be simulated for each group of properties insured by a specific insurer. To do so requires knowledge of the hydrology, topology, and surface geology of the region in question, together with propagation equations for earthquakes of different types and detailed models of expected damage to each type of structure, given the intensity of shaking in the vicinity of the structure.

Imagine now a model incorporating all of these features and with sufficient data on the underlying geology of the region and the precise location of every property to allow an assessment for each of the 10,000 events, and for each structure in the insurer's book of business. Weighting the probabilistic outcomes of these assessments by the recurrence probability of each of the events leads, after a great deal of computation, to the probability distribution of annual losses that can be expected. Combining this with premium and financial information allows the insurer to obtain a very detailed picture of the risks it faces from various segments of its insured population.

Such models allow, for the first time, a detailed assessment of the impact of underwriting policies (e.g., increasing or decreasing deductible levels for catastrophe risks) and the costs and benefits of reinsurance and other risk transfer mechanisms. Piecemeal actuarial approaches do not provide anywhere near the precision of catastrophe simulation models. The resulting improvements in the quality of information for understanding, pricing, and controlling such risks have virtually transformed the insurance market for catastrophe risks in the 1990s. These models are now routinely used by such diverse parties as insurers, reinsurers, capital market investors, government agencies, and regional and local emergency response agencies. Catastrophe models have become, in effect, a credible representation of the very complex and nested reality of the economic effects of natural disasters. Coupled with updated global weather models (as discussed earlier), these models also provide the means for assessing in real time the likely economic and business impacts of particular events (e.g., a large hurricane about to make landfall on the East Coast) in aggregate or on a particular insurer.

The electric utilities industry is also developing new approaches to address systemic complexity. Companies in the industry have established electronic bulletin boards for posting supply and demand information between large demand points on the grid (e.g., industrial customers and local distribution companies) and generators. This information is used for contracting among participants in the wholesale market as well as for determining spot market prices based on the normal logic of supply and demand.

Suppose that a generator or transmission provider in this market is attempting to determine the return on an investment in new generation or transmission capacity. Traditionally, this type of decision would have involved a standard investment analysis, using available information on costs and expected asset utilization and revenues. Both costs and revenues typically would be assessed under fairly aggregate conditions and under several scenarios, but using rather simple spreadsheet modeling. These simple methods often missed key factors, such as nonobvious transmission constraints, that would affect costs and revenues.

Optimizing Power Pools.   In the 1990s, new modeling methods were introduced to simulate the operation of the electric generation pool under various scenarios of demand and competitive entry. These models require an analysis of demand in various regional markets connected to the pool and the logic for dispatching electricity in the pool. Since transmission constraints play an important role in determining such dispatch, these too must be faithfully modeled. Coupled with the availability of evolving historical data (lots of it!) on suppliers and wholesale customers, the result of such modeling has been an order-of-magnitude increase in the ability of managers to assess the profit impact of their investment and trading strategies under alternative institutional and regulatory rules and competitive strategies.[13] Without these new modeling methods, such an assessment would be considerably more uncertain.

In general, these advanced simulation and optimization models reflect the complex, systemic interactions among different parts of the system. Decision makers can simulate outcomes under different scenarios and explore the rich interactions among different parts of the system. Artificial agents can explore, on behalf of the decision maker, literally billions of alternative strategies.[14] Just as in the famous victory of IBM's Deep Blue chess-playing program over the reigning world chessmaster Garry Kasparov in 1997, this sheer computing power can lead to improved understanding of both good and bad strategies, provided the model that is being optimized is a reasonable representation of reality.

There are always limitations in the time and resources that can be devoted to such activities, which means that even with complete information (which is never possible) there is a limit to the precision of this modeling. For this reason, judgment and accountability will always be the realm of the decision maker. Still, this approach can support a more informed assessment of systems in which there are complex interactions. It also can allow significant improvements in communications among multiple parties attempting to negotiate a joint strategy or investment that will be affected by such a system.

Navigating Multistakeholder and Environmental Complexity

In addition to data and systemic complexity, a third major source of complexity results from the interactions of multiple stakeholders, including competitors, regulators, and public interest groups. These mutual dependencies and the necessity for agreed-upon rules have been described as "co-opetition" (cooperation combined with competition).[15] For example, in electric power, it would be impossible to design equipment or operate the power system without standards on frequency and voltage levels. Such standards, once established, allow generating companies to compete without destabilizing the system. In insurance, professional associations, such as those governing actuaries and accountants, establish standards that allow continuing developments of the science underlying insurance, and without which insurance professionals would not have a working vocabulary. Beyond these foundations, however, the increasing complexity of markets requires considerably more cooperation to provide the basis for market competition.

We see this clearly in the developing rules for business networking and e-commerce.[16] These markets demand a significant degree of standardization (on interface protocols, on privacy, on computer languages) to deliver improved efficiency in coordinating supply and demand. Cooperation in establishing these standards is required before the competitive games can begin. In many sectors, public interest groups and regulation have made nonmarket forces a critical determinant of market success by insisting that enterprises need not only an *economic franchise* to operate, but also a continuing *social franchise*. The latter is only assured if the enterprise operates within certain standards of expected conduct.

What these standards are depends on the outcome of an ongoing, complex social process between industry, the public and public surrogates such as regulators and lawmakers. For companies doing business internationally, the problems of predicting and evaluating actions of such public stakeholders, as well as the actions of other global competitors, increase exponentially. Coping with such environmental complexity has triggered new approaches to decision making, just as with data and systemic complexity. These new approaches range from cross-industry working groups and technical committees to scenario planning and experimental economics.

Listening to Stakeholders.   In insurance, a critical issue in the area of catastrophe protection has been the interaction of consumer groups and the insurance industry. Historically, consumers have had little trust in the integrity and fairness of some policies of the insurance industry, especially in the catastrophe lines, where pricing and underwriting policies for hurricane and earthquake risks have been very controversial. To understand, monitor, and perhaps influence consumer and regulatory opinions on appropriate public policies toward catastrophic risks, insurers and reinsurers now invest heavily in listening to consumers and nongovernmental organizations, mapping their views and participating in groups intended to influence the course of public policy.

The traditional approach to laws and regulations has been called by some the "Decide, Announce, Defend" approach, in which companies unilaterally determine their perspectives, announce them, and defend them against all parties, public and private. The new approach considers the multiple stakeholders in insurance markets as having legitimate alternative points of view that must be understood, tracked and perhaps influenced, but which cannot be completely controlled.

The key is to link this external stakeholder mapping process to company strategy. When this multiparty approach is coupled with detailed knowledge of historical trends and outcomes, provided by the types of data and systems modeling described earlier, a company can integrate and communicate its market and investment strategies to all affected stakeholders in a responsible manner. For example, the electric power industry is using technical committees from all its varied stakeholders to set standards for pool operations, market structure, transmission planning, regulatory reviews, and other key elements. This integration is a natural consequence of the fact that sudden changes in the institutions governing electric power transactions could lead to catastrophic failure. But it also reflects the attempts of market participants to reduce the transaction costs of change and to gain an understanding of how other stakeholders are likely to react.

Behavioral Approaches.   In addition to such consensus-building activities, evaluation of multistakeholder interactions in competitive strategy also are being supported by new behavioral approaches. These include the use of role playing, together with long-range simulation models of the type described earlier, to determine who will be the winners and losers under various scenarios and to evaluate alternative competitive and regulatory strategies. Such strategic gaming is similar to war games in the military, but is now backed up by sophisticated simulation tools to evaluate the outcomes of actions. A typical strategic simulation game would take participants through ten years of choices, with the consequences of decisions evaluated on a yearly basis by an appropriate simulation vehicle.[17] A more formal approach to evaluating such strategic gaming is the use of experimental economics. For example, controlled experiments have been used to investigate the likely performance of alternative approaches to structuring auctions and pool rules for electric power.[18] The point of these experimental approaches is that often theoretical predictions about the performance of institutions like auctions do not hold up when actually implemented. For example, sealed bid auctions (in which bidders submit sealed bids for an object and the highest such bid wins) have some nice properties in theory. They are often avoided in practice, however, because of the appearance of manipulability, buyer remorse, and other subjective and qualitative issues. If there are any such problems, people will avoid the auction in question. Thus, when setting up an Internet-based auction or selling platform for, say, reinsurance contracts or for bulk power sales, issues of perceived fairness, transparency, and understandability of auction rules are at least as important as efficiency properties of the auction procedures used. The result is that experimental approaches and extended prototyping of such systems are prudent investments, and often this requires a realistic simulated environment to mimic the real phenomenon of interest during the development phase of such systems.

Behavioral approaches such as experimentation and role playing recognize the complexity of the environmental interactions between different participants and the great difficulty of capturing these in credible analytic models. When integrated with the data and systemic approaches described earlier, managers can integrate the complexity of complex data sets with the equally complex factors of human behavior. This allows them to create a significantly richer understanding of the environments in which they must compete.

NEW APPROACHES TO DECISION-MAKING STRATEGY

The new tools and approaches discussed are leading to a model of decision making focused on options and flexibility rather than on the precise evaluation of choice alternatives. In essence, the decision maker is preparing to make correct choices in the future rather than on nailing down the decision in advance.

There are three basic ingredients to this new approach, sharing a common thread that emphasizes shaping the conditions for choice before the precise decision context is fully known. These three aspects of complexity, while presented separately here, are actually interrelated, creating further wrinkles in developing the infrastructure to support effective decision making:

- *Building the information base.* The use of data warehousing and data mining, illustrated in the above examples, together with powerful evaluation vehicles based on optimization and simulation models of grand scope, provide the basis for a much richer and more precise informational base for decisions.

- *Identifying constraints.* The calculus of real options theory has underlined the importance of assuring that today's decisions are directed at assuring a rich menu of possibilities for tomorrow's decisions.[19] This is reflected not only in options to improve, delay or cancel projects but also in investments to assure a proper constraint set and a reasonable information base for future decisions.
- *Strengthening organizational capabilities.* The fact that managers need powerful decision support and data management tools to function adequately dictates that organizations as a whole require new skills and capabilities to design and implement these tools.

This new approach to decisions has emerged in the last decade because of the increasing difficulty of making business decisions and legitimating them to sophisticated internal and external stakeholders. These new approaches have made some progress in addressing this problem based on advances in information technology. Nevertheless, these changes in decision-making strategy do not reflect a displacement of man's very human capability to plan ahead. The focus of such planning has now shifted, however, from evaluating isolated decisions to creating business platforms to enhance and support an entire decision context.

Given the relentless development of technology, complexity can only be expected to increase. This promises to lead to more intense and complex challenges for decision makers, but as the discussion above indicates, will also put more powerful tools into their hands for addressing these decisions. Continued changes will also mean that flexible approaches will become even more crucial for managers as the environment of decision making becomes so complex that working out all the details of decision contingencies before the fact is neither feasible nor desirable. Managers will increasingly need to prepare the groundwork and capabilities for choice and use these capabilities to confront and deal with the moving targets as they appear in real time.

CHAPTER 8

MANAGING FRAMES TO MAKE BETTER DECISIONS

PAUL J.H. SCHOEMAKER
The Wharton School

J. EDWARD RUSSO
Johnson Graduate School of Management
Cornell University

The frames we use to view the world determine what we see, locking us into certain ideas and shutting out new possibilities. We need to actively manage our frames to make better decisions.

We thank John Carroll, Harry Davis, Paul Kleindorfer, Milind Lele, Nanty Meyer, John Oakes, and Ann Marie Ott for their helpful comments on earlier drafts. Special thanks go to Doug Dickson and Margo Hittleman for their editorial advice.

*The test of a first-rate intelligence is the ability to hold two opposite ideas
in mind at the same time and still retain the ability to function.*
                                   —F. Scott Fitzgerald

*Managers use frames to simplify reality—choosing which aspects to focus
on and which to ignore—but these frames can also create blindspots and
traps. For example,* Encyclopedia Britannica *framed its business as print
publishing and failed to quickly recognize and react to the growing market
for CD-ROM encyclopedias. The authors explore the power and pitfalls
of frames, as well as strategies for better managing frames. These strategies include conducting a frame audit, identifying and changing inferior
frames, and using a variety of techniques for reframing. By recognizing
and using frames, managers can utilize the efficiencies of frames in simplifying complex problems while avoiding the blindspots created by them.*

Assume you are the vice president of
manufacturing in a Fortune 500 company that employs over 130,000 people with annual sales exceeding $10 billion. Due to the recession as well as
structural changes in your industry, one of your factories (with 600 hun-
dred employees) is faced with either a complete or partial shutdown. You
and your staff have carefully narrowed the options to either:

A. Scale back and keep a few production lines open. Exactly 400 jobs
will be lost (out of 600).
B. Invest in new equipment that may or may not improve your competitive position. There is a one-third chance that no jobs will be lost but
a two-thirds chance that all 600 jobs will be lost.

Financially, these options are equally attractive (in expected rate of return). The major difference is the effect of the decision on the plant workers, who have stood by the company for many hard years without unionizing.
Which option would you choose if these were your only alternatives?

Having presented this hypothetical dilemma to hundreds of senior managers, we find that most choose option B. Typically, they are loathe to accept a sure loss and are willing to take the chance that no jobs will be lost.

But consider what happens when we present the same options through a different frame:

A.' Scale back and keep a few production lines open. Exactly 200 jobs will be saved (out of 600 threatened with layoff).

B.' Invest in new equipment that may or may not improve your competitive position. There is a one-third chance that all jobs will be saved but a two-thirds chance that none of the 600 jobs will be saved.

In this case, most of the managers make the opposite choice, selecting option A'. What is the difference between the two versions? Only the framing of the situation. In the first formulation, the options are framed as losses, and in the second, as gains. The presentation of the problem shapes the outcome. Many savvy managers will take a 180-degree turn depending on how the consequences happen to be framed. Yet, most managers are not conscious of the frame or how it influences their decisions.

Frames determine how we see the world. (See box for a more precise definition of frames.) Managers allude to them often when they talk about "thinking outside the box," "shifting the paradigm," or "not being on the same page." Yet most managers are unaware of the cognitive frames that underlie their own perceptions and decisions. And even fewer know how to *systematically* use framing—or, more specifically, the skills of *reframing*—in ways that can foster organizational success. This chapter synthesizes multiple views of framing and their relevance to managers.

Frames are crucial because they simplify and focus our attention on what we deem is most relevant, making it possible to decide more quickly and efficiently than with widespread attention. Frames reside in our mind and control what information is attended to and, just as important, what is filtered out. Through a process of pattern matching, people try to match new experiences to patterns from their past experience. This is especially important in situations that demand quick action and can be very efficient in situations in which the underlying context has not changed much. We need these mental structures, and associated processes such as pattern matching, to help our minds make useful connections and not be distracted by irrelevant ones. They structure our thinking.

What Is a Frame?

A frame is a stable, coherent cognitive structure that organizes and simplifies the complex reality that a manager operates in. Many frames reside in memory and are usually evoked or triggered automatically. The terms *frame* and *framing* have their origin in cognitive science and artificial intelligence (AI), and refer to the mental representations that allow humans to perceive, interpret, judge, choose, and act.[a]

We consider three types of frames: problem frames (used to generate solutions), decision frames (used to choose among clear alternatives) and thinking frames (deeper mental structures based on years of experience). In decision making, Daniel Kahneman and Amos Tversky[b] brought the concept of decision frames to great prominence by demonstrating that changes in the surface features of the decision frame (such as framing the outcome as a gain versus a loss) can alter choices, as shown with the framing of the options for the layoff decision problem at the opening of the chapter.

Frames are related to mental models and paradigms, but are less complete than mental models and less widely held than paradigms:

- *Mental models.* Peter Senge defines mental models as people's deeply held images of the world.[c] We can think of each mental model as a rich network of concepts and relationships that captures a mental construct such as a car, a computer, or something more abstract such as a restaurant.[d] An adult brain contains thousands of mental models that have developed over decades of education and experience. In addition to models for objects (such as a car, computer, or house), we also possess mental models for constructs such as the boss, a legal contract, leadership, democracy and so on. Much of managers' special knowledge about their business may be represented as a collection of mental models. Frames are the essential elements of mental models. Like the frame of a house, they define the shape of these models, even if the models themselves are fully furnished with more details. Because frames are simpler than full mental models they are easier to deal with.

- *Paradigm.* A paradigm is a widely shared mental model that groups of people use to define their reality.[e] Thomas Kuhn's original notion of a paradigm views it as a mental structure that is broad, encompassing, and largely invisible to those within it. Frames, in contrast, entail fewer elements and can be highly personal or confined to a specific domain.

134

What Is a Frame? (Continued)

Furthermore, frames can be more easily exposed, understood, and re-aligned in a limited time. This is why we focus on frames rather than paradigms (or mental models).

---

[a] Marvin L. Minsky, "A Framework for Presenting Knowledge," in *The Psychology of Computer Visions*, ed. P. Winston (New York: McGraw-Hill, 1975).
[b] Amos Tversky and Daniel Kahneman, "Prospect Theory: An Analysis of Decision Under Risk," *Econometrica*, 47 (1979), pp. 263–91.
[c] Peter Senge, "The Leader's New Work: Building Learning Organizations," *Sloan Management Review* (Fall 1990), pp. 7–23.
[d] For more on mental models see Rob Ranyard, *Decision Making: Cognitive Models and Explanations* (Routledge, New York/London, 1997) or C. Marlene Fiol and Anne Sigismund Huff, "Maps for Managers: Where Are We? Where Do We Go From Here?," *Journal of Management Studies* 29, 3 (1992), pp. 267–285. The classic references to mental models and their cognitive functions are: *Mental Models: Towards a Cognitive Science of Language, Influence and Conciousness*, ed. Dedre Gentner and Albert L. Stevens (Erlbaum, Hillsdale, NJ, 1983) and Philip N. Johnson-Laird, *Mental Models* (2nd ed.) (Harvard University Press, Boston, 1983).
[e] Thomas S. Kuhn, *The Structure of Scientific Revolution* (University of Chicago Press, 1970).

But sizing up a situation based on past patterns can be disastrous if there have been significant changes in the decision context. Because we accept these simplifications as reality, frames can also create blindspots and be very hard to challenge.

IMPRISONED BY FRAMES

The choice of frames is not an idle exercise. The wrong frames can have significant negative consequences for companies. Encyclopedia Britannica thought it was in the book business until it woke up to find it was really in the knowledge and information business, which had gone digital. In 1989, Britannica was booming, with $627 million in sales of its $1,300 sets of encyclopedias. By 1994, its sales had dropped 53 percent. Why? Other encyclopedia companies were developing CD-ROM alternatives, which made content more exciting, less expensive, and easier to use. Britannica's management, unfortunately, had framed the company as a book publisher, and consequently offered only a very limited electronic license of the series' content. By the time the company's leaders realized the full impact of CD-ROM on their business, they had neither the money nor time to develop new technology or new license partners. Their large sales staff was dedicated to selling the print product. In 1995, CEO Peter Norton was forced to resign.[1] Britannica suffered a near-death experience because they were locked into the wrong frame.

Even with the right frames for a particular time or place, firms very often find themselves trapped by their own success. Like actors who become typecast in a single role, a company's reliance on a frame that was effective in the past can inhibit healthy change. Several decades ago, Federal Express virtually created the U.S. overnight delivery system through a radical shift in the way package delivery was framed. Its winning approach called for a dedicated fleet of planes, a single central hub, standardized procedures for processing packages, and an image campaign that equated the firm with guaranteed on-time delivery. But when FedEx exported its system to Europe in the late 1980s, it was spectacularly unsuccessful. A single hub in Brussels added costly customs delays. Differences in national cultures frustrated FedEx's attempt to standardize its procedures. European firms shipped intercountry less frequently than U.S. firms do interstate. And finally, the European market failed to exhibit the kind of growth the U.S. market had experienced, a crucial factor in this high fixed-cost business. The bottom line: annual losses as high as $200 million. In 1992, the company scrapped its intra-European express delivery, laid off 6,600 employees and closed more than 100 European facilities. It took a $254 million restructuring charge and lost $114 million for that year.[2]

These two examples illustrate how senior executives missed key changes in their environment. It is difficult in hindsight to unravel the myriad causes of a particular pattern of failure. The origins of such executive failures can be numerous, ranging from bad luck, to misdirected incentives, to a flawed strategy. Nonetheless, we believe that in these cases, previously successful corporate leaders got stuck in a narrow way of looking at their business environment. They did not factor significant new considerations into crucial strategic decisions. We believe they failed, in large measure, because of key mistakes in framing.

FRAMING TRAPS

Frames influence our thinking by simplifying issues. The price we pay for this benefit is distortion. As Albert Einstein noted, "we should make things as simple as possible, but not simpler." Frames create highlights and shadows, focusing our attention on certain aspects of a problem while leaving others in the shadows. Frames also distort by imposing mental boundaries on options, for example when a manager's domestic frame precludes global expansion. Finally, frames distort by establishing yardsticks and reference points, as we discussed in the example of company layoffs at the opening of the chapter (which can be assessed from the reference point of a loss or a gain).[3]

These distortions can cause communication problems within a company. Consider the frames of three separate functional groups within a major U.S. pharmaceutical manufacturer (Figure 8.1). When middle managers within the R&D group talk about what is important to them (and, implicitly, to the company), they naturally focus on long-term strategic direction, stock price, and the firm's human capital and intellectual property. Marketing managers, on the other hand, highlight customer needs, revenue generation, competitors, and the company's "face" to the world. While there is some overlap between the frames (speed to market, competitors, and therapeutic needs are highlights in both the R&D and marketing frames), the overlap is limited, and most of the highlights of any one frame lie in the "shadows" of the other. And there is only one aspect shared by all three frames: the importance of speed to market. These different frames made it very difficult circa 1992 for people from different functional backgrounds or cultures to communicate with each other in this pharmaceutical company. Since then, there have been some changes made to these frames, such as economic value added (EVA) being important in all three frames.

The mechanisms by which frames exert their influence on our thinking are complex and only partly understood. Nonetheless, their effects are clearly visible in the form of well-documented mental traps. We discuss

Figure 8.1
Overlaps among Three Functional Frames

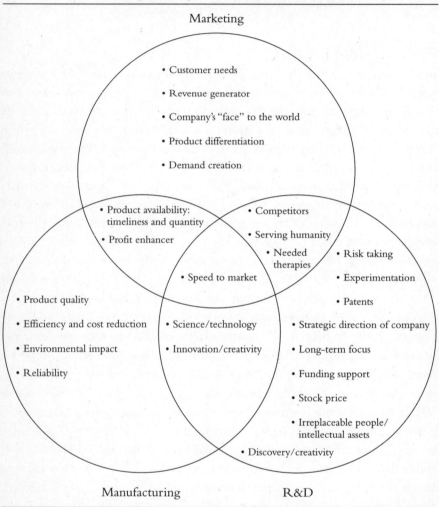

Marketing

- Customer needs
- Revenue generator
- Company's "face" to the world
- Product differentiation
- Demand creation

- Product availability: timeliness and quantity
- Profit enhancer

- Competitors
- Serving humanity
- Needed therapies
- Risk taking
- Experimentation

- Speed to market

- Product quality
- Efficiency and cost reduction
- Environmental impact
- Reliability

- Science/technology
- Innovation/creativity

- Patents
- Strategic direction of company
- Long-term focus
- Funding support
- Stock price
- Irreplaceable people/ intellectual assets
- Discovery/creativity

Manufacturing

R&D

three related traps that are especially pernicious for managers and those they supervise (see Figure 8.2).

Frame Blindness

Being unaware of our frames poses an enormous risk. All too often, managers look out at the world through one mental window and fail to notice the views offered by other windows. They may operate from outdated frames (using a domestic frame when the industry is globalizing, for example) or try to solve a marketing problem by using a sales frame. Worse yet, they may not even realize they are doing so.[4] We refer to this as *frame blindness.*

One company switched its yardstick for its salesforce bonus from total revenues to growth of market share. This grow-our-share frame was meant to provide an incentive to beat competitors (the desired highlight) rather than beat last year's sales (the old highlight). This new frame, however, caused substantial conflict between the sales and marketing organizations. While the marketing group set prices, the salesforce proposed

Figure 8.2
How Frames Can Limit Effectiveness

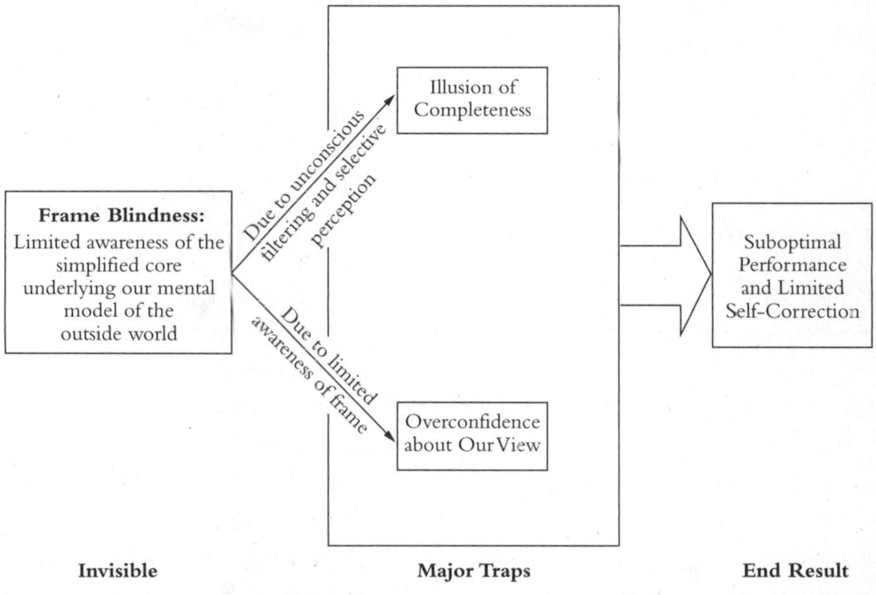

| Invisible | Major Traps | End Result |

pricing changes (since they were closer to specific customers and followed competitors' prices). The salesforce wanted to grow market share by lowering prices, which ate away at the profits for which the marketing group was accountable. The executives who instituted the switch to the "grow our share" frame were blind to the major conflicts it would cause between sales and marketing.

The Illusion of Completeness

Managers who do not understand that they are operating from a particular frame (with its distinct highlights and shadows), may erroneously believe that they "have the complete picture." It is the illusion of completeness, rather than the existence of frames per se, that is the real culprit. No frame is complete; each one highlights and hides different aspects of the situation at hand.

A strategy consultant frames your difficulty as a strategy problem, an organizational development consultant sees the same situation as an OD problem, and an information technology consultant is likely to propose a new information system. What is striking here is not just the incompleteness of any one perspective, but the sincerity with which these consultants believe that their own frame fully captures the problem and provides the very best solution.

Be on guard about the false sense of completeness that any frame will offer. Try to see the gaps and limitations of the frame as well as why it fits.

Overconfidence

Most of us suffer from a well-documented tendency to overestimate what we know, which contributes to our tendency to overvalue the relevance of our own frames and undervalue the relevance of others.[5] IBM, whose traditional frame for making and selling computers was that of vertical integration, has become a classic example of frame-based overconfidence. IBM developed its own circuitry, platforms, operating system and applications software, as well as a first-class salesforce and high-service channels. As a consequence, the company's leaders failed to recognize direct mail opportunities for selling personal computers. There were people at IBM who did recognize the potential importance of direct mail, but overconfidence in their existing frames and the illusion that they saw the complete picture caused bright people to filter out opposing voices, just as in the Encyclopedia Britannica example.

Frame Conflict

Different frames, and the associated overconfidence instilled by them, create the potential for conflict. These frame conflicts can generate outright hostility, accusations of private agendas or questions about competence. For example, as today's U.S. healthcare system undergoes fundamental changes, physicians and hospital executives have a very different view of the challenges. In a typical physician's frame, doctors are independent service providers who use the resources of hospitals, laboratories, specialists, and so on to help patients. In the business frame embraced by a growing number of management-trained hospital executives, doctors are an asset of a well-managed hospital. Hospitals are businesses that offer their customers many medical services, one of which is access to physicians. What gets lost is that each of these frames contains highlights *essential* to the provision of high-quality, cost-effective medical care. Ultimately physicians and health-care executives will have to understand elements of each other's frames, and together develop a new, more robust frame that incorporates elements of both. This will require constructive and deep dialog—a meeting of both the heart and minds in which profound differences in views, interests, and values may be bridged. Many companies are turning to cross-functional teams as an antidote to myopic thinking and frame blindness. These teams can also serve a valuable role in identifying and addressing frame conflicts.

MANAGING FRAMES TO AVOID THE TRAPS

How can managers avoid these and other traps? Managers can consciously control their frames, rather than to be controlled by them—and even use framing to their advantage. An old story about a Franciscan priest and a Jesuit priest illustrates the gentle art of frame control. Both were heavy smokers and somewhat troubled about their human frailty, especially about smoking when praying to the Lord. The Franciscan decided to see his prefect and asked: "Father, would it be permitted to smoke while praying to the Lord?" The answer was a resounding no. The Jesuit also sought counsel, but framed his question somewhat differently: "Father, when in moments of weakness I smoke, would it be permitted to say a prayer to the Lord?" The answer: "Yes, of course my son."

We next identify three key steps for taking charge of your frames.

1. See the Frame by Conducting a Frame Audit

You cannot manage your frames if you cannot see them, and like water to a fish, frames are usually invisible to us. A frame audit begins with surfacing your own or your organization's frame or frames, understanding the frames of others, and developing an appreciation of newly emerging frames.

Surface Your Frames.   One of the best ways to surface your frames is to present them visually. Figure 8.3 illustrates this process with the mental model of a pharmaceutical R&D executive. (Remember that mental models are much broader than frames.) In the center circle is the frame of drug discovery, science, innovative products, and experimentation. The R&D manager sees the world through this lens. Issues such as speed to market and status of competitors' products, which would be central to marketing or strategy executives, are in the outer circles. Exercise 1 (see box) describes how to generate these visual representations of your own frames and mental models. More complex representations are possible as well, such as system dynamic models.[6]

Understanding the Frames of Others.   The process of examining the frames of different stakeholders should make you more aware of frame overlap and conflict. A second exercise (see box) can help you become more aware of the frames of your boss, colleagues, competitors, customers, regulators, and key partners. To understand other people's frames, you might ask yourself, "What matters most to them? What do they talk about most often?" Ask also, "What do I naturally consider that they rarely mention? What messages do they seem to filter out?" The first questions reveal their highlights; the second, their shadows. Effective communication and dialog

Figure 8.3
Simplified Mental Model of a Pharmaceutical R&D Executive

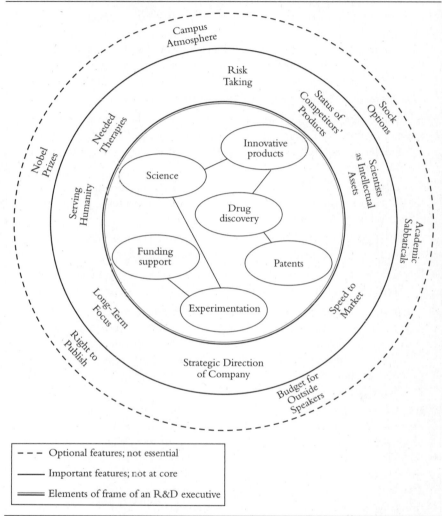

```
- - -  Optional features; not essential
────  Important features; not at core
════  Elements of frame of an R&D executive
```

require a thorough understanding of other people's frames of mind. In one case, when we conducted the first exercise, it became apparent to all that some key objectives and areas of focus were missing from the inner circles of most of the functions and departments presented in the group. For example, the IT group gave insufficient attention to customer satisfaction or

Exercise 1: Surfacing Mental Models and Frames

In many discussions or meetings it is crucial that various parties thoroughly understand each other's mental models or at least the core frames. This exercise invites participants to contrast their perceptions of present and future frames in a domain of interest. For illustration's sake, assume that a company wants to better understand the frames of key stakeholders such as its customers, distributors, suppliers, and competitors.

A: Using parallel breakout teams, we start with a characterization of the traditional frames of these groups. Each team is assigned to study just one stakeholder group and asked to draw three concentric circles that capture the following:

Inner circle. List those objectives, concerns, or notions that traditionally have been most central to this stakeholder's interests, perspectives, and ways of thinking (see example in Figure 8.3).

Middle circle. List those elements that are important but not at the very core of this stakeholder's traditional frame of mind.

Outer circle. List those elements that are tertiary in importance to this stakeholder, within the traditional view of the industry.

Hint. The elements you list should correspond to what a set of interviews or recordings of internal meetings would reveal as being most central, secondary, or tertiary in the minds of the stakeholder group you are assessing. This part of the exercise is *descriptive*. Figure 8.3 shows an example of these concentric circles from the perspective of a pharmaceutical executive.

B: After having de-briefed the mental snapshots of the traditional frames of mind of the four key stakeholder groups, we are ready to engage in a more projective exercise that tries to anticipate what these pictures may look like, say, five years out. It should already be evident that new concepts (such as the Internet, alliances, globalization, etc.) are entering the dialog. This exercise is an opportunity to discuss and arrange these new ways of thinking in terms of their constituent elements and their relative importance. By its very nature, part B of the exercise entails conjecture and imagination, since participants need to contemplate what the world may be like in five years and what new priorities, concerns, or concepts may arise. *Example:* In the manufacturing frame of mind of the 1950s, such notions as cost efficiency, mass production, plant safety, unions, and automation were foremost on the minds of plant managers. Today, such concepts as quality, supply chain management, environmental compliance, flexible production, and global purchasing are more often at the core.

Exercise 2: Know Your Own Frames (and Those of Others)

Indicate how frequently you rely on the frames listed when addressing business problems in the categories shown. Put an H, M, or L (denoting High, Medium, or Low frequency of use) in your column and that of someone else. Also ask a colleague to score how they see your frame preferences. You may be surprised. Add to the list any other personally relevant framing domains, such as family-work balance, approaches to leadership, view of strategic alliances, and so on.

Yourself   Other

1. **Functional frames** for general business
   problems:
   —*Research and development* perspective
   —*Engineering or manufacturing* perspective
   —*Marketing and sales* perspective
   —Other (*finance/accounting; legal/regulatory;
   strategic planning; human resources; public
   relations*)

2. Your view of **customers** (or distributors)
   —An *adversary* whose gain is your loss
   —A *partner* without whom you can't exist
   —Other perspectives

3. Your view of **competitors or rivals:**
   —*Other firms* offering the same product/service
   —*Any party reducing your profit* (e.g., suppliers,
   substitutes, customers, government, employees)
   —Other views

4. Your usual approach to business **negotiations:**
   —A *battle* resulting in clear winners and losers
   —A *journey* where most parties can come out
   ahead
   —Other approaches

5. **Organizational frames** for complex problems:
   —Organization viewed as a *family*
   —Organization viewed as a *sports team*
   —Organization viewed as *military unit*
   —Other (e.g., *machine; garden; orchestra*)

6. Your view or approach to (*fill in*):
   (List different approaches or views here.)

competitive benchmarks; and the legal department ignored profit considerations most of the time. As one participant put it, it suddenly hit her
what the problem was in her department: poor frames. As people special-
ize in functions and departments, they often lose sight of the big picture and
what really matters to the company. General Motors—which suffered its
share of mental blindspots in the past—is one company that has since instituted a very effective frame audit strategy that is used whenever complex
issues arise or cross-functional teams meet.[7]

Appreciate Emerging Frames.   Frames do not stay the same. Every field
experiences innovation. How other people are currently changing the way
they frame important questions may illuminate something that your frame
keeps you from perceiving. For example, the war or sports frame in negotiations (win-lose) is giving way to a new frame (win-win) that looks at negotiation as joint problem solving where both parties can achieve most, if not
all, of their goals. Study new frames such as virtual organizations (in contrast to traditional physical organizations), learning cultures (organizations
focused on learning in contrast to performance cultures) or co-opetition
(managers simultaneously competing and cooperating in contrast to strictly
competitive frames) to see what their highlights might add to your own view.

2. Identify and Change Inadequate Frames

Managers often use frames that are outdated, or just plain wrong, to "solve"
their problems. But how can we identify a poor frame, given that our
frames filter what we see and then create an illusion of completeness? The
answer—which we acknowledge is easier said than done—is: We must constantly challenge our own frames. Outlined next are three tactics for effective frame challenge.

Are Your Frames Effective?   The first challenge to pose to your frame is
whether it is effective. Does your current frame get the job done? Among
the questions that can help you assess the effectiveness of your frame are:

1. Does your frame prompt you to ask the right questions most of the
   time?

2. Have you tested or challenged your frame, or have others tried to do so?
3. Does your frame help you resolve tough issues decisively?
4. Is your frame easily communicated to and understood by others?
5. Do key stakeholders accept your frame as a guide to joint action?
6. Is your frame sufficiently simple (without being too simple)?
7. Is your frame adaptable to change?
8. Does your frame generate solutions that achieve the desired results?
9. What are some notable failures of your frame? Where did it lead you astray?
10. In which cases did your frame allow you to see the forest for the trees?
11. What are some of the deeper assumptions that underlie your frame?
12. What is the origin of these assumptions in your past experience?
13. How do the frames of those you admire differ from your own?
14. How have you improved your framing skills over time?

Observe the Symptoms of Frame Misfit.   Poor results, surprises (violations of expectations), inconsistencies, and difficulties communicating with others are indications of a weak frame. Consider the possibility that your frame may be wrong or, at least, not perfect! Experiment with an opposing frame. For example, if your frame says customers care mostly about price and only secondarily about service, try the opposite approach and see what happens. Give yourself a chance to be proven wrong. In building his advertising empire, the late David Ogilvy went as far as to run ads he thought would probably not work just to test his own theories about advertising. (He would pull the failing ads quickly, and at little cost.) Or ask people who usually disagree with you: "How do you see it?" "What am I overlooking?"

Question Your Reference Points.   Ask yourself where your own reference points, or those used in your company, actually come from. What contributes good versus bad performance to you? For some time, Ford has been adamant about *not* comparing its quality to that of its two domestic rivals, but instead focuses on being the best in breed, which includes Japanese and German car companies, among others, in its comparisons.

Recognize Your Key Assumptions.   Bringing your organizational frames to the surface helps you to understand what type of thinking dominates your organization. It's likely that some of these assumptions are explicit, while others exist below the surface. For example, GM's assumptions about itself and the world in the 1970s presumed an isolated U.S. market, an abundance of cheap gas, dominance of styling over technology, alienated workers due to unions, and little social unrest. These assumptions, which worked when technology was simple and gas was cheap, kept the company from noticing the many signals that the world had changed. Recognize how your assumptions direct your attention and lead you to filter information. Ask yourself whether changing an assumption would change the preferred course of action, or whether changing several assumptions, in an internally consistent way, would create entirely new scenarios.[8]

3. Master Techniques for Reframing

Once you have surfaced your frames and identified potential weaknesses, you then need to develop the capacity to synthesize and create new frames. There are several elements to this final skill, but much of its success relies on challenging your frames and those of others, and on having a repertoire of frames to work with. The box below provides a set of questions and issues to consider in building new frames.

Given that different frames highlight and obscure different aspects of a situation, you must select the right frame for the problem at hand rather than using a particular frame out of habit, convention or, worst of all, having it imposed by others. When stuck in a critical meeting or facing an important problem, use the following reframing techniques to expand your perspective and help you "think outside the box." Besides offering more options, they also may change the kind of information you want to gather, and help you combine frames.

Use Multiple Frames.   Experiment with different frames and compare the solutions you develop. Place yourself in a different environment. To renew their perspective on the business, the Hyatt Hotel Corp. sends senior executives out to work in every position from room service to check-in clerk once a year.

A Toolkit for Better Framing[a]

Strategies	Key Questions to Ask
1. *Focus on the Objective:* Identify the specific results you desire.	√ What should the solution achieve? What tangible results do we expect? What problems must be solved by the solution?
2. *Consider Key Stakeholders:* Identify the requirements of those who will make or break the success of the solution.	√ What is needed to ensure agreement and commitment to a solution? Who are the key players? What are their interests and constraints?
3. *Identify All Constraints:* Identify all limitations you must accept.	√ Are there any schedule or resource constraints to consider? Critical dates? Time, cost, or staffing limitations? Which constraints are negotiable and which are non-negotiable?
4. *Analysis of Assumptions:* Surface and challenge all important and implicit assumptions and constraints.	√ What important assumptions are we making, including implicit or hidden ones? Are these appropriate and realistic? What other assumptions are possible?
5. *Yardstick Analysis:* Examine any bias or incompleteness in performance measures.	√ Are the metrics we use biased or incomplete in any way? What am I not measuring that might be important? Is my judgment based on facts or inference?
6. *Reference Point Analysis:* Examine the basis for whatever benchmarks you are using.	√ What reference points am I using? What other reference points might apply? How do different reference points affect my perceptions?
7. *Get Other Views:* Ask experts, customers, suppliers, etc. for their inputs.	√ Consult with people whom you respect or who have prior experience with this problem. Encourage them to challenge your problem definition and assumptions.
8. *Assess the Mental Images:* Evaluate metaphors, analogies or illustrations.	√ What images do I repeatedly use to describe the situation or explain people's behavior? In my conversations or presentations at meetings? In my memos and other written work?

(continued)

A Toolkit for Better Framing (Continued)

Strategies	Key Questions to Ask
9. *Create a Joint Frame:* Include the important elements from each perspective.	✓ Which alternative perspectives are most important to consider? What are the important elements of each frame? Can we prioritize them? How should these elements be represented in our decision or problem frame?
10. *Portfolio Perspective:* Combine the various options to explore their net effects.	✓ List the sets of options that can be implemented concurrently and evaluate the net result of these combinations, rather than the component results.
11. *Consider Implementation:* Identify what will be needed to ensure the solution can be implemented successfully.	✓ What factors relative to implementation should be considered? What resources and problems are expected? What criteria should be included to ensure a smooth implementation?
12. *Prospective Hindsight:* Imagine you are in the future and the decision has failed. Then ask, "In which ways was the problem perhaps misframed?"	✓ What is highlighted or hidden by each frame? Which frames seem most useful? Which capture the most important elements? Which should promote understanding and communication?

[a] These tools were drawn from *Mastering Tough Decisions,* a proprietary decision training program developed by J. Edward Russo and Paul J.H. Schoemaker, with the help of John Oakes (see www.thinkdsi.com for details).

You can also think about how others might frame a particular problem. How would a marketing manager define the problem? An engineer? An entrepreneur? A regulator? Someone from a different industry? Someone from a different culture? Even someone from a different era? Assembling people with different backgrounds (and presumably, different frames) can surface a broader range of ideas, help see into the shadows of existing frames, develop alternative frames, or at least, stretch existing frames.

For example, after British Petroleum (BP) had failed repeatedly to find a profitable way to produce oil from its Andrew field in the North Sea, it shifted its frame and approach.[9] With the support of CEO John Browne, the development team invited seven key contractors into the problem-solving effort, a major departure from established practices. Normally, the contractors would bid on the project once it had been fully developed by BP's staff. The best approach BP had come up with carried a projected cost of $676 million to develop this geologically complex field. Once the contractors got involved, every problem, aspect, and assumption was examined. Breakthrough solutions were found from drilling horizontal wells, to cost sharing, to offshore construction of an integrated deck. The end result was a new budget for the project of $560 million, with penalties for overruns and bonuses for savings. As it turned out, the project came in just below $444 million and was completed six months ahead of schedule.

Of course, such cross-functional teams are not without their own problems, particularly when team members are oblivious to the issues of framing, frame blindness, and the lack of completeness inherent in their individual views.

Look for Ways to Align Frames. Try to align your frames with those of others. Frame blindness nearly derailed a joint venture by Raychem Corporation and a business partner, both telecommunication equipment manufacturers who dominated their respective and complementary niches. The alignment of both companies' frames proved critical to their joint success.[10]

In early 1993, Raychem and its partner had independently developed a sealed station protector, part of the technology needed to connect telephone lines to each other. Recognizing the opportunity to build on each other's reputation, they decided to form a joint venture to develop, manufacture, and market this product together. But as so often happens in joint ventures, conflict in the meeting room demolished a plan that looked great on paper. Engineers from both companies wanted to preserve as much of their own existing designs as they could. Neither group wanted to reveal significant shortcomings to the other because of fear of giving away design secrets.

By finally agreeing to an open discussion of the advantages and disadvantages of both designs, the teams uncovered a key difference in perspective. Raychem had long focused its expertise on exceptional grounding technology, exceeding the industry standards in that area; its partner, while meeting industry standards for grounding capabilities, had developed its expertise on the sealing needed to prevent moisture from degrading the equipment.

Once they had refocused the discussion from the differences in design to the differences in expectations (frames), the two teams were able to analyze the quality of their individual frames. They then created a better frame by combining the critical highlights of each one. Applying this new frame to the two designs, they found that neither would have passed muster in the market. The new frame resulted in a new design, which ended the impasse, saved about $250,000 in tooling and two person-years in design costs and protected their market position. Furthermore, the new frame can be applied to future joint venture projects.

Change Metaphors to Regain Control of a Frame.   Whenever someone uses descriptive imagery or a strong analogy to define a problem, be on guard: you are about to be framed. The connections that will automatically fire in your brain are dictated by this outside suggestion. Try to shift the metaphor to redefine the problem. During World War II, some U.S. government agents questioned the loyalty of Japanese-Americans by demanding: "Whom do you want to win, America or Japan?" Some Japanese-Americans, recognizing that the framing of this question was "war" or "battle" or "fight-to-the-death" tried to shift from a military frame to a family frame. They responded: "Whom do you want to win when you see your mother and father fighting? You just want them to stop fighting."

To regain control of a frame, challenge it with alternative images, then see which ones fit best. Many times, you will find that a combination of elements from several different frames offers the best picture of a problem.

Challenge Others' Reference Points.   A worker at a Texas company confronted a manager about the firm's 5 percent annual wage increase. The worker felt the raise was small compared to the company's 12 percent increase in profits that year. Instead of accepting the worker's reference point, the manager challenged it. "What were the wage increases at our competitor across the street?" he asked. The answer: "3 percent." Then he added: "And do they offer our employment security ?" "No." By shifting the reference point and adding new dimensions (such as the non-salary benefit of job security), he defused the problem and took control of the frame.

Stretch a Frame.   It is often easier to get others to stretch their frame, rather than to totally change it. Prior to 1992, the R&D and manufacturing divisions of the pharmaceutical company described in Figure 8.1 had frames that focused primarily on quality. By beginning to talk about speed-to-market as an attribute of quality (and in the process, generating the notion of quality-speed), corporate leaders were able to stretch three functional frames to include an additional highlight. Since then, they have stretched the frame yet further, introducing economic value added as another key attribute, and are now talking about quality-speed-value.

Build New Frames for New Situations.   Be aware of situations in which a radically changed business environment necessitates the construction of an entirely new frame. Most successful entrepreneurs challenge existing frames and set out to demonstrate that the new environment favors a new or better business theory. Corporate leaders also can construct new frames to help an existing company thrive in a new business environment. In response to advertising's declining share of marketing budgets, an international advertising agency decided to move the company toward offering integrated marketing services. To succeed long-term, the company had to switch its entire strategy from a traditional *advertising* frame to an *integrated marketing,* and even a *consulting* frame. These three frames entail very different approaches to defining the scope of work, the pricing of services, and the management of the client relationship.

Speak to Others' Frames.   People often cannot see or hear anything that lies outside their frames. You need to speak in their frames. Often, failure to convince someone of your point of view occurs because your frame differs from theirs. Learning how to align your message with your listener's frame can move them from opposition to buy-in. Howard Perlmutter at the Wharton School has developed an interesting framework to encourage deep dialog among organizational stakeholders.[11] He identifies various dialog deficits that limit effective communication, such as lack of trust, cognitive misperceptions, or false assumptions. In addition, he recommends seven types of processes that can improve and deepen dialog within organizations, ranging from bridging to bonding to blending. This framework of deep dialog encompasses both the cognitive aspects of communication, such as frames, and the affective and cultural elements as well.

FRAMING FROM THE TOP: IN CONCLUSION

In addition to the tools and approaches described here, reframing also requires a willingness to live with discomfort for a while. This may be a small sacrifice in light of the costs generated by mental inertia in highly competitive settings.

Become *brutally realistic.* Collect disconfirming evidence. Ask other people (especially those who usually disagree with you), "How do you see it?" "What am I overlooking?" You won't always like what you hear. No matter how disturbing it is, use this feedback to improve your frames. Don't view it as criticism, but reframe it as a gift.

Appreciate people's *emotional commitment to their frames,* especially if core values are involved, people usually need considerable time to adapt. Recognize the stages of denial, anger, despair, acceptance, and rebirth. A CEO who was trying to reframe his organization once confessed to us as he was correcting his own impatience, "I forget how many times I have to repeat the message."

Complex issues can seldom be solved within a single frame. We believe that it is the unique responsibility of the senior manager to see that an organization, and those within it, are working from appropriate, robust frames.[12]

In fact, the higher a person rises in an organization, the more time should be spent on framing (and reframing) key issues. In a complex and uncertain world, senior managers can't be expected to choose the alternative that, in hindsight, always produces the best possible outcome. But good senior managers *can* be expected to ensure that the entire organization frames questions thoughtfully, that the dominant frames used throughout the organization are appropriate and updated as needed, and that complex decisions are evaluated through a variety of alternative frames.

To do so, managers must learn to recognize the limits of their own frames and to appreciate the value of other perspectives. They must learn how to recognize and challenge other people's frames (defensive frame control) and master techniques to help others to accept better frames (proactive frame control).

Ultimately, this is where management differs from leadership. Managers operate within an existing frame and execute; leaders ask the deeper questions, provoke new ideas and operate across frames, moving the organization from an old frame to a new one. Effective leaders challenge old frames, envision bold new ones, and contrast the two very clearly.

PART III

MULTIPARTY DECISION MAKING

"Okay, 60 million. But only
because of the candlelight."

While the right setting may not hurt negotiations, clinching the deal is usually far more complex than providing candlelight. Part III looks at decisions in the context of negotiations and other multiparty interactions. How can you strengthen your position and bargain for advantage? How can you avoid being led astray by dim lighting

and deceptions? What influence does your reputation have on your partner's actions? What impact do new technologies such as e-mail and the Internet have on the bargaining process? Part III shines new light on a number
of issues.

In Chapter 9, Colin F. Camerer and Teck H. Ho use game theory to examine how decision makers learn, and how they can teach their partners in
the course of multiple rounds of decisions. In Chapter 10, Steven Glick
and Rachel Croson explore how the reputation you bring to the negotiating table affects the deal you walk away with. In Chapter 11, Maurice E.
Schweitzer examines the different types of lies in negotiations, their impact
on decisions and ways to spot them. In Chapter 12, G. Richard Shell looks
at how e-mail, the Internet, and other communications technologies are
changing negotiations. These channels can lead to grave misunderstandings and unexpected consequences, but negotiating technology also offers
the potential for facilitating better bargains.

CHAPTER 9

STRATEGIC LEARNING AND TEACHING

COLIN F. CAMERER
HSS, Caltech

TECK H. HO
The Wharton School

Like the movie *Groundhog Day*—in which actor Bill Murray plays a character who keeps reliving the same day in Punxsutawney, Pennsylvania, until he learns from the experience—decision makers learn from repeated experience, affecting their future choices.

159

A man who carries a cat by the tail learns something he can learn in no other way.

—Mark Twain

Decision makers learn from experience and this learning affects their future decisions. But how? Using game theory, the authors explore how people factor in the payoffs of past decisions in their current choices. The authors introduce the concept of experience-weighted attraction (EWA) to explain how people learn from their experience. Sophisticated players can use this concept to learn which strategies work and "outguess" their rivals. And by understanding how rivals and customers learn, managers can take actions that "teach" rivals and customers what you want them to believe—reassuring partners and intimidating competitors.

Every decision is influenced by learning. The price a firm bids in a B2B auction, a complicated wage-bonus package offered to an executive, and the scale of investment in new business are all influenced by what has worked in the past. Airlines have struggled for years to coordinate industrywide pricing practices, effectively teaching one another to stabilize fares and keep airplanes full, while skirting laws against explicit collusion. Firms figure out how to balance risky portions of compensation packages (such as options and company stock) with fixed salary portions, to both motivate employees and keep them happy during a stock market downturn. Internet buyers clicking through Web sites use trial-and-error learning to figure out how to get what they want from the Web site. Firms also try to teach customers through advertising, service experiences, and so forth.

Understanding how customers learn is invaluable for evaluating marketing strategies. Understanding how rivals learn is crucial for developing competitive strategies. How do managers learn from their own experiences and from one another to make these decisions? How can they effectively teach customers and rivals to affect their decisions?

THEORIES OF LEARNING

Learning is a change in behavior based on experience. How do managers learn? According to economic theories, idealized decision makers run through complicated calculations to derive an optimal decision. But in practice people typically learn by trial and error. Firms try out a group bonus scheme one year, and abandon it if productivity does not improve. Construction companies bid on contracts and learn to build in expected cost overruns after losing money. Firms learn that hiring friends referred by current employees improves morale and productivity, and reduces turnover; so they increase their inside-hiring bonus. Financial markets learn, cyclically, whether initial public offerings (IPOs) are good investments or not. And consumer products companies learn whether a successful yogurt brand name can be used to umbrella-brand ice cream, chocolate, or pudding.

In all these cases, not only are people and firms learning how to do better, but what they are learning depends on what others—consumers, competitors, regulators—are doing.

There are three primary theories of how this kind of interactive learning takes place:

1. *Reinforcement.* From the 1920s to the 1960s psychologists asserted that the primary way animals and people learn is by reinforcement. If actions are positively reinforced, they are taken again; if they are negatively reinforced, they are not taken again. Reinforcement is undeniably important, especially for learning by animals and children, and for certain kinds of human learning that derive from the "old" part of the brain (e.g., learning what to fear, and developing drug addictions). But later research in psychology showed that humans—and even pigeons—are sensitive to whether actions they did *not* take would have yielded positive reinforcements. Reinforcement theory omitted this kind of learning from the road not taken.

2. *Belief learning.* Beginning in the 1950s, learning theorists proposed that managers learn by developing a precise guess (or belief) about what other managers will do, based on observations of the past actions of those managers. Then managers choose a strategy that will yield a good payoff if their belief proves to be right.

3. *Experience-weighted attraction (EWA).* Experience-weighted attraction learning theory improves upon these two leading theories by combining their key features. It is based on the concept that strategic choices have different "attractions" for managers (as reflected in a

numerical value), based on past experience. The EWA theory is embodied in a mathematical model,[1] which is beyond the scope of this chapter, although we highlight its key features.

The concept of attraction incorporates *both* the extra reinforcement based on a manager's experience and the beliefs about the actions of others.[2] The way in which attractions are adjusted to reflect learning is based on three factors: consideration, change, and commitment, as discussed in more detail next.

The EWA, reinforcement, and belief theories have been compared in 31 separate sets of data from experiments (conducted by us, as well as six other researchers). In 90 percent of those studies, EWA explained and predicted what people actually chose more accurately than either of the other theories. Experiments also show that players achieve higher payoffs by using the EWA model to forecast the strategic behaviors of others.[3] For example, in one study, 43 of 54 players using EWA earned more money than counterparts not using this approach.

Learning Styles: Consideration, Change, and Commitment

Different managers learn from their experiences in different ways. These different learning styles—and the attraction levels assigned to different strategies—are based on three factors: consideration, change, and commitment.

Consideration Index.   People hate missing a plane by five minutes more than they hate missing it by an hour, because they can more easily imagine ways they would have caught the plane; consideration of a missed opportunity is far stronger for a near miss. In the EWA theory, the consideration index is a measure of the relative weight people give to foregone payoffs in past decisions, or how vividly they imagine lost value from missed opportunities. If their imagination is hazy, lost value does not weigh very heavily in learning. If, however, there is powerful emotional regret, as when the passenger is standing at the gate watching the plane taxi onto the runway (or a competitor lands a big account you spent months wooing), consideration will be a much more significant factor in learning.

Consideration of lost opportunities is also embedded in legal principles such as negligence. In an accident, the party who had the "last clear chance" to avert the accident is usually held liable, because it is easiest to imagine the accident being avoided by that party's last-second action. Economists often refer to the value of a lost opportunity as an "opportunity cost." When the consideration index is higher, managers switch more quickly to the strategies they wish they would have picked, minimizing their opportunity cost or regret.

Smart learners have a high consideration index, which means they are actively considering what they should have done after every move. Learners with a low consideration index can get stuck using a strategy that is not necessarily bad, but is not nearly as good as alternative strategies.[4] In artificial intelligence programs that help machines to learn, clever programmers avoid getting stuck with suboptimal outcomes by having the machine experiment periodically.

Change Index.   The second factor that affects the attraction of past strategies is the manager's perception of how rapidly the environment is changing. When change is rapid, players attach little weight to old experiences, because what worked years ago (or months, in Internet time) is irrelevant. When the environment is stable, managers can learn over longer periods, weighing previous successes and failures equally. In this case, managers can use a long history of payoffs to choose a strategy.

In learning, information is like machinery. The change index determines the obsolescence policy for disposing of old information, much as companies develop obsolescence policies for replacing old equipment. When technology quickly makes machinery obsolete, managers retire old machinery and upgrade quickly; when obsolescence is slow, they hold onto old machinery longer. When the world is changing rapidly, you should "retire" past experience more rapidly. This advice implies that different businesses in a single firm should be learning at different rates. Think of a restaurant that begins to advertise and accept reservations on its Web site. Learning about how to operate the Web site requires very rapid adjustment and learning (which implies forgetting about what worked a year or two ago). But knowing how to train waitstaff and buy fresh produce and seafood benefits from the wisdom of many years of experience.

Commitment Index.   The third factor that affects learning is how quickly managers lock in on a strategy that has performed well. If, for example, a given strategy has produced consistently high payoffs, and the environment is relatively stable, then it makes sense to commit to choose that strategy all the time. But if the relative performance of strategies seesaws back and forth, and the environment is changing rapidly, then it is a mistake to commit too strongly to one strategy.

In the EWA theory, commitment is expressed by judging a strategy based on its cumulative performance, simply totaling up all its successes. If attractions are cumulative payoff totals, then a strategy that is good enough to be chosen often will pile up more and more wins, compared to lesser strategies that are not tried much. This process is like the opposite of handicapping a horse race. To make a horse race even, the best horses are forced to carry more weight to slow them down. But suppose you wanted to guarantee that the best horse wins. Then you would want to give less weight to the fastest horses, to give them an advantage based on previous successes. Similarly, suppose you were deciding which scientist in your R&D lab to devote resources to. During an initial trial period, you might judge new scientists by their average output. Then it makes sense to commit more resources to the scientists who did well initially, and judge scientists by their total output.

The EWA theory specifies a precise mathematical way in which past experiences are combined using the consideration, change, and commitment indices. These indices correspond to different learning styles. For example, a manager who is constantly second-guessing and pointing out mistakes has a high consideration index (which is good for learning, but may have other organizational costs such as demoralizing workers and discouraging risk-taking). A manager who always surfs the latest trend has a high change index; one whose mantra is "if it ain't broke don't fix it" has a low change index.

SOPHISTICATED LEARNING

Sophisticated players are aware of the learning process. They use an understanding of how others learn—and the factors of consideration, change, and commitment—to anticipate the decisions of their competitors. Even if they don't apply the formal EWA model in their decision making, they use this deeper understanding to outguess their competitors and coordinate with partners.

All decision makers become more sophisticated over time. In our experimental studies, we find that a small fraction of players are sophisticated learners, but that fraction grows as subjects play similar games repeatedly. They learn about how to play better and also to anticipate how others are reacting and learning.

How does the presence of sophisticated players affect competitive interactions and outcomes? To explore this issue, we examine a well-known competitive game—the beauty contest.

Beauty Contest Games

Economist John Maynard Keynes once compared investment in the stock market to a kind of beauty contest popular in British newspapers in the 1920s.[5] In these contests, a newspaper printed pictures of 100 people and asked readers to name their favorites. All those who chose the face that proved to be most popular were eligible for a prize. Keynes pointed out that the goal was not to pick what *you* considered to be the prettiest face, but to pick the face that *the most people* would pick. He noted that stock market investment is similar—just substitute "hottest stock next week" for "prettiest face." While Keynes' metaphor is nearly 80 years old, it is perhaps no more apt than in the modern-day era of tech stocks valued by "new paradigm" principles.

Based on this idea, researchers have developed a type of competitive game called the "beauty contest." The game has been studied on three continents with several samples of sophisticated adults, including economics PhDs, CEOs and corporate presidents,[6] and readers of business publications including the *Financial Times*.[7] It illustrates some important properties of strategic thinking in naturally occurring settings.

In the beauty contest game we analyze next, a group of players simultaneously choose numbers between 0 and 100. The player whose number is closest to two-thirds of the average wins a fixed prize. Since all players should choose two-thirds of what they think the average number will be, any kind of introspective reasoning will lead to lower and lower numbers. A typical player might reason as follows: Suppose the average is 50. Then I should choose 33. But if everybody does that first step of reasoning, then the average will be 33; so I should choose two-thirds of that, which is around 22. But if everyone chooses 22, should I choose two-thirds of 22? Where does this thinking stop?

In standard game theory, there is no natural stopping place until one reaches the *Nash equilibrium,* the point at which all players' strategies are profit-maximizing best responses to one another. In this case, the Nash equilibrium is zero. This assumes all the players are acting rationally, according to the dictates of game theory.

In practice, however, everyone is not rational, nor do we expect them to be. Some might be confused and choose around 50, or just choose a lucky number. Others will do one step of reasoning and pick 33. Others will do two steps and come down to 22. The number of levels of reasoning people are likely to use is a question that can only be answered by psychology and observation, rather than by pure mathematics. (The early game theorist Tom Schelling said that many questions in game theory cannot be answered by pure logic. Those questions can only be resolved by putting people in strategic situations and watching what they do, much as you cannot prove a joke is funny until you tell it and people laugh.) Furthermore, a smart player's goal in the game is to be one step smarter than the average person, *but no smarter!*

Experiments on the beauty contest game have shown a surprising amount of regularity. Figure 9.1 shows some distributions of choices from four interesting groups of subjects. Each interval is a range of five numbers (1–5, 6–10, and so forth). The height of each bar represents the proportion of subjects choosing numbers in that interval. It is easy to see that initial choices are widely dispersed and centered somewhere between equilibrium (in this case, 0) and 50. The average tends to be between 20 and 35, so that choosing a number between 14 and 25 would give you a better-than-average chance of winning. These numbers correspond to one or two steps of reasoning from the presumed average of 50. In fact, about a dozen experimental studies have shown, with very different strategic situations and different subjects, that people typically engage in one to two steps of reasoning. One group of subjects are Caltech undergraduates, who have spectacular analytical skill (and know that their peers do, too); they choose numbers about one step closer to the equilibrium than the other groups—CEOs, portfolio

Figure 9.1
Distribution of Choices

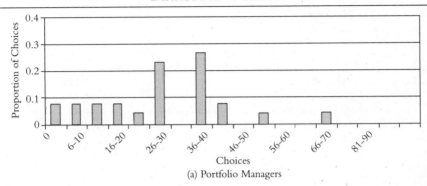

(a) Portfolio Managers

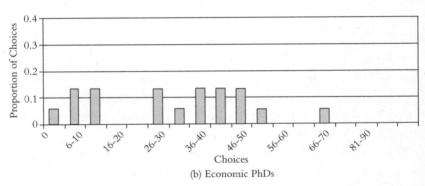

(b) Economic PhDs

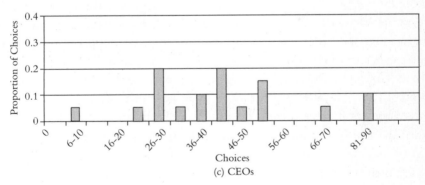

(c) CEOs

(continued)

Figure 9.1 (Continued)

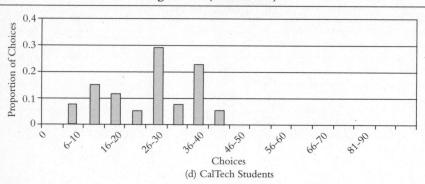

Choices
(d) CalTech Students

managers, and economics PhDs. Players learn as they continue to play. When the game is repeated, numbers gradually converge toward the equilibrium prediction of zero. That prediction is useful as a long-run benchmark, but it is not very helpful for explaining the trajectory of learning or for giving advice on how to play in the first few periods. Fortunes can be made and lost getting to equilibrium.

What happens when sophisticated players enter these games? In any given game, some players are very sophisticated and others are not. The sophisticated players understand the learning process. Suppose the average in one period is 30, so that choosing 20 would have been a winning number. In the next period, most players tend to choose 20, but sophisticated players guess others will choose 20 and choose ⅔ of 20, around 13, leapfrogging ahead. (In the Internet economy, the trick is not to be one step ahead of the competition, but always planning for the next step after that one.) The more sophisticated the players, the more rapidly the group will converge toward the equilibrium point of zero. But what is important is that the sophisticated players will lower their number if they believe other players are unsophisticated. Remember, they are trying to anticipate how others will act. For example, if these sophisticated players could actually use the EWA model to predict every player's choice in every period, they would know how to make better choices and would win more often.

Figure 9.2a shows the distribution of actual choices by subjects who played the game 10 times. The axis on the front left shows intervals of

Figure 9.2
The Predictive Power of Experience-Weighted Attraction Learning Theory

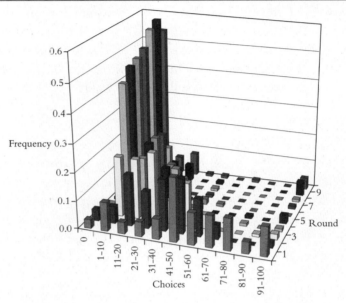

(a) Actual Choice Frequencies in Beauty Contest Games

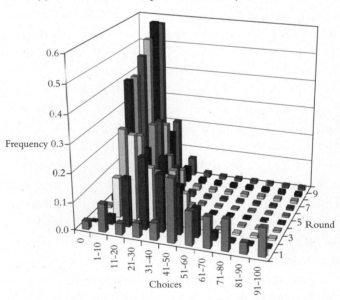

(b) Predictions of EWA Theory in Beauty Contest Games

numbers players might pick. The right axis is the period of the game (from 1 to 10). The proportion of players choosing lower numbers grows and grows across the 10 repetitions—that is, the bars representing low-number choices grow taller and taller—as they learn. Figure 9.2b shows statistical predictions of the EWA theory (that is, what players are predicted to do). The two graphs look very similar, which means that the theory is doing a good job of predicting how players will actually learn.

STRATEGIC TEACHING

This same process used by managers to *learn* from past experience can also be used to *teach* rivals and customers. If a sophisticated player thinks other players are adaptive and will respond to their recent experiences, it can then shape those experiences to its own advantage. The sophisticated player has an incentive to choose strategies in the current period that affect how the adaptive players respond in future periods, if those responses benefit the sophisticated player. We refer to this as *strategic teaching*.

Strategic teaching goes on all the time in business. For example, Wall Street security analysts tend to hammer the share price of a company that reports disappointing earnings—below what was expected. Managers have an incentive to manipulate expectations for earnings as best they can (using accounting methods to keep some potential earnings "in their pocket"). They are effectively trying to teach the Street that earnings will be low so analysts will be pleasantly surprised when the earnings come out higher.

In this process, it is important to understand what a rival is learning from your teaching to avoid teaching too much or too little. Think about a supplier trying to reassure a new client of its goodwill by providing extra goods, lowest price guarantees, and so forth. Some clients will easily learn that the supplier is trustworthy, so repeated concessions to establish trust are a waste of money (the supplier is over teaching). Other clients will never quite trust the supplier, so it may be better to sever the relationship. The EWA model offers a way to quantify what another firm or person is learning from the current strategy.

There are many other important potential applications of the idea of optimal teaching. In economics, it is well established that a spurt of unexpected inflation can lower unemployment (this is called the *Phillips curve*). As a result, policy makers who benefit from lower unemployment—such as a sitting administration just before a presidential election—are always tempted to increase inflation. Policy makers who take a long view—such as a Federal Reserve Board chairman with a long-term perspective—would like to build up credibility with the public by keeping price inflation low for years at a time. This certifies his ability to resist the temptation to inflate. In our terms, the policy makers have an incentive to teach the public that inflation will be low in the future. This basic idea has been used to explain the substantial shift from the high double-digit inflation of the 1970s in the United States, to a more recent post-1985 drop in inflation.[8]

Another example is the pricing of goods that fall in price rapidly, such as computers and new high-tech products like cellular phones and personal digital assistants. In these markets, consumers may delay purchase if they believe prices will fall rapidly. Since firms would like to sell goods earlier rather than later, they have an incentive to teach consumers that prices will not fall that rapidly, so they will buy right away.

The Prisoners' Dilemma

A sophisticated player who is teaching other players may even deliberately choose a bad strategy in the current period, if choosing that strategy yields a better return in future periods. In a sense, the current period choice is an "investment" in educating the other players, which pays off for the teacher in the future. To explore this, consider the well-known example of the repeated prisoners' dilemma.

In the prisoners' dilemma, two prisoners are arrested. They have the choice of either cooperating with one another or defecting and ratting on the other. If they cooperate, they each receive an equal payoff of 3, as shown in Table 9.1. If one defects and the other doesn't, however, the defector is then rewarded with a payoff of 5 while the betrayed partner is left with zero. If both defect, then they both end up with 1. The dilemma is

Table 9.1
Prisoners' Dilemma Payoffs

	Cooperate	Defect
Cooperate	3,3	0,5
Defect	5,0	1,1

that both players can do better if they cooperate. But if they cannot be sure what the other player will do, they are better off defecting. At least that guarantees a payoff of 1 and perhaps of 5. In the repeated prisoners' dilemma, players engage in this same game over several sessions. Players usually cooperate in the initial periods. Then one of the players defects as the end draws near, and both players defect until the last round. How can we explain this?

Strategic teaching explains it by assuming that some players are adaptive, and learn, while others are sophisticated and try to teach the adaptive players to cooperate. If the teachers can convince the adaptive learners to cooperate, then everybody can get payoffs of 3 for several periods.

How does the teaching work? The sophisticated player starts by cooperating, choosing a strategy that maximizes the sum of the current payoff and expected future payoffs (assuming the adaptive players learn from what the sophisticated players do in the beginning). Suppose the adaptive players start out with equal initial attractions on cooperating and defecting, so they are equally likely to choose either one. If the adaptive students choose to defect, they earn 5, and are likely to continue to defect in the future.

Anticipating this, the sophisticated teacher may well give up, and both players defect throughout. More interestingly, suppose the adaptive player starts by choosing to cooperate. Then both players earn a payoff of 3, but this also reinforces defection (since they know they would have earned 5 if one had defected). Thus, strategic teaching can explain why there is mutual cooperation for several periods in the repeated prisoners' dilemma. But how does it explain the fact that cooperation usually breaks down a couple of periods from the end? Remember that sophisticated teachers maximize the sum of their current payoff and expected future payoffs (knowing how their current actions "teach" the adaptive players). When the end draws near, there are not many future periods of cooperative payoffs left, and the strategic teachers are tempted to defect to earn the largest payoff of 5. How likely adaptive players are to switch to defect will depend on the amount of cooperation they encountered previously. Thus, it pays for sophisticated teachers to cooperate until close to the end, to build up the chance that an adaptive player will still cooperate in the last period (even after a defection), and to defect a couple of periods before the end.

Strategic teaching is sometimes beneficial for both players—as when one firm tries to reassure a business partner, who learns from the firm's past behavior that it can be trusted in the future and that trust enables the two sides to do business profitably. In other cases strategic teaching benefits the teacher by enabling the teacher to exploit or manipulate the student who is learning. Examples include developing a reputation for aggressively pricing when there is new competition.

CONCLUSIONS

An important component of good strategic advice is a theory of learning. Learning is important because in many naturally occurring strategic situations players do not know their payoffs at all; therefore, they can learn more from experience than from deduction and calculation. Understanding how others learn also is important because sophisticated players who know how others learn can stay a step ahead of them. Sophisticated players can teach others what to expect in the future, in a way that often benefits the teacher.

Since its discovery about 50 years ago, game theory has been hailed as *the* mathematical language for analyzing social situations. Unfortunately, an obsession with mathematical details of how rational players would play a game after careful introspection have kept game theorists from tackling the more practically useful question—how do people actually play? And knowing that, how *should* people play? The EWA theory was created because other learning theories left out important pieces of this puzzle. We also had a nagging sense that the two most prominent kinds of learning— learning by reinforcement of successful strategies, and learning by forming beliefs about other players' behavior and responding to them—might have something fundamental in common. Furthermore, we know statistically from analysis of 31 experimental data sets that leaving out any of the three learning-style features (consideration, change, and commitment) falls short in explaining how people actually learn.

Implications

What are the implications of this theory for managers? In any competitive interaction, look for opportunities to teach and to learn from the situation. Game theory can help you think through the dynamics of multiple rounds of interactions. Don't just look at the impact of poor choices but also consider the impact of regrets over choices that were not taken.

- *Learn how to learn.* As you become more sophisticated in your learning you will better be able to make your own decisions and outguess your competitors. Understand how the three factors of consideration, change, and commitment affect learning. For any given decision, identify how these factors will influence your learning about it and decide what learning style is best. Considering the opportunity costs of all strategies you have not tried is generally wise. Applying a low change index is smart when the world is changing rapidly, but drawing on a large span of experience (i.e., a high change index) is smart when the world is relatively stable. Committing strongly to a particular strategy is wise only if you become convinced from its string of successes that no other strategy is likely to prove better.
- *Understand learning patterns of others.* Knowing how competitors respond to experience enables firms, in principle, to stay one step ahead. Recent evidence from academic studies of financial markets shows that investors tend to underreact to certain kinds of events in the short run, and overreact in the long run. These patterns open up the possibility that a theory of how investors learn could enable investment managers to beat the market.[9]
- *Assess the sophistication of other players.* Determining whether other players are sophisticated or not offers insights into the strategies you should take with them. If players are unsophisticated, how can you use teaching strategies to educate them in the direction you want to go?
- *Try using a statistical model.* While we have left out the mathematical details of the EWA theory, applying it statistically may improve a firm's ability to forecast learning of others. Many statistical models are used in business, like the Black-Scholes options pricing formula (and many subtle versions of it), models forecasting consumer purchases, and models forecasting interest rates and other macroeconomic variables. These models are successful because they combine variables in very precise ways, which sharpen managerial intuition. A variant of the EWA theory was applied by one of us (Ho) and Juin-Kuan Chong[10]

to predict consumer choices of ice cream, diapers, and other consumer products. The theory assumes that people learn what brands they like by trial and error and generalize from experience with one brand to related brands which are similar. The analysis used 130,000 choices by consumers and was able to predict choices about 10 percent better using only one-fifth as many variables as the previous "best practice" model. (Ten percent is a small improvement, but in consumer forecasting even a 1 percent increase adds value.) A large supermarket chain rushed the model into their business immediately (before Ho and Chong's paper was even published in a journal!).

Learning has become a central focus of organizations. But less attention has been spent on the process by which people learn—particularly from their own experience and that of others. The EWA learning theory is a powerful tool for strategic decision making for two reasons: First, it enables a company to stay a step ahead of competitors by predicting what they will do. Second, it enables a company to teach competitors how the company will behave in the future, which is useful for both creating trust among partners, and signaling toughness to competitors.

CHAPTER 10

REPUTATIONS IN NEGOTIATION

STEVEN GLICK
Boston Consulting Group

RACHEL CROSON
The Wharton School

Negotiators are more likely to use hard-line tactics against partners who are perceived as "cream puffs" and against "tough" negotiators.

A good reputation is more valuable than money.

—*Publius Syrus*

Many executives place a high value on their reputations. What few under-stand is how these reputations—good and bad—precede them and affect the character of their negotiations. The real value may be realized not so much in having a sterling reputation but in actively managing your own reputation to prepare for future negotiations and in tailoring your negotiating tactics to the reputations of others. This chapter offers insights, based on original re-search, on the impact of reputations in negotiations. In general, negotiators are more likely to use hardball tactics with both tough partners (defensively) and cream puffs (offensively). Similarly, they are more likely to use concil-iatory approaches with middle-of-the-road negotiators than with either tough negotiators or cream puffs. The authors also discuss ways managers can be-come more effective negotiators by tailoring their tactics to the reputation type of their partners and how they can actively shape their own reputations.

Real estate developer Donald Trump has a well-publicized reputation as a hard-line negotiator. In an article de-scribing his negotiations with the Taj Mahal Casino Resort's bondholders, Trump's advisors tell how after a deal is agreed upon, he always comes back requesting something more.[1] Well-informed counterparts, familiar with his reputation, are prepared for this tactic and anticipate it in deciding how many concessions to make during the preagreement stage. Similarly, Trump has a reputation for storming out of negotiations in the middle of talks. An anonymous participant in the bondholders negotiation said, "You know Donald's going to get up and leave, you just don't know when."[2] Once ne-gotiators develop reputations for hardball tactics like these, counterparts change their tactics and strategies to accommodate.

Clearly reputation plays a pivotal role in Trump's negotiations. But you might question whether this is more the exception than the rule. After all, how often do negotiators develop discernible reputations that their nego-tiating partner would be aware of? Not everyone is as well known as Don-ald Trump. How does a more positive reputation for negotiating affect the behavior of partners?

Our research finds that reputations are built quickly in negotiating com-munities. We also found that these reputations strongly affect the strategies used by negotiating partners. This chapter summarizes our research in this area and provides advice for the negotiating manager on reputation development and management.

NEGOTIATION COMMUNITIES

You don't have to be a famous real estate tycoon for others to be familiar with your negotiating tactics. Negotiating partners who interact on a repeated basis, or communicate with people who do, develop reputations. Our research suggests that even lesser known players become as familiar to each other as neighbors in a cul-de-sac through repeated interaction and information sharing.

One of the best examples of such a *negotiation community* is the Silicon Valley, where an active technology trade press helps to generate a rich flow of information, a prerequisite to reputation building. Supplementing this information exchange is a large, energetic network of venture capitalists and angel investors, who gain knowledge of particular individuals' negotiation tactics while providing financial and advisory support to hundreds of fledgling companies.

If the entrepreneurs, angels, and venture capitalists maintained exclusive relationships, there would be little potential for, or interest in, information exchange. However, just the opposite is true: Joint ventures, coinvestments, and overlapping relationships are the norm, providing almost infinite potential for information sharing.

The strength of this negotiation community is highlighted by a number of interviews with its members. One entrepreneur who recently secured funding from Kleiner Perkins, one of the Valley's most prestigious venture capital firms said in an interview: "The VCs [venture capitalists] talk continuously. Because they coinvest or might be coinvesting in the future, they share information all the time on entrepreneurs as well as on each other. Reputation becomes incredibly powerful."[3]

The same entrepreneur confirmed the importance of both first-hand reputations (those developed as a result of direct experience) and second-hand reputations (those developed as a result of hearing about someone else's experience) when considering negotiation tactics. For example, when negotiating with several venture capitalists for second-round financing, this individual weighted some venture capitalists' second-hand reputation (acquired via a trusted angel) as significantly as his own first-hand reputation (acquired via the entrepreneur's own experience).

Within a single firm, the potential for repeated interactions and reputation formation is even greater. For example, each time a European pharmaceutical company launches a product, headquarters and the U.S. subsidiary must decide who will foot the bill for medical marketing studies, which can cost tens of millions of dollars. After a few such launches, the executives at headquarters and the subsidiary have firmly established negotiating reputations. Within and across functions, managers constantly negotiate budgetary allocations, product responsibilities, and compensation arrangements.

Both across and within firms, repeated interaction and open communication create negotiation communities. Reputations born and raised within these communities go on to play significant roles in future negotiation processes and outcomes. How do these communities develop and how do they affect negotiations?

YOU HAVE A REPUTATION—WHETHER YOU KNOW IT OR NOT

In negotiation communities, almost everyone has a reputation, even if it is sketchy and second hand. This prevalence of reputations is a direct result of the degree of information exchanged within the community. "If you are hooked into the right network, and have the right people on your side, you can find out an incredible amount about the person you are negotiating with," noted the Silicon Valley entrepreneur.

A study of 105 graduate and undergraduate students enrolled in a negotiations course at the Wharton School demonstrated the speed with which reputations are established within a negotiation community. As part of the course, students negotiated with each other and conducted debriefing sessions with their classmates. Reputations quickly developed and spread among the students as to who was what type of negotiator. Clearly, the classroom setting and prescribed pattern of interaction accelerated information sharing and reputation development. However, in other key dimensions, the negotiation community created in the classroom closely mirrors those found in the business world.

In this study, we asked students to rate their negotiating partners based on five reputation types. They were organized from least cooperative (most confrontational or toughest) to most cooperative (softest):

1. Liar/Manipulator: Will do anything to gain an advantage
2. Tough but Honest: Very tough negotiator but doesn't lie, makes few concessions
3. Nice and Reasonable: Will make concessions/be conciliatory
4. Cream Puff: Will make concessions/be conciliatory regardless of what you do
5. No Particular Reputation

Reputations can be formed based on either first-hand experience or second-hand experience. First-hand reputations come from negotiating yourself with the person in question; second-hand reputations are based on information about the negotiating experiences of others. Since we are interested in both types of reputations, we did not distinguish between the two.

An analysis of each participant's ratings revealed remarkable agreement about the reputation of each negotiator. We used a chi-squared test for individuals to examine whether the ratings he or she had received were statistically different than an equal distribution. For 78 percent of the negotiators (82 out of 105), a reputation was identified as being statistically significant. This result is consistent with observations from interviews in actual negotiation communities in the business world, such as Silicon Valley, that reputations are discernable and robust.

This first study demonstrates the existence of negotiation reputations within a group of individuals. But what impact do these reputations have on the actions of partners? In a second study, we examined the effect of these reputations on the negotiation process and the tactics used.

HOW REPUTATIONS AFFECT NEGOTIATING TACTICS

During a lengthy negotiation with one of the country's largest Internet access providers, one media executive described how he modified his tactics to counter his negotiating partner's emerging behavior pattern and reputation. "He was a consistent counterproposer," the executive said. "It became apparent that we needed to come in with a more extreme position than we actually hoped to leave with because the counterproposal process would predictably force us towards the middle."[4]

Similarly, for the Silicon Valley entrepreneur mentioned earlier, the reputation of the party on the other side of the table plays a large role in determining posture and tactics. "If someone has a strong reputation for being straight and honest, then negotiation partners will be less inclined to delay. The reaction is more 'shut up and take whatever deal this person is offering.' In the interest of reducing transaction costs and saving time [critical in an industry where business models are outmoded every six months], we'll just go ahead and do the deal."

Previous researchers studying negotiations have examined the tactics chosen by negotiators as a function of their own knowledge of the tactics,[5] their emotional state,[6] gender,[7] or time pressure.[8] Our research shifted the focus to the other side of the table. How does the reputation of the negotiating *partner* affect tactics used? We found that negotiators use different tactics based on the reputations of their counterparts.

A subset of 75 of the business students who had participated in the first study on reputation communities participated in a second study on the impact of these reputations. Negotiators were provided with a list of tactics and asked to indicate which of those they would use or had used against counterparts of varying reputations:

1. Beginning with extreme demands
2. Threatening to walk away from the negotiation
3. Evading the questions of your counterpart
4. Asking pointed questions of your counterpart
5. Sharing information voluntarily
6. Making unilateral concessions

The first four of these tactics are "hardball" tactics, typically used in distributive (win-lose) negotiations—beginning with extreme demands, threatening to walk, asking pointed questions of your counterpart, and evading your partner's questions. The last two are tactics more appropriate for integrative (win-win) negotiations—sharing information voluntarily or offering unilateral concessions.

Figure 10.1 summarizes the proportion of subjects reporting they would use a particular type of tactic against a counterpart of varying reputations. Against liars, 61 percent of respondents reported using distributive tactics, while only 9.8 percent used integrative tactics. Against tough negotiators, 48.7 percent used distributive tactics and 35.1 percent integrative tactics. Against nice negotiators, only 30.2 percent used distributive tactics while 64.2 percent used integrative tactics. And against cream-puff negotiators, 40.3 percent used distributive tactics while only 26.7 percent used integrative tactics.

Generally, negotiators were more likely to use hardball, distributive tactics against counterparts with tough reputations and to use integrative tactics against counterparts with softer reputations. Thus, for example, if Carol knew Bill was a particularly tough negotiator, she might be more likely to begin her negotiation with an extreme demand.

Interestingly, however, reputations did not influence the tactics used in a uniform way. Confrontational tactics were more likely to be used against "tough" negotiators (for defensive reasons), but *also* against "soft" negotiating types (for offensive reasons). These tactics were not often used against participants with reputations for moderate negotiating styles.

Figure 10.1
Frequency of Tactics against Varying Reputation Types

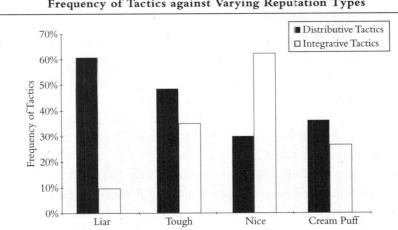

Similarly, integrative (win-win) tactics were used more often against participants with moderate negotiation styles than against either tough or soft negotiators. For example, 53 percent of the respondents said they begin with an extreme demand when facing a liar/manipulator and 40 percent against a tough but fair negotiator. Subjects were statistically significantly less likely to use this tactic against negotiators who were nice and reasonable (20 percent). However, the incidence of using this tactic rose to 47 percent against a cream puff negotiator.

We speculate that the first two uses of this tactic are defensive; in order to hold your own against a liar or tough negotiator you need to begin with extreme demands. In contrast, the latter use of this tactic is offensive; starting with an extreme demand will often yield benefits against a cream puff. Against a nice and reasonable negotiator, however, beginning with extreme demands may spoil the negotiation atmosphere.

We found a similar but inverted relationship between tactics and reputations for integrative tactics. For example, subjects were reluctant to share information voluntarily with either tough negotiators or with cream puffs (44 percent and 33 percent respectively). Significantly more subjects (83 percent) were willing to share information with nice and reasonable negotiating partners. Here, we speculate that the reluctance to share information with tough or manipulative negotiators is defensive, and the reluctance to share information with cream puffs is offensive.

Managing Your Reputation

Given the reactions of negotiating partners to your reputation, shaping and managing your own reputation can have a significant impact on negotiations. Donald Trump's tough negotiating posture has changed the way partners approach negotiations with him. It is impossible to say how a different negotiating style might have worked in his particular situation and industry. In entering negotiations, you need to ask: What is the most effective style to achieve my desired goals?

While this is a complex decision, and one that is likely to be highly sensitive to your industry, our studies indicate that if your goal is to elicit cooperation and integration from partners, you might want to avoid appearing either too hard or too soft. Developing a moderate reputation is most effective. On the other hand, if it serves your purpose to draw out tough tactics from partners—maybe to throw them off balance or force them to overcommit to a position—then taking either an aggressive or an extremely soft position will elicit the desired response.

The other side of this challenge is deciding how you will respond to the reputations of others. The reactions we identified are general tendencies, but they can be overcome by a sophisticated negotiator. Do you want to take advantage of a cream puff rival? Do you want to meet a hardball negotiator with hardball tactics? Sometimes negotiators can reshape the tenor of negotiations by doing something unexpected. You may want to reconsider your natural reactions next time you are at the negotiating table and instead react consciously and strategically.

Finally, you can use this information to decide to reshape your own reputation for the future. In some industries, individuals need moderate, cooperative negotiating reputations to be invited to the table at all. "The understanding and mutual respect that companies develop as a result of repetitive negotiations is an important asset," said the CEO of a large New England telecommunications infrastructure, whose company's growth has depended largely on a series of successful, high-stakes negotiations. He indicated that strong reputations for honest dealing and seeking mutual benefit enabled him and his partners to develop complex integrative solutions.[9]

A bad reputation, or even the lack of a good reputation, can lock negotiators out of positive outcomes in some industries. In Silicon Valley, where time to market is often in shorter supply than money, a significant constraint on businesspeople is often space on the calendar to negotiate with a long list of potential business partners. Our Silicon Valley entrepreneur indicated, "If we don't have an indication of positive reputation on some VC, we just won't even begin dealing with him." In this environment, a positive reputation is not simply an asset, but a basic precondition of doing business.

On the other hand, Donald Trump still gets invited to the table, despite his reputation for toughness—and probably, quite often, *because* of it. A tough negotiator is respected in some circles. Ronald Reagan credited the U.S. reputation for toughness against the Soviet Union as a crucial posture in finally achieving strategic arms limitation agreements. Sometimes a tough reputation has great value in setting the stage for negotiations or even bringing a partner into negotiations. So what might be perceived as a "bad" reputation in one context could be an asset in another.

Because you are always building your reputation, your decision about what to do at the negotiating table affects more than the negotiation at hand. Negotiation reputations are built over time; each round of negotiations affects the reputation you take into the next one. When choosing tactics during a negotiation, managers must estimate not only the impact of the tactic on the outcome of this particular negotiation but also the impact of the tactic and its effect on reputation. This impact might vary depending on the industry and the norms. For example, our Silicon Valley entrepreneur noted, "It is critical to get to a big win–win, because each outcome is going to determine your own reputation going forward." In other industries, having a reputation for being tough may be the desired asset. Understanding the impact of reputation on future negotiations can help managers select the appropriate trade-offs between choosing tactics this time and developing their reputations in the future.

CHAPTER 11

DECEPTION IN NEGOTIATIONS

MAURICE E. SCHWEITZER
The Wharton School

Can you detect a lie? One study found that 28 percent of negotiators lied about a common interest issue during negotiations, while another study found that 100 percent of negotiators either failed to reveal a problem or actively lied about it during negotiations if they were not directly asked about the issue.

I thank Richard Shell and Robert Gunther for helpful comments.

Truth is the most valuable thing we have. Let us economize it.
                                                    —*Mark Twain*

During the course of negotiations, people often misrepresent information to gain at least a temporary advantage. For example, a seller may fabricate the existence of another interested buyer or a buyer may misrepresent the price and availability of an item from a different vendor. The author explores different types of lies, their impact on negotiations and decision making, and the inherent difficulty negotiators face in detecting falsehoods. The chapter concludes with prescriptions for contending with the use of deception by others and for managing the use of deception within your organization.

In 1994, Textron was in labor contract negotiations with the United Automobile Workers Union (UAW). Both prior to and during the negotiations, the UAW asked Textron about its intentions to subcontract work with nonunion workers. Textron assured the UAW that they had no plans to subcontract work, and the parties reached an agreement. Shortly after the contract was signed, Textron unveiled plans to subcontract work. In actuality, Textron's management had developed plans to subcontract work prior to the negotiation. This intention was substantiated by internal company documents, and the UAW subsequently sued Textron for negotiating in bad faith. The UAW lost the lawsuit. The court determined that if the issue of subcontracting was critical to the UAW, they should have included a clause regarding subcontracting in the contract.[1]

Managers often have incentives to lie, and in the Textron case, management derived, at least in the short run, benefits from telling a lie. How can negotiators avoid falling victim to the use of deception by others?

At the individual level, when are people more or less likely to lie in negotiations? In one case, attorney Richard Bonczek had worked at DuPont for 24 years. He was interested in leaving DuPont and interviewed with Carter-Wallace for a position in their legal department. As the interview process progressed, he negotiated for his position title, salary, and benefits. Ultimately, Carter-Wallace extended Bonczek an offer "contingent on the completion of reference checks." Upon receiving the offer letter, Bonczek resigned from his job at DuPont. When Carter-Wallace initiated a background check, however, they learned that Bonczek had misrepresented both his title and his salary at DuPont. Carter-Wallace then withdrew its offer, leaving Bonczek unemployed.[2] (Bonczek subsequently filed a lawsuit against Carter-Wallace and lost.)

In companies, how does organizational culture encourage or discourage deception? A 1992 investigation by California state regulators concluded that Sears automotive employees performed unnecessary repairs 90 percent of the time. The California regulators discovered that the company had given automotive service advisors aggressive goals for selling parts and services. These findings prompted Sears' chairman Edward Brennan to announce that the "goal-setting process for service advisors created an environment where mistakes did occur" and that they would be "dumping the sales system, effective immediately."[3]

Deception of some kind is an inherent part of human interaction. We tend to be overconfident in our ability to detect deception and often prefer not to consider the possibility that we are being deceived as we negotiate and make important decisions. This chapter examines the potential for deception and some ways to avoid it and manage it within your organization. Why do people decide to deceive? How common is deception? Why is deception so hard to detect?

THE HONEST TRUTH ABOUT LYING

Are people lying to you in negotiations? There is a very good chance that they are. One study found that 28 percent of negotiators lied about a common interest issue during negotiations,[4] while another study found that 100 percent of negotiators either failed to reveal a problem or actively lied about it during negotiations if they were not directly asked about the issue.[5]

People are generally more comfortable telling lies of *omission,* by not revealing information, than lies of *commission,* by actively misrepresenting information. Some ethicists argue that lies of omission and lies of commission are morally equivalent if the outcomes and the liar's intentions are the same.[6] As a practical matter, however, the intentionality of omissions is difficult to judge, and the law typically holds negotiators more responsible for lies of commission than lies of omission.[7]

The Subject of Lies

In addition to distinguishing between lies of omission and lies of commission, lies also can be classified according to the type of information misrepresented. Broadly speaking, negotiators can misrepresent their reservation price, their interests, their intentions, and material facts:

- *Reservation prices.* Lies about reservation prices are very common. So common in fact, that negotiators should never rely on the claims their negotiation partners make regarding their bottom line or reservation price. The law echoes this sentiment, and lies concerning one's "bottom line" do not usually constitute fraud.
- *Interests.* Negotiators also frequently misrepresent their interests and intentions. For example, a negotiator may misrepresent a common interest as a conflicting interest to extract concessions.[8] In many cases, negotiators have compatible interests that are difficult for both parties to recognize. A buyer and a seller may both prefer an earlier closing date for the sale of a property. After a seller expresses her preference for an earlier closing date, however, a strategic buyer might misrepresent his interest, and claim that a later closing date would be more convenient for him, but that he could accommodate the seller if she made other concessions.
- *Intentions.* Negotiators can also bluff about their intentions. This tactic was used successfully by David Cohen, the deputy mayor of Philadelphia, during labor negotiations with most of the city's blue-collar workforce in 1992. The city of Philadelphia had engaged District Council 33, the union that represented most of the city's workforce, in a contentious and protracted negotiation. The city had asked the union to make significant wage concessions. During the negotiations, Cohen solicited and received several bids for privatizing trash collection. Though Cohen never intended to privatize trash collection, he knew that this issue was important to the union and that he could "concede" this issue in exchange for other concessions. In the final hours of negotiations, the city and union negotiators reached an agreement—the unions agreed to wage concessions and the city conceded the issue of privatizing trash collection.
- *Material facts.* Lies about material facts are almost always more serious. Most negotiators consider lies about material facts to be unacceptable.[9] These lies constitute fraud whenever a negotiator makes a "knowing misrepresentation of a material fact on which the victim

relies that causes damage."[10] Not all lies about material facts fit this definition. For example, a home buyer is obligated to exercise reasonable prudence and hire a title search firm rather than rely on the verbal assurances of a seller when a seller states that she has "good title" to her home.

Lies have also been categorized according to the object of the lie. Lies can be told about oneself (e.g., "I have substantial experience handling an order of this size"), about the target (e.g., "You look great in that suit"), about another person (e.g., "Your partner is trying to steal your business"), or about an object or event (e.g., "This contract is likely to generate a substantial number of referrals").

Finally, we can distinguish between lies according to whether the primary motivation of the lie is to promote one's own interests (self-oriented lies) or to promote someone else's interest (other-oriented lies). Other-oriented lies are often used to make others feel at ease. A negotiator may claim that "now is a great to time to meet" or "we would be happy to meet that request," when in fact the opposite is true.[11]

Many lies, such as other-oriented lies, can actually facilitate the communication process. In this chapter I focus on self-oriented lies about material facts, intentions, and interests that can harm the negotiation process.

DECIDING TO LIE

Why do people decide to lie and how are lies incorporated into the decision process? One might look at the decision through a simple cost-benefit framework. As the benefits of lying rise and the costs of lying fall, negotiators become more likely to lie.[12] Consistent with this model, one experiment found a direct link between incentives and deception; subjects who were offered a larger incentive to misrepresent a forecast were more likely to lie.[13]

This cost-benefit calculation, however, is far from straightforward. While the benefits of deception are often apparent, assessing the expected costs of deception is more complicated. First, a negotiator must estimate the probability that the deception will be detected. These estimates may be biased in a number of ways. For example, a negotiator who has been successful using deception in the past may be overconfident in her ability to use deception in the future.

Second, a negotiator must estimate the costs of detected deception. These can include both legal and reputation costs. In high-profile and repeated negotiations these costs can be quite high. In other cases, however, these costs can be surprisingly low. For example, in some industries, repeated interaction is low and negotiators can operate effectively with a tarnished reputation. House negotiations are almost always a single-shot transaction between a buyer and a seller. In these cases, a buyer may bluff and declare $300,000 to be her "firm and final price" with relative impunity. If the seller responds by claiming that his last offer of $310,000 is his final price, the buyer can capitulate and pay $310,000. In this case, the buyer loses credibility with the seller, and the seller would reasonably discount any future claim she might make regarding her "firm and final price." However, since the buyer and seller are unlikely to interact with one another in the future, this loss of credibility is not very important for the buyer.

A final cost negotiators may bear for telling lies is the potential for feeling guilt or remorse. The degree of guilt is subject to a great deal of individual variation. In general, the expected costs of telling lies in negotiations are higher when the target is more likely to detect the deception, the target is more likely to be vengeful, the relationship is repeated, and the visibility of deception is high.

Further, the *framing* of outcomes in terms of gains or losses can influence the *perceived* costs of using deception. For example, suppose a management team is engaged in salary negotiations with a union. The union states an initial demand for a 10 percent wage increase and the management team flatly rejects their demand. Suppose that after protracted negotiations, both sides agree to a 4 percent wage increase. In this case, the 4 percent increase can be viewed by the union as either a 4 percent *gain* relative to their current wage or a 6 percent *loss* relative to their initial demand of 10 percent. The current wage rate *or* the 10 percent increase serve as reference points in this example.

Several other reference points may exist, such as last year's wage increase, the rate of inflation, or the percentage increase other unions received. In general, any negotiation can be viewed in terms of gains (e.g., maximizing profits) or losses (e.g., minimizing costs), and different reference points can be cued relatively easily.

What makes the gain/loss distinction important is the way in which gains and losses are evaluated. People are more willing to take risks in the domain of losses than in the domain of gains. This "risk shift" may increase a negotiator's propensity to lie since the decision to use deception is often a risky choice. Compared to outcomes negotiators attain from telling the truth, negotiators typically attain better outcomes from successful deception and worse outcomes from unsuccessful deception.

Loss aversion may also influence a negotiator's propensity to lie. For example, most people consider the pain of losing $100 to be greater than the pleasure of gaining $100. Over the domain of losses, negotiators may work particularly hard to reduce losses or breakeven. While this additional effort can be constructive, it also may lead negotiators to cut corners. (Schoemaker and Russo discuss framing issues in more detail in Chapter 8.)

Justifying the Use of Deception

In addition to the difficulty of weighing the costs and benefits of deception, many negotiators will buffer themselves from the emotional costs by finding a justification for their use of deception. Although guilt and remorse may restrain negotiators from lying in egregious situations, most people readily justify their own use of deception, and work to avoid feeling guilt and remorse both prior to and after using deception.

Some negotiators justify their own use of deception in terms of self-defense, on the grounds that they were lied to in the past or that they may be lied to in the future.[14] For example, in a car purchase negotiation, buyers often preemptively suspect that sales agents will employ unethical tactics, and consequently employ unethical tactics themselves. This cycle of suspicion and deception can build upon itself. In a study involving incentives for deception, people with larger incentives were not only more likely to lie themselves but also were more likely to expect others to lie as well.[15]

Negotiators are also more likely to justify their distortion of information when that information is not known with certainty.[16] For example, some values, such as the amount of another offer, are known more precisely than others, such as the estimated cost of renovating a property. Sellers have incentives both to understate the cost of necessary renovations to a property and to overstate the value of another offer. In general, however, negotiators are more likely to bias the values they report for elastic (uncertain or

ambiguous) values, such as renovations, than for inelastic values, such as
the amount of another offer.

GUARDING AGAINST DECEPTION

If deception is so prevalent in negotiations, how do you guard against it? One
option is to be more vigilant in identifying signs of deception. Table 11.1
lists a number of diagnostic cues that indicate deception. This list, however,
warrants three important caveats. First, none of these cues is perfectly correlated with deception. Second, despite the abundance of available cues,
most people are not very good at detecting lies, and third, most people are
overconfident in their ability to detect deception.

As Table 11.1 suggests, most deception cues are nonverbal. In fact, people who are good lie detectors tend to focus on a number of nonverbal cues
such as facial expressions.[17] Consequently, negotiators attempting to detect deception should focus on nonverbal behaviors and listen carefully to
how things are said in addition to what is said.

This finding also suggests that different media, such as the telephone or
e-mail, limit a negotiator's ability to detect deception. On the other hand,
access to visual cues may also help deceivers tell lies. One study found that
negotiators were actually more likely to misrepresent a common-interest
issue via videoconference than via telephone.[18] In this case, liars could access
and update their beliefs about the target's gullibility with visual access better than they could without visual access. Consequently, visual access (via
videoconferencing or in person) may enable negotiators to be more successful in telling certain types of lies.

Finally, even if both verbal and nonverbal cues are available, most people
are not very adept at detecting deception.[19] The best defense against deception is taking steps to reduce the likelihood that people will use deception in
the first place. This can be done before, during, and after negotiations.

Before Negotiating

- *Prepare your questions.* First, negotiators should identify missing information and prepare to ask the same or similar questions multiple
  times. This repetition will reduce elastic justification and curtail lies

Table 11.1
Cues to Detect Lies

Vocabulary Cues

    "to tell the truth"

    "let me be honest with you"

Verbal Cues

    Use of more negative statements

    Irrelevant information

    Overgeneralized statements

    Fewer words in response to questions

    Lack of spontaneity

    More speech errors, grammatical errors, slips of the tongue

Vocal Cues

    Speech hesitations

    Changes (usually elevation) in pitch

    Reduced rate of speech

    Longer response time to questions

    Increased use of pause fillers (e.g., uh, er)

Visual Cues

    Less gesticulation, less head movement

    Increased blinking

    Increased use of self-adapters (nervous habits, e.g., scratching, twiddling)

    Pupil dilation

    Flushing or blanching of the skin

    Increased sweating

    Changes in respiration

    False smiles: asymmetrical, no movement around the eyes and forehead

    Conflicts between emblems (e.g., head nod) and verbal statements (e.g., nod yes when responding no)

    Conflicting microexpressions (brief lapses in facial expression)

Adapted from K. Fiedler and I. Walka, "Training Lie Detectors to Use Nonverbal Cues Instead of Global Heuristics," *Human Communication Research* 20 (1993): 199–223.

of omission. In many cases, carefully worded questions can yield valuable information—even from the way questions are deflected.

- *Evaluate motivations.* Negotiators should analyze their negotiation context and their negotiation partners. This analysis should include an evaluation of whether their negotiation partner is losing money, what their partner's goals are, what incentives their partner faces in completing a transaction, and the importance to the partner of preserving his reputation. Changes in these factors are likely to increase or decrease the likelihood that people will use deception.
- *Increase costs of deception.* Negotiators should consider options for increasing their partner's costs of using deception. For example, consider either transforming a single interaction into an opportunity for repeated business or involving a prominent third party, even nominally, in the transaction.
- *Consider the setting.* Before negotiations begin, consider the setting and communication medium. Most diagnostic cues for detecting deception are nonverbal, and different media such as face-to-face communication, videoconferencing, the telephone, and e-mail will influence whether or not negotiators will use deception.
- *Avoid overconfidence.* Finally, be vigilant. Spend time and resources checking important background information.

During Negotiation

- *Establish trust.* Negotiators should work to establish a foundation for trust at the beginning of the negotiation process. Work to convince your negotiation partner that you will not use deception. This tactic will reduce the possibility that others will employ defensive justification.
- *Shift the frame.* Negotiators can adopt frames or points of reference in a number of ways. In some cases, reference-point adoption is very subtle. For example, a manager in a labor negotiation might implicitly adopt a loss frame if others communicate this frame. In general, the communication process can be used to influence reference-point adoption both prior to and during a negotiation.[20] Consistent messages such as "I cannot accept lower profits" or "I cannot accept higher costs"

have been demonstrated to successfully influence other negotiators' frames.

- *Ask direct questions.* One study found that subjects were significantly less likely to lie when asked a direct question. In the study, when sellers were asked a direct question, 61 percent revealed the problem, 39 percent lied by commission, and none lied by omission. When sellers were not asked a direction question, none of the sellers revealed the problem, 25 percent lied by commission, and 75 percent lied by omission.[21]

- *Listen carefully.* Be sure that the person providing information is in a position to know that information. In addition, after you ask questions, listen carefully. This includes listening both to what is and what is not said.

- *Pay attention to nonverbal cues.* Nonverbal cues are more revealing than verbal cues. As you listen to responses to important questions, focus on visual clues such as increased blinking, changes in respiration, and reduced gesticulation. Some evidence suggests that people can be trained to detect lies, and that some types of professionals, such as Secret Service agents, are better than others at detecting lies. In general, however, bear in mind that detecting lies is very difficult, and that many people are overconfident in their ability to detect deception.

- *Keep records and get things in writing.* During the negotiation keep a record of claims others make. If certain information is particularly important to the deal, put things in writing, inspect records, and insist on guarantees. The importance of this last step is underscored by the Textron example at the opening of the chapter. The union had assurances from the company that they would not hire contract workers, but the union never got those assurances written into the contract.

After Negotiations

- *Manage your reputation.* Take a long-term perspective of negotiations. Develop relationships and a reputation for treating people fairly and honestly. In addition, consider developing a reputation for penalizing dishonesty. Although developing these reputations can be costly in the short run, in repeated and high-profile cases they are likely to pay off in the long run.

- *Don't gloat.* Finally, always be modest. Never gloat over unexpected gains, and never convey the impression that you have "won" a negotiation. Related to this advice, following a negotiation never reveal additional confidential information, such as the most that you would have been willing to pay. These revelations can fuel feelings of injustice and harm future relationships. Perceptions of fairness are fragile, and often enough people will remember losses and attempt to even the score next time.

MANAGING DECEPTION IN YOUR ORGANIZATION

It is not just your negotiating partners that may be susceptible to the use of deception. You and other negotiators on your side of the table also will be tempted to use deception. For most people, the advice never to lie is overly simplistic. But how do you keep the temptation to be deceptive from harming current negotiations and your long-term reputation?

To set a standard of being absolutely free of all lies of omission is unrealistic. Negotiators who honestly represent their bottom line or correct every mistaken impression their counterparts have, are likely to find themselves seriously disadvantaged. On the other hand, lying whenever it is convenient to do so is clearly not an acceptable alternative either (at least for legal if not moral reasons). As Shell[22] suggests, aim high in setting your ethical standards, and apply your standards consistently throughout your negotiations. Previous scholars have suggested that negotiators consider Golden Rule questions such as "How would you feel if everyone behaved this way?" or "Would your mother approve of your behavior?"

In many cases, setting a standard is easier than adhering to it. Negotiators are often tempted to misapply their ethical standard. The short-term gains from deception can be large, and deception often succeeds. In the long run, however, your reputation and your conscious will be better served by consistent honesty.

As you negotiate or empower others to negotiate on your behalf, you should consider a number of factors that influence the deception decision process:

- *Set goals carefully.* As noted in the Sears automotive example at the opening of the chapter, setting aggressive goals may lead to more deceptive behavior.[23] Managers, employees, and even athletes work harder when motivated by difficult, but realistic goals. Essentially, once goals are adopted people view any outcome short of the goal as a loss. Research has found that challenging goals motivate both constructive and unethical behavior—including lying and cheating.[24] Negotiators with difficult goals are likely not only to bargain more contentiously, but also to bargain less ethically.
- *Monitor decision making in the loss domain.* Like goal setting, framing outcomes in terms of losses can motivate people to bargain more aggressively, and perhaps less ethically.
- *Assess underlying uncertainty.* In general, the more uncertain and ambiguous the information is, the more likely people are to communicate that information in a self-serving way.[25] Consequently, negotiators should assess the underlying certainty with which information is known. Similarly, when negotiators fail to ask questions or ask ambiguous questions, they are much less likely to learn relevant facts. Direct, specific questions curtail deception.[26]
- *Pay attention to self-perceptions and norms.* Self-perceptions and norms also guide the use of deception. Certain contexts such as the sale of a used car may cue different norms and expectations that facilitate the self-justification process. Creating a culture that clearly stresses the norms of honesty and fairness may help reduce the likelihood that negotiators will engage in unethical behavior.
- *Prepare carefully.* Many negotiators misapply their ethical standards because they are ill prepared. Many lies are "responsive" lies told under pressure. When confronted with a difficult or unexpected question, many negotiators become anxious and use deception. To avoid this predicament, you should prepare by anticipating difficult questions, by practicing replies, and by considering follow-up questions

you are likely to be asked. You do not need to answer every question, but take the time you need to respond when you do.

- *Look for justifications.* In addition, anticipate your own justification process, such as defensive and elastic justification, in your own use of deception. Evaluate your actions from a neutral perspective and encourage your employees to do so as well.

While we might wish all interactions to be completely open and honest, deception is an inherent part of human communication. There will always be missing information and differences in attitudes regarding what should or should not be revealed. Consequently, managers should take specific steps to curtail the use of deception by others, and consider guidelines for managing their own temptations to use deception.

CHAPTER 12

ELECTRONIC BARGAINING: THE PERILS OF E-MAIL AND THE PROMISE OF COMPUTER-ASSISTED NEGOTIATIONS

G. RICHARD SHELL

The Wharton School

The computer can sometimes come between negotiators—creating a variety of potential pitfalls—but computer programs also can offer powerful decision support to improve deal making.

A computer does not substitute for judgment any more than a pencil substitutes for literacy.

—Robert McNamara

Information technology, particularly the Internet, has changed the nature of negotiations. On the one hand, technology creates new pitfalls because of greater isolation, informality, and decreased "bandwidth" compared with face-to-face negotiations. On the other hand, e-mail can give negotiators who dislike face-to-face conflicts and employees at lower levels in corporate hierarchies a more even playing field. It can also encourage a less emotional approach to negotiations and facilitate coalition building. Finally, new technology can be used to assist in negotiations, leading to better outcomes. The author examines the impact of e-mail and other electronic channels on negotiations and offers insights on ways to take advantage of the power of technology while avoiding its perils.

Not long ago, an up-and-coming manager in an executive MBA program—we'll call him John—told a sad but instructive story about using e-mail at work. This student was fast approaching his graduation date. After two years of continuous study on weekends while working full time, John decided to ask for a promotion and raise.

John's boss, a hypercompetitive individual with little patience and even less time for mentoring, asked John to make his case for a promotion via e-mail. John, a basically shy, technically oriented person, was happy to comply. He sent a short, punchy message describing a major organizational problem at the firm, suggesting a new position to fix this problem, and asking for a big increase in salary for taking the new job. John was actually pretty proud of himself for being so direct and assertive about this issue.

John heard nothing for a few days. Then, the boss summoned him to a meeting attended by the entire senior team. To his complete astonishment, however, John did not get the promotion he wanted. Instead, he was fired.

After receiving John's e-mail, his boss had circulated it to his senior management team and asked for input. This group included a vice president whose performance was called into question by John's analysis and who had clashed with John in the past. Prompted by John's adversary, the group had come back with a swift, unified opinion: John's request was arrogant and his analysis showed that he lacked both understanding of and commitment to the boss's "innovative" new strategy. Two years of weekends attending the executive MBA program had left John without allies at the senior level. With no one speaking up for him, John's career at the firm was over.

John's punchy e-mail, which circulated even more widely in the wake of this disaster, handed his office enemies a potent weapon. And John's MBA graduation dinner became a rueful seminar on the dangers of using e-mail to address delicate issues of office politics. The *Wall Street Journal* has reported similar tales of woe from e-mail users across the corporate spectrum.[1]

THE PANDORA'S BOX OF TECHNOLOGY

New communication technologies change the nature of interactions and relationships. When the telephone was invented in the late nineteenth century, it created many new opportunities for people to do business at a distance. But the telephone also gave birth to novel and unwelcome commercial practices. A new word—*phonies*—arose to describe con artists who used the visual anonymity and auditory intimacy of the telephone to launch fraudulent schemes against customers, suppliers, and consumers.[2] Similarly, electronic mail has spawned a new term, *flaming,* for the vitriolic messages that seem to be encouraged by the isolation of the medium. New technologies change the communications that flow through them.

The Internet and its associated computer technologies have given managers powerful new tools for communications and negotiations. These innovations offer many benefits to managers, but also present new perils, as illustrated by John's story. These technologies tend to encourage communications that are impersonal, informal, and lacking in context. Managers need to be aware of these potential pitfalls to mitigate them. The first part of this chapter examines some of these challenges and potential solutions.

On the other hand, technology can be a tremendous ally in negotiations, if it is used effectively. The second half of the chapter looks at the way information technologies, particularly the Internet, are helping to improve negotiations. Electronic dispute resolution sites, such as Cyber$ettle.com, are helping to ease and optimize the resolution of disputes in the insurance industry. As I will show, other negotiation support systems that help managers prepare for or conduct negotiations can also produce better bargains than unassisted negotiations.

NEGOTIATING ON E-MAIL: THINK BEFORE YOU CLICK

John did not realize it, but he was making a strategic choice when he agreed to make his pitch for a promotion via e-mail. John saw only the pluses: E-mail provided a simple, direct way to communicate his analysis and enabled him to avoid a face-to-face confrontation with his combative boss on a sensitive matter.

But John discovered there were risks associated with using e-mail to negotiate. Thousands of people make similar, equally ill-considered strategic communication decisions every day in our networked world. With more and more business correspondence now flowing via e-mail on electronic channels,[3] business managers are tempted to treat this medium interchangeably with a variety of face-to-face and telephone communication links. John's experience and a lot of research suggest this is unwise: You should think before you click.

Pitfalls of Electronic Communications

How are electronic interactions different from face-to-face communications? Among the negative implications of using electronic channels are:

- *More clashes.* Some of the earliest research relevant to e-mail negotiations examined group decision-making processes in networked environments. Scholars discovered that groups linked via computers that were trying to resolve sensitive issues experienced more conflict than was the case with people in conventional face-to-face meetings. One study noted that in face-to-face meetings, the second group member to address a topic often agreed with some aspect of what the first speaker said, with the third expressing still more agreement. In electronic groups, by contrast, opinions diverged more than they converged. Each speaker expressed a more extreme and unique position

than the preceding speaker, leaving the group with the problem of resolving sharply conflicting positions. When a group was charged with
arriving at a consensus decision on a contested matter, electronic communication became a liability.[4]

- *Longer decision processes.* Another finding was that networked groups
  took longer to reach decisions than did comparable groups using face-
  to-face communication. One study found that it took approximately
  four times as long for a three-person group to make a decision electronically than it did when people met face to face—and up to 10 times
  as long for a four-person group.[5]

- *More extreme decisions.* When time is short, computer-mediated
  groups tend to reach more extreme or polarized decisions than do people in conventional meetings, perhaps because electronic communication does not provide rapid means of finding the subtle compromises
  and linkages between ideas needed to blend proposals.[6]

Moving from the group decision setting to studies looking directly
at electronic bargaining, scholars have found that e-mail negotiations,
especially between strangers, are associated with higher impasse rates
and more competitive behavior.[7] And experiments with prisoners'
dilemma games requiring cooperation and trust between parties show
that e-mail communication is much less successful than face-to-face
communication in establishing win–win attitudes among negotiators.[8]

IMPROVING E-MAIL NEGOTIATIONS

Given these pitfalls, what can managers do to become more effective online negotiators? It will help if we begin our search for "best practices" by
probing more deeply into the underlying reasons why e-mail causes negotiating problems in the first place.

Three Problems: Isolation, Informality, and Bandwidth

Three characteristics of online communication appear responsible for many
of the problems associated with e-mail negotiating: interpersonal isolation,
a sense of informality when composing messages, and the "text only" focus
associated with reading written messages on a computer screen.

First, people compose and receive e-mail negotiation messages in isolation from one another, and isolation dampens interpersonal awareness. Even before e-mail, researchers had discovered that people negotiating solely through an exchange of written messages behaved more bluntly and competitively than did face-to-face negotiators.[9]

E-mail communication suffers from a similar isolation effect. A series of studies on e-mail have shown that people using it feel less empathy for others, less guilt about their own behavior, less concern with how their behavior compares with others, and less constrained by the usual social conventions surrounding interpersonal communication than do people communicating face to face.[10]

The magnitude of such effects varies widely, but the direction is usually the same—toward more assertive communication styles. One need go no further than an electronic chatroom to confirm this. Hidden behind their screen names, even shy, self-conscious individuals can be transformed into bold, loquacious, even belligerent chatroom regulars. At the extreme, people become e-mail flamers, using aggressive and even obscene language to convey their emotions.[11] This can become a special problem in negotiation when the serial monologues comprising an e-mail negotiation exchange become hostile and then escalate toward an impasse.

The second characteristic of online communication that causes problems in negotiation is what researchers label e-mail's informality.[12] E-mail (as compared with writing a letter or a formal memorandum) encourages senders to treat communication as a casual event designed simply to convey information—like leaving a Post-it note on someone's desk or computer. One sign of this informality is the increased number of spelling and grammar mistakes in e-mail compared with other forms of written communication.[13] For many people, therefore, the typical electronic message reads more like a telegram than a richly textured, personal letter. In the context of negotiation, informality encourages bluntness and transaction-orientation, both of which can be easily misinterpreted as exhibiting a lack of personal concern about the other party.

The third characteristic of e-mail that causes bargaining problems is the narrow bandwidth through which one's meaning is conveyed. An e-mail message consists entirely of text rather than the rich combination of words, tone, gestures, and facial expressions in face-to-face communications.[14]

Opinions about the other individual's mood, motives, goals, and preoccupations must be based on the literal words a negotiator sees on the screen. And researchers have demonstrated that only a small fraction of the total meaning of spoken communication (some estimates place it as low as 7 percent) comes from the literal meanings of words.[15]

Sophisticated e-mail users have devised various strategies to overcome e-mail's bandwidth limitation. Special emotive symbols such as exclamation points, smiling faces, and the like (called *emoticons*) can denote feelings. But even if negotiators use emoticons, there is still no interaction allowing a message sender to know, as senders do in real-time conversations, that his or her intended meaning has been received. There are, in short, no electronic substitutes for the nods, confirming vocal sounds, and questioning looks that people use to show they understand or want more information regarding what is being said by someone else. Without this continuous feedback loop, the chances of misunderstanding inevitably rise.

Two Solutions: Explicit Schmoozing and Emphasis on In-Groups

Isolation, informality, and bandwidth pose barriers to effective negotiation, but they are surmountable barriers if negotiators make an effort to create a context for the negotiations. Negotiators who schmooze before negotiations or identify with their partners as part of an in-groups can overcome some of the inherent problems of online negotiation.

To illustrate how these strategies can affect negotiations, researchers staged an e-mail negotiation contest between MBA students at their respective schools.[16] Sixty-eight students from the Kellogg School at Northwestern University negotiated against the same number of students from Stanford. Twenty-nine additional pairs were made up of students drawn entirely from Stanford. None of these negotiators knew anything about their bargaining partners except the school they attended. All the parties were given the same negotiation problem. All were restricted to using e-mail to close their deals.

Prior to negotiating, students received an information packet that included the negotiation case and the e-mail address of their counterparts. In addition, half of the pairs received some extra information about their counterparts designed to help personalize the online negotiation experience: black-and-white photos, some biographical information such as prior schools, hobbies, and so on, and a dictionary of 11 emoticons to use when negotiating. These negotiators were also instructed to hold one electronic getting-to-know-you session with their bargaining partner before they started the actual negotiation.

The results showed that special attention to the personal side of negotiation, including schmoozing and common group affiliation, helped overcome the inherent limits of e-mail's isolated, text-only world. Only 6 percent of the between-school groups who held the getting-to-know-you preliminary session deadlocked and failed to reach an agreement, as compared with 29 percent of the pairs that did not schmooze. Subsequent analysis of the communication patterns of the deadlocked negotiators revealed that the failure to establish interpersonal rapport was a key factor in their poor performance.

The rapport problem was not much of a factor when both negotiators hailed from the same in-group. Of the 29 Stanford-only pairs who negotiated with each other, only 3 deadlocked—1 getting-to-know-you pair and 2 pairs that did not schmooze. Apparently, the knowledge that the other side was part of the same, self-identified in-group helped overcome the risk of impasse almost as much as did the getting-to-know-you session.

Similarity Principle and Liking Rule.   This study demonstrates the particular importance in e-mail negotiations of two social psychological phenomena associated with effective negotiation: the *similarity principle* and the *liking rule*. The similarity principle describes our tendency to be receptive toward other people based solely on their similarity to us in dress, appearance, background, group membership, and so on.[17] Con artists the world over use the similarity principle to trick targets into trusting them based on factors such as dress or the same school ties, but similarity serves a useful, ice-breaking function in many negotiating situations. The Stanford-only negotiating pairs had the benefit of this principle, as did the getting-to-know-you negotiators from different schools who discovered similarities in the photos and background information they received prior to negotiating.

The liking rule derives from another, even more obvious truth: We prefer to say yes to requests made by people we like as compared with those we do not like.[18] Schmoozing helps establish (or reestablish) the conditions of personal liking by giving people a chance to show concern and curiosity about each other. The getting-to-know-you communication session helped set the stage for the liking rule to work its magic—and thus for a relatively productive encounter to follow.

The lesson of this study? It pays to go out of your way to establish both similarity and interpersonal liking when you must solve a negotiating problem with someone online. Even explicit schmoozing that might feel somewhat artificial given the informality of e-mail will probably help smooth the path toward agreement. And an emphasis on common group membership and other similarities helps, too.

The Need for Face Time. Although in-group similarity can mitigate problems of electronic negotiations, managers cannot count on it to remove all the barriers of e-mail. While managers negotiating with others inside their own firm benefit from an in-group identification, they still find challenges when their interactions are primarily through e-mail. Research has shown that organizations that increase their use of e-mail to communicate within the firm experience a marked decline in face-to-face interactions. This leads to more misunderstandings as people lose opportunities for casual meetings and interpersonal schmoozing.[19] The firm must then create self-conscious occasions for people to interact on a person-to-person basis to regain the benefits of linking them via e-mail.

Lucent Technologies recognized the importance of face time when it set up a 500-person work group to design a very complex new fiber-optic telephone switch.[20] With engineers on three continents and in 13 time zones working on this project, e-mail was the dominant method of communication. Such projects may not look like negotiations on the surface, but they rapidly become such as different groups moving at different speeds begin to assert conflicting agendas and priorities. This project was no exception and significant disputes and misunderstandings arose as the program developed.

E-mail amplified these differences, and frayed tempers began to turn into costly delays. In the face of fierce deadlines and growing pressures, the leaders of the two main work teams wisely decided the best way to *save time* was to give their engineers more "real time" with each other. Lucent flew teams of widely dispersed engineers to common locations for relatively brief, face-to-face meetings. As reported in the *Wall Street Journal,* "More than anything else, it was sheer physical presence—face time—that began solidifying the group." Interpersonal relations were renewed, misunderstandings cleared up, and the product shipped by its deadline.

USING ELECTRONIC NEGOTIATIONS TO ADVANTAGE

E-mail poses challenges for negotiators, but the news about e-mail negotiations is not all bad. E-mail negotiations help encourage detachment, add time for reflections between rounds, and allow shy or lower-level negotiators to be heard. There are genuine advantages to be gained from each of these characteristics:

- *Encouraging detachment.* Separating people who have a hostile relationship or who enjoy making themselves an issue in negotiation can be a benefit to the overall process. In its advertising, a Web site called Cyber\$ettle.com that provides lawyers with a venue for settling insurance claims touts the fact that "the parties communicate only via computer," thereby eliminating "wasteful personality conflicts, fruitless and unnecessary disagreements, as well as posturing and positioning." And my own laboratory work on negotiation has shown that shy people who genuinely hate to negotiate often relax and enjoy the process much more when they can send offers and counteroffers via a computer screen instead of having to confront another person.
- *Adding pauses for reflection between rounds.* In addition to removing face-to-face conflict from the negotiations, e-mail also can ensure there is time for careful reflection between negotiation rounds. At the negotiating table, many negotiators get caught up in the intensity of negotiations and take positions that they might not have taken on more careful reflection. Because e-mail is asynchronous communication, pauses are built in. The challenge for negotiators is to use these pauses to compose constructive, effective messages.
- *Encouraging equal participation.* One of the most well-established research findings about e-mail is its tendency to break down systems

of organizational hierarchy and status. E-mail encourages more equal participation by everyone in networked groups.[21] Studies have shown that lower level employees feel less inhibited when sending electronic messages to higher level employees than is the case when low-status individuals must meet superiors in face-to-face meetings.[22] And people—such as the disabled, the shy, or those with language difficulties—who might otherwise be excluded or marginalized in conventional meeting contexts can participate as equals in networked environments.[23] These findings suggest that e-mail may be a superior medium for encouraging input regarding a firm's goals and bargaining positions for a front-line negotiating team, even if the negotiation itself is being carried out by conventional means.

Using In-Groups to Build Electronic Coalitions

Electronic communications have also been used to quickly develop powerful negotiating coalitions around issues. Far-flung strangers who share a common cause or group affiliation are special beneficiaries of e-mail's broadcast function when trying to build and maintain a coalition pushing for a common goal.

The following example from labor negotiations is instructive. In 1997, after repeated rounds of tough, face-to-face negotiations, the union representing American Airlines' 9,300 pilots agreed to a new collective bargaining agreement with the company. No sooner had the union leadership endorsed this agreement, however, when a handful of Miami-based, renegade pilots calling themselves "Pilots Defending the Profession" launched a campaign to persuade the union membership to reject the proposed agreement.

Their organizing methods were distinctly high-tech—and took both the company and the union leadership by surprise. Faced with the problem of mobilizing dissent among pilots based all over the United States, the renegades first assembled an e-mail list of as many union members as they could. Using this list, they sent broadcast messages to the rank and file pointing out the weaknesses in the agreement and asking members to forward the e-mail broadsides to like-minded colleagues. Within days the renegades had communicated their message to virtually all union members and had the e-mail addresses of most of their supporters. It is hard to imagine how telephone or fax communications alone could have matched the speed with which this coalition formed around a unified, articulated position.

At the same time, the pilots launched a sophisticated Web site featuring economic data, color charts, questions and answers on pay and pension issues, and detailed position papers criticizing the proposed deal. This Web site served as the common meeting space for the coalition, and the people running it were able to track both how many union members visited it and how many times management logged on. The renegades supplemented their electronic strategies with a toll-free telephone number and public appearances at key union meetings.

The results were stunning: Within a very short period of time, the pilots rallied enough colleagues to reject the proposed deal, sending the dispute to arbitration. It was a major demonstration of how e-mail and the Internet can be used to build and maintain an effective, nationwide coalition.[24] Organizers leveraged their in-group identification as members of the union to build a nationwide coalition. Similar electronic strategies have worked to facilitate labor disputes, political interest group organizing, and community-based coalitions in the United States and elsewhere in the world.[25]

The success of such efforts has strategic importance for the future. For example, it will likely become increasingly important to control e-mail lists of potential coalition partners. By the same token, an organization faced with a "dissident from within" will gain significant leverage from denying dissenters the use of e-mail as an organizing device. The fairness of such limiting tactics will probably be tested in court as e-mail coalition building becomes a "normal" way of voicing concerns.

Impact of E-Mail on Optimizing Negotiations

Let's pause for a moment to review where we have come so far. First, e-mail poses some significant communication barriers that can interfere with effective negotiation. Problems such as the separation of communicators from one another, the tempting informality of e-mail communications, and the narrow bandwidth through which meaning is conveyed all work against effectiveness. E-mail negotiating can be more competitive, take longer, and deadlock more often than analogous, face-to-face negotiations. But electronic communications also have benefits: They liberate otherwise shy negotiators, promote more equal exchanges of information between people at different status levels within networked organizations, and give people time to consider their messages between negotiation rounds. As the American Airlines pilots story illustrates, e-mail also creates new tactical opportunities. Broadcast messages can identify coalition partners and help keep them informed, rallying them into a unified bargaining coalition.

The possible benefits of e-mail as a negotiating channel have prompted scholars to ask another question. Does e-mail's cool, message-focused environment enable those negotiators who can overcome the risks of misunderstanding and impasse to achieve more *optimal* agreements? Preliminary research indicates that e-mail has neither a positive nor negative effect on achieving optimal agreements. But computers do have potential as support systems for helping negotiators prepare.

Before exploring these questions, we need to consider for a moment what scholars mean when they speak of an optimal negotiation outcome. The simplest illustration of this concept comes from Mary Parker Follet's classic story of two sisters and an orange.[26]

Two sisters both wanted an orange but could find only one. They bargained over who should get it. After arguing for a bit, they cut the orange in half.

This was a perfectly fair outcome, but it was not an optimal one based on the sisters' underlying needs. As it turned out, one sister had wanted the orange to make orange juice and needed only the inside pulp of the orange. The other was cooking a pie and needed just the peel. Had they shared information about these underlying needs before dividing the orange in half, they might each have gotten all of what they needed. Instead, each got only half of what they needed and threw the rest away.

Negotiation scholars speak of deals being optimal when, given a mix of needs, priorities, and goals, the parties reach agreements that are hard to improve upon by engaging in further trading. Even after they divided the orange in half, for example, the sisters could have optimized their deal by making one more trade: If you give me the pulp from your part of the orange, I'll give you the peel from mine. Expert negotiators are always on the lookout for these sorts of win-win trades that make one or both sides better off—without making either worse off.

Does e-mail help or hinder efforts to optimize negotiation outcomes as compared with face-to-face negotiating? To answer this question, a colleague and I asked 34 pairs of first-year Wharton MBA students to negotiate a buy-sell scenario face to face and enlisted an equal number of pairs to use conventional e-mail to do the same case. Hidden in the scenario was an optimal tradeoff between two issues. Exactly 4 of the 34 pairs *in each condition* made the optimal trade-off. To our surprise, it made no difference whether they were negotiating face to face or over e-mail.

Another study yielded similar results.[27] The investigator had 33 pairs in the face-to-face condition and 44 pairs negotiating on e-mail. She used a case in which there were a number of different ways both parties could do better by sharing information, being creative, and trading on differences. Once again, negotiators in the two conditions performed about the same in optimizing their outcomes.

The results of these experiments confirm that optimal deals are very hard to reach no matter how people communicate. E-mail probably helps some people negotiate better than they would in person, but others do worse. The net result is a wash.

But is this the end of the story? Computer and network systems have enormous capacity to assist humans in making many types of complex decisions. But the e-mail systems used in these experiments made no use whatever of these capabilities; they just carried messages back and forth. Might it still be possible for electronic negotiators to surpass face-to-face negotiators by making use of specialized features designed for computer and network negotiation systems?

Anyone researching a major purchase such as a new car or house on the Web, for example, quickly learns that negotiating tips are a common click-on service provided by many e-commerce Web sites. And businesses such as Cyber$ettle.com (discussed next) provide more than a pipeline for communication. They use computing technology to structure the communication process and facilitate outcomes.

The prospect that computer systems might help negotiators optimize deal making has prompted another important line of electronic negotiation research: the search for Negotiation Support Systems. The final section discusses this subject.

Using Negotiation Support Systems to Improve Outcomes

In addition to spawning e-mail disaster stories, the Internet is giving birth to a host of innovative, consumer-oriented "electronic bargaining tables." Firms such as Priceline.com and eBay.com provide auction-like systems under which people post prices for items ranging from antiques to airline tickets and seek partners who wish to transact with them. One of the more interesting developments of this sort involves the use of the Internet to provide a bargaining platform for settling legal cases.

The U.S. insurance industry pays some $34 billion annually in legal and other expenses associated with administering and processing claims.[28] Small, contested personal injury matters are a special problem because the costs of a trial usually dwarf the money damages sought by the plaintiff. Insurance companies cannot afford to gain a reputation for paying whatever the plaintiff demands in these cases, but they are reluctant to spend hundreds of thousands of dollars litigating them.

A firm mentioned earlier called Cyber$ettle.com is one of several companies competing to reduce the costs of settling such claims by creating a Web-based, dispute settlement process for plaintiffs' attorneys and insurance adjusters. Here is how it works. An insurance company seeking to settle a particular claim logs on to Cyber$ettle's Web site, registers the case for settlement, pays a modest fee, and enters three confidential (and progressively more generous) offers to resolve the matter. Cyber$ettle then notifies the plaintiff's attorney via e-mail that the case has been registered and invites the plaintiff to participate in a binding settlement process. The plaintiff must respond within a specified time period by entering up to three demands of his or her own.

Once the plaintiff has input at least one demand, the computer system conducts a settlement round. The first round consists of a simple comparison of the plaintiff's most aggressive demand with the least generous offer posted by the insurance company. If the two numbers overlap—or are within either 30 percent or $5,000 of each other—the case settles.

In the case of an overlap, the plaintiff's demand becomes the outcome. If the numbers are within the 30 percent or $5,000 range, the case settles at the mid-point between the parties' two numbers. If there is no settlement in the first round, the plaintiff is invited to make a second, somewhat lower demand, which is compared with the second, somewhat more generous insurance company offer. This process is repeated through three rounds.

In addition to the up-front registration fee, Cyber$ettle receives a bonus payment for every case that settles successfully. Several firms, including one called ClickNsettle.com, have opened their own Web-based case settlement clearinghouses.[29] Each such site uses a slightly different settlement algorithm, but the process is similar to that used by Cyber$ettle.

Cyber$ettle and its competitors are examples of Negotiation Support Systems, electronic systems that go beyond carrying messages back and forth and actually structure the negotiation process. Negotiation Support Systems take three different forms: preparation systems, process support systems, and interactive bargaining systems.

First, there are preparation systems that support individual negotiators or bargaining teams before negotiations begin or between negotiating rounds. These systems do not involve any between-party or e-mail communication at all. Rather, they are a specialized type of individual decision support system for use in negotiations.

Preparation systems range in complexity from the bargaining checklists provided by new car Web sites, to decision tree and multiattribute utility assessment software adapted to negotiation settings,[30] to specialized expert systems giving users hypertext access to negotiation concepts and advice.[31] Commercially available preparation systems include software products such as Negotiator Pro and Win Squared.[32]

The second type of Negotiation Support System provides what scholars call *process support*. These systems operate at or in lieu of a bargaining table, usually structuring the interaction in such a way as to encourage optimization. Cyber$ettle is an example of a process support system.

The third type of Negotiation Support System, interactive bargaining systems, combine elements of the first two types. They provide computerized, expert preparation assistance and then link negotiators on a network, allowing them to negotiate on their own via e-mail but prompting them toward optimization in various ways. Two such systems are SmartSettle[33] and

Negotiation Assistant. I am one of the designers of Negotiation Assistant (along with Professor Arvind Rangaswamy of Penn State University), so I will use that system as an example of how an interactive bargaining system works.[34]

Negotiation Assistant structures a three-stage negotiation process. First, it prompts negotiators to use a private, structured, multistep preparation process based on additive utility assessment and multiattribute issue analysis. In essence, users rank various issues and options, giving them numerical scores that reflect their own unique preferences. Second, negotiators log on to a common computer network or the Internet and negotiate with one another by sending either e-mail messages or formal offers (or both) back and forth. One feature of the system is its ability to score offers coming from the other side using a negotiator's own numerical values for various issues and options. This score appears on the screen at the same time the party receives any formal offer from the other party. The system also gives outgoing offers a score using the same, confidential scale. Thus, a negotiator can compare the value of his or her last offer against the value of the last bid received from the other party.

The third stage of the process occurs after the parties have reached a binding agreement. This is the postsettlement phase. At this point, Negotiation Assistant will (with the consent of both parties) scan both sides' initial inputs to see if there are trades that might make at least one of them better off without making the other worse off (in terms the parties' initial, private utility assessments). If the parties agree to continue, Negotiation Assistant will display these potential improvements. The parties are free to either agree to a set of improvements or go back to their binding, original agreement.

To see which, if any, of these features actually improved optimization, we tested Negotiation Assistant with Wharton MBA students under four different negotiation conditions: face to face, e-mail only, Negotiation Assistant preparation followed by face-to-face negotiation, and Negotiation Assistant preparation followed by Negotiation Assistant's special form of electronic negotiation. For each condition, we offered our negotiators cash awards of $100 to each buyer and seller who got the best deal for their side. I reported the results of the pure face-to-face versus pure e-mail conditions earlier in the chapter—both of these groups reached the same, relatively poor (4 out of 34 pairs) results in terms of optimality.

What about the two conditions in which Negotiation Assistant played a role? We had hoped, for example, that our computerized postsettlement phase would prompt many negotiators to opt for better deals than they had reached themselves. To our dismay, however, few negotiators elected to adopt the suggestions made by the computer. Why? It turned out that our negotiators changed their minds about what mattered to them during the negotiation process. The system could not stay current with these changing values, so its suggestions at the end of the bargaining process were often outdated. Sometimes our subjects raised their original values for issues after fighting hard to win them; other times the value went down because the other party gave up an issue too early and too easily. Occasionally people were persuaded to alter their prenegotiation values based on arguments made during the negotiation. Finally, some negotiators were just too tired of bargaining by the time they reached an agreement to use the postsettlement stage. E-mail negotiations, as pointed out earlier, can take longer than face-to-face negotiations to reach the same result.

Nevertheless, the negotiators who used Negotiation Assistant did significantly better jobs optimizing than those who did not. Whereas only 11 percent (4 out of 34 pairs) of those who negotiated without assistance optimized their deals, some 35 percent (12 out of 34) of those using Negotiation Assistant to prepare followed by a face-to-face negotiation made optimal tradeoffs. And e-mail negotiators did even better with the Negotiation Assistant support, with 44 percent (15 out of 34) of the pairs reaching optimal deals through the system's special e-mail link.

In other words, Negotiation Assistant's structured preparation process helped a lot and its structured bargaining process helped a little more. With better information about *their own preferences,* people tended to hold out more vigorously for their goals and insist on the tradeoffs that benefited both sides, regardless of the methods used to communicate. The special scoring display system we devised apparently helped our Negotiation Assistant e-mail negotiators keep their goals in mind even better.

The lesson of the Negotiation Assistant experiments is a useful one: Negotiation Support Systems are probably more valuable as tools to help negotiators prepare than as tools to structure the bargaining process. Where process systems have been successful, as the Cyber$ettle system appears to be, this success may stem more from the systems' ability to simplify and streamline negotiations—giving 24-hour access to a decision maker, for example—than from "optimizing" them.

CONCLUSIONS

Our tour of the research on both e-mail bargaining and Negotiation Support Systems yields some intriguing hints regarding the prospects and perils that await negotiators in the electronic age. By understanding the strengths and weaknesses of the use of technology in negotiations, managers can use it more effectively. Here are a few closing tips for effective use of these tools to achieve negotiation goals.

Tips for Electronic Negotiators

1. *Think before you click. E-mail may not be the best negotiation medium for resolving sensitive matters.*

Research reveals that the isolation, informality, and the narrow bandwidth of e-mail communication make it a risky medium for use in sensitive negotiations. Messages often appear more assertive than a writer intends. Electronic negotiations over complex matters tend to take longer than would be the case using another communication method. And, where touchy, political issues are concerned, remember that the broadcast feature of e-mail makes it easier for unintended audiences to see your offers and arguments.

Choose your communication channels carefully. Before you click on the "send" button, therefore, ask yourself whether you might better achieve your goal at less risk by using the telephone or attending a face-to-face meeting. If someone initiates a negotiation with you using e-mail when you suspect that e-mail will cause problems, do not reply via e-mail. Use the telephone instead. If they persist with another e-mail message, call them again. Explain that you have found e-mail to be a difficult medium for solving complex problems. Tell them you prefer a communication method that allows you to better understand their problems. Finally, craft your e-mail negotiation messages as if they were going to be reviewed and interpreted not only by the intended recipient, but also by all third parties interested in your discussion. If you cannot convey your ideas operating under this restriction, think twice about using e-mail.

2. *Remember, human beings with feelings will receive your message. Go out of your way to soften your language. Refer to personal information and/or compliment the other party, if appropriate.*

Don't be too quick to get down to business when you negotiate online. Make sure you add contextual information about yourself, your assumptions, and your desire to learn more about the other side's point of view. If possible, make your e-mail negotiations part of an ongoing relationship that includes personal and telephone interaction so missing context information will be filled in naturally. Remember the example of Lucent's development team. They needed face time so their online time would be productive.

3. *Take advantage of the broadcast feature of e-mail to build coalitions and keep your allies informed about what is going on.*

On the positive side, remember that the broadcast feature of e-mail can be a powerful tool in building effective bargaining coalitions. The use of e-mail by the renegade American Airlines pilots against their union shows just how quickly and efficiently electronic resources can be brought to the aid of skilled negotiators. If you are trying to build support quickly for a proposal, use e-mail to rally your allies.

4. *Everyone can benefit from becoming more skilled at e-mail negotiations. But shy people, those at lower rungs in corporate hierarchies, and those who strongly dislike interpersonal confrontation may benefit most from learning to rely more on e-mail to conduct negotiations.*

Research shows that e-mail encourages more equal participation in organizational life by those lower down in traditional hierarchies. Also, shy, conflict-averse people feel more comfortable negotiating via e-mail than face to face. They gain time to think between moves and do not have to face the reaction on the face of their counterpart when their offer does not accommodate the other's demands. These people should pay special attention to honing their e-mail negotiation skills.

5. *Preparation and analysis can benefit from expert Negotiation Support Systems.*

Web-based Negotiation Support Systems for negotiation and dispute resolution will likely proliferate in the future. Research suggests that such systems can provide convenient and helpful assistance at the preparation stage of negotiations that can pay off in optimizing final results.

6. *Negotiation Support Systems providing specialized, structured bargaining processes are best reserved for simple, secure interactions solving specific types of repeated negotiation problems between parties in preexisting commercial relationships.*

The creation of negotiation preparation software products and such innovative services as Cyber$ettle.com and ClickNsettle.com demonstrate that there is very real value to be gained from structured, electronic negotiations if the conditions are right for their use.

Forward-looking firms should be investigating the use of such systems to facilitate routine negotiations with customers, suppliers, and others within their relationship networks. A system like Cyber$ettle, for example, could be established between equipment manufacturers and their component suppliers to set price and delivery terms for standard items that are bought and sold between the same parties on a frequent basis.

A cautionary note is in order, however. Firms should make sure to provide tight security during periods when opposing parties are logged into common networks or servers. It did not take long for the phonies to exploit the telephone, and information pirates will play a similar role as more and more dealmaking goes online.

PART IV

IMPACT OF DECISION MAKING ON SOCIETY

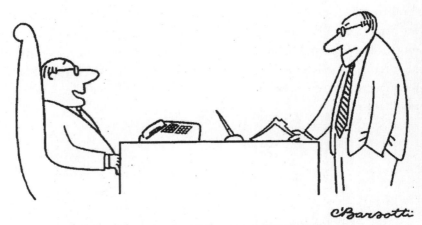

" OH! YOU MEAN IS THIS DECISION RIGHT IN THE ETHICAL SENSE?"

Decisions about health care, the environment, and other broad issues are among the most complex and important facing our society. How do decision makers understand and react to these decisions and how are their choices different from individual decisions? This section explores a variety of topics.

In Chapter 13, John Hershey and David A. Asch explore the tricky challenges of designing medical testing, when individuals may not react to test results as they initially anticipate. Instead, they may use the tests to keep their options open or change their minds after receiving the results. In Chapter 14, Julie Irwin and Jonathan Baron explore how values such as environmental protection or quality health care affect decisions. They find that sometimes people's "protected values" are not so protected. In Chapter 15, Howard C. Kunreuther explores the conflicting positions of individuals on high-risk, low-probability events such as an earthquake or flood. Before the event happens, people underinsure against it, and after it happens they tend to overinsure. In Chapter 16, Felix Oberholzer-Gee examines how decision makers tend to follow the crowd, for example, not buying a piece of real estate that has been on the market for a long time. These "information cascades" can be efficient, but can also lead to lemming-like outcomes. Finally, in Chapter 17, Mark V. Pauly explores the inconsistencies between public and private decisions. People call for eliminating deductibles publicly but accept them in their private decisions. They call for stricter environmental policies but then refuse to pay for them in their purchases.

CHAPTER 13

A CHANGE OF HEART: UNEXPECTED RESPONSES TO MEDICAL TESTING

JOHN HERSHEY
The Wharton School

DAVID A. ASCH
Philadelphia VA Medical Center
Leonard Davis Institute of Health Economics
University of Pennsylvania

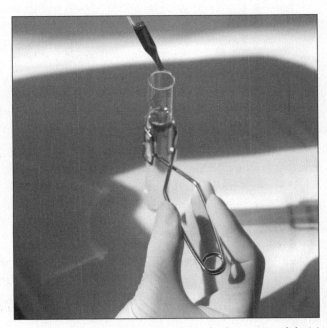

The results of medical tests may not always lead to expected decisions by patients. The tests are sometimes used not to reach a "logical" decision as much as to keep options open, find reassurance, or put off difficult decisions.

One day Alice came to a fork in the road and saw a Cheshire cat in a tree. "Which road do I take?" she asked. His response was a question: "Where do you want to go?" "I don't know," Alice answered. "Then," said the cat, "it doesn't matter."

—*Lewis Carroll*

You got to be careful if you don't know where you're going, because you might not get there.

—*Yogi Berra*

Powerful DNA testing can now identify the genes associated with many specific diseases. But is it cost effective to test the entire population? And when the results of the testing are in, will patients actually act on this information as expected? Using examples of diagnostic testing in medical decision making, the authors explore behavioral factors that influence how patients respond to these tests. Among these factors are a desire to keep options open, find reassurance, or put off difficult decisions. As society weighs the costs and benefits of testing and as managers conduct testing and analysis in preparation for their own corporate decisions, this chapter offers insights on how these behavioral factors affect costs and outcomes.

Imagine you have poor vision, correctable with glasses, and you are tentatively scheduled for an operation that can restore your eyesight to perfect vision. The operation is scheduled for next week, but you are having second thoughts. You are faced with the decision illustrated in Figure 13.1. The operation offers a 99 percent chance of restoring your vision to 20-20 but a 1 percent chance of causing serious eye damage. You can cancel the operation and continue to live with your current poor vision.

There is a $2,000 test that can be performed now that can refine your prospects at the time of the operation. If you perform the test, there is an 80 percent chance that the test will reveal that you are such a good candidate for the operation that you are virtually guaranteed of success. But there is a 20 percent chance you will not be so fortunate. In this case, you will now face a decision of whether to go through with an operation next week with a 95 percent chance of success.[1]

Figure 13.1
Nicholas and Alexandra—Eye Surgery Test

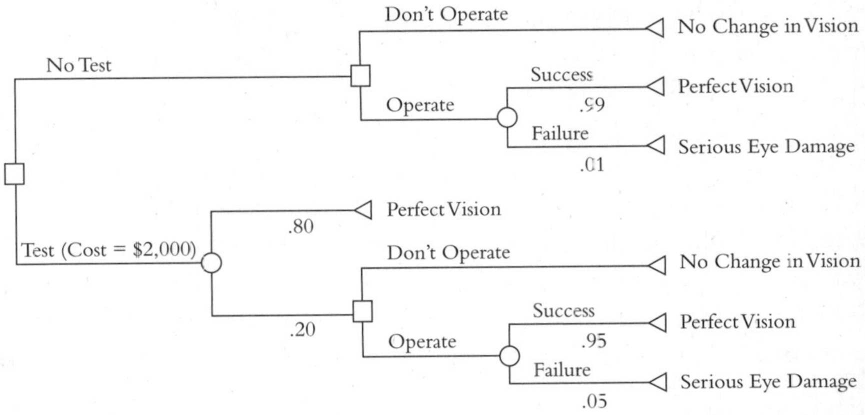

The tree is read from left to right. A square node indicates a choice is to be made. A round node indicates outcomes that result from chance.

Like many decisions, this one can be structured as a series of sequential choices. Each choice is made in the light of new evidence. Should you pay for the test? When you have the results, you are then faced with the decision of whether or not to go ahead with the procedure. In making the decision, you may be aided by an analyst (in this case, the doctor and laboratory) who attempts to clarify the probabilities of future outcomes or capture the decision maker's relative preferences (or utilities). This analyst attempts to find a way to maximize the expected utility for the decision maker.

But the actual process people use does not always conform to this structured model. Sometimes decision makers react to such tests in unexpected ways or use them for purposes that would not be predicted by straightforward utility models. People may have other goals in making the choice that are not fully understood by the analyst, such as valuing the opportunity to rule in or rule out some outcome with certainty.[2] Alternatively, they may unknowingly misrepresent their preferences when the decision plan is first charted. An option that seems good in the abstract may be rejected in reality. People may so underestimate the likelihood of some contingencies that they fail to think through the next steps they would take. Or they may simply change their minds.

DEFYING THE MODEL

Suppose you are a doctor with two patients, Nicholas and Alexandra, each of whom faces the decision about eye surgery testing presented earlier. Both patients say they would without question take their chances on the operation if the probability of success were as high as .99. But they differ when the probability is .95.

Nicholas, after considerable thought, decides he would go through with the operation even if the test were to turn out badly. Perfect vision is just too valuable for him. In this case, the test option can be collapsed to a 99 percent chance of success and a 1 percent chance of failure, the same odds he faces with no test. Since the test costs $2,000, it appears that the test should be rejected, since its outcome appears to have no bearing on the decision to operate.

But Nicholas wants to perform the test anyway. He suggests two reasons not usually considered in a prescriptive analysis. First, testing offers a high probability of early reassurance that the operation is going to be a success. The test could save him from what would otherwise be an anxiety-filled week. He also expresses the view that it is hard to think about the tough follow-up decision when it is just hypothetical. There is only a 20 percent chance he will actually face this decision, and he reserves the right to change his mind. In sum, Nicholas displays two behavioral phenomena not usually considered in decision analysis—*valuing options that offer early reassurance* and *valuing the ability to avoid or delay making difficult trade-offs.*

Alexandra decides that if the test turns out badly and she were to face a 5 percent chance of failure, she would probably forego the operation. Her problem comes down to a choice between no testing and a testing option that can be reduced to an 80 percent chance of getting perfect vision and a 20 percent chance of no change in vision. She decides to go ahead with the $2,000 test.

But Alexandra offers a separate problem for prescriptive analysis. Imagine she agrees to perform the test, and the test turns out badly. Before the test, she was certain that she would not proceed in this case. Now, however, she confronts the new odds of success for the first time as a clear reality. After reconsidering the decision, she decides to take her chances with the operation anyway. During the implementation of Alexandra's preferred strategy, she has *changed her mind* about her preferences. From a prescriptive viewpoint, this third behavioral phenomenon is particularly troublesome. Had Alexandra's real preference been known in time, she could have been advised to save the cost of the test. As it turns out, she is going to have the surgery regardless of the test result. Note that Nicholas chooses the test partly because he *may* change his mind, whereas Alexandra might regret having chosen the test precisely because she *does* change her mind.

SOCIETAL DECISIONS ABOUT MEDICAL TESTING

A maxim in medical decision making is that "if you are not going to change your actions after learning the results of a test, you should not do the test in the first place." As the decisions of Nicholas and Alexandra indicate, this prescriptive advice may conflict with the actions of real decision makers. They may pursue information, even if it is unlikely to affect their ultimate decision.[3] Patients may value options that offer early reassurance; they may value the ability to avoid or delay making difficult tradeoffs; and they may change their minds. For example, in the face of a positive test result, patients may reject the indicated treatment plan and proceed much the same as they would have with a negative result. Similarly, a policy analyst making a recommendation for a population must not ignore behavioral responses to carefully charted prescriptive advice.[4]

But how should the analyst proceed? What is the analyst's obligation as a benevolent agent?[5] Should the analyst insist on compliance with stated *ex ante* preferences of the patient? Surely not, so long as the subsequent preferences are as carefully considered as the initial ones. You wouldn't force Nicholas to have the operation if he has changed his mind or prevent Alexandra from having the operation just because she thought she wouldn't want it at the outset. Another approach is to follow the prescriptive path, but to "check in" from time to time to see if preferences have changed. But if these changed preferences are then acknowledged and accepted, the final sequential strategy chosen might well be suboptimal compared with a path that had anticipated and accounted for the decision maker's vacillation. Of course, this latter path is only known for sure in hindsight.

Still another approach is to incorporate formally the possibility of noncompliance into the model. That is, at critical decision points in the prescriptive model, decisions are replaced by probabilities of action. Here, the prescriptive model recognizes the descriptive reality that decision makers change their minds. But the model is not *purely* descriptive because it still recommends a best policy, albeit one that recognizes less-than-perfect foresight about future actions. The benevolent agent maximizes the *ex ante* expected utility of a principal who doesn't yet know her true preferences. The agent estimates them based on a combination of what the decision maker can reveal and the agent's experience with others who have gone before.

In the following discussion, we propose such a hybrid approach that incorporates estimates of the probabilities of behavioral responses in prescriptive decision analysis. This is not the purely prescriptive approach that yields the outcomes one expects for options that must be followed to completion. And it is not a purely descriptive approach that simply records what people do, based on their intuitions or past experience. It is a hybrid approach, one that balances what people say they want to do with what they are likely to do.

Screening for Cystic Fibrosis

While the eye surgery case was focused on an individual decision, societal decisions about testing are much more complicated. Should society or insurers pay for testing? Which tests? What are the costs and benefits of each approach? How can the unpredictability of patient responses affect these costs and benefits?

For example, many alternative genetic screening strategies have been developed for detecting carriers of cystic fibrosis (CF) mutations. Approximately 1 in 25 Caucasians in the United States carries the gene for CF, and approximately 1 in 2,500 babies born is affected. If both reproductive partners are carriers, one in four of their children will have CF. Most children with CF are born to couples without a family history who learn they are carriers only through the birth of an affected child.

The discovery of the CF gene has offered the possibility of screening a population to identify these carriers in advance. Parents could find out before they have the child, and even before they conceive, that they are carriers and their children are at higher risk. But these tests are expensive and there are hundreds of distinct mutations of the gene, so most DNA-based screening procedures test for only five or ten of the most common mutations representing in aggregate about 85 percent of carriers.[6] But are even very good screening tests justified in low prevalence conditions?

There is an even trickier issue than the cost and accuracy of the screening. This is the very controversial issue of what parents do when they receive the results. Many plausible strategies may be constructed using different decision rules for proceeding to further testing or deciding whether to continue a pregnancy.[7] In turn, these strategies yield different clinical and economic outcomes. Thus, the clinical and economic questions are not only whether widespread CF carrier screening should be done but also how it should be done.

We analyzed the costs, benefits, and outcomes of a range of testing strategies. (Previous models of CF carrier screening have considered only one or a few alternative screening strategies and they have not considered the effects of screening beyond a single pregnancy.)[8] Our model used a tree structure to reflect alternative clinical strategies, the probabilities associated with chance events given each strategy, and the clinical and economic consequences of those chance events. The model initially considers only single gestations carried by women with no independent reason for undergoing amniocentesis other than the possible results of CF carrier screening. The model also initially considers only women with identifiable reproductive partners who can be screened if necessary.

We examined 15 different ways of performing population CF carrier screening based on various combinations of the following tests: standard mutation analysis, expanded mutation analysis, Microvillar Intestinal Enzyme Analysis (MIE), and Prenatal Diagnosis with Amniocentesis. The standard mutation analysis identifies the mutations that account for about 85 percent of CF carriers.

Not only can the choice of the test be varied, the process for testing also can be varied. Members of a couple may be screened in parallel or in series. For example, in one parallel strategy, DNA from both partners is obtained and tested and the couple proceeds to prenatal diagnosis with amniocentesis if both partners are found to screen positive. In one sequential strategy, one partner is screened first; DNA from the second partner is obtained and screened only if the first partner screens positive; and the couple proceeds to prenatal diagnosis of the fetus only if both are positive.

Figure 13.2
Sample Decision Tree for CF Testing

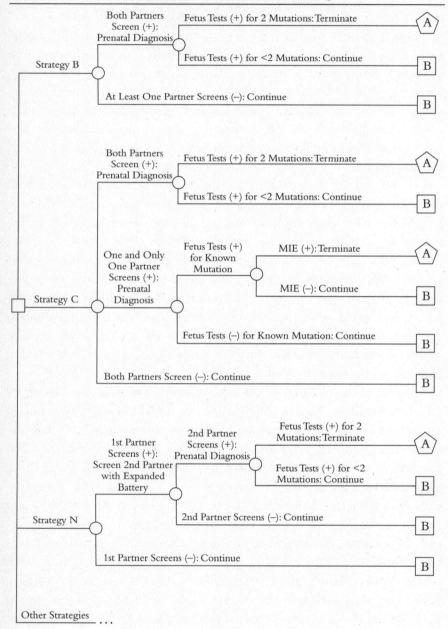

Figure 13.2 (Continued)

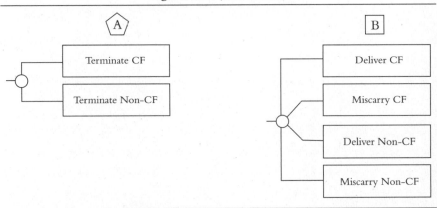

The tree uses the same conventions used in the tree in Figure 13.1. Each pregnancy can either be terminated (subtree A) or continued (subtree B). If it is terminated, it might have led to the birth of a child with CF or without CF. If it is continued, it might lead to a miscarriage or to a delivery, and in either case might be affected with CF or not.

As an alternative to simple sequential and parallel strategies, we also consider a "couple-screening" strategy.[9] DNA samples are collected from both partners (as in parallel strategies), but testing is performed sequentially and results are reported at the level of the couple. For example, couples in which the first partner tests positive and the second partner tests negative are designated "screen negative." In this strategy, couples in which one partner screens positive and the other negative are not notified and so these couples will not suffer the anxiety they might if they had full information.

The decision tree for three of the alternatives is shown in Figure 13.2. Three possible outcomes were considered: the child could be delivered, the pregnancy could be terminated, or a spontaneous miscarriage could occur. In each of these three cases the child could be affected with CF or not, resulting in a total of six possible clinical outcomes.

The prescriptive model in this case begins by assuming that all couples who identify a fetus inheriting two CF mutations (and thus will have CF) will terminate the pregnancy. Given the ethical issues this assumption raises, as well as the inherent complexities of responses to testing that we saw with Nicholas and Alexandra, this is a significant oversimplification, as discussed next.

Costs, Benefits, and Outcomes of Testing

Among the key societal questions about these alternatives are: How effective are they? What do they cost? Are they worth it? Table 13.1 summarizes the results of each of the 15 alternatives as well as a base case (A) in which no testing is done.[10] Each strategy was evaluated according to its overall cost and the distribution of a hypothetical cohort of 500,000 pregnancies. Table 13.1 shows the number of pregnancies falling into each of the six clinical outcomes and then evaluates the total cost from a societal perspective and the cost per CF birth avoided relative to the no-screening alternative (A).

The range of cost per CF birth avoided (relative to A) runs from D with a cost of $930,000 to N with a cost of $367,000. As shown in Figure 13.3 strategies A, N, J, P, C, G, and E present an efficient frontier: Screening programs to the upper left of the frontier are inefficient either because they cost more or because they are less effective at reducing CF births compared to strategies on the frontier. Of these efficient options, these results suggest that the lowest cost per CF birth avoided is achieved with screening strategy N. In this strategy, partners are screened in sequence and, if the first partner is positive with a standard battery, the second partner is screened with an expanded test designed to detect more mutations.

The lowest cost per CF birth avoided may not be the most important measure. In six of the strategies (C, E, G, J, M, P) the frequency of terminations of unaffected pregnancies and spontaneous abortions attributable to amniocentesis are unacceptably high. The only strategies seriously considered were the remaining ten, for which these risks are quite small.

Although the overall cost-effectiveness ratios for the screening strategies are sensitive to many inputs to the model, the relative rankings of the strategies are generally stable. Expanding the effectiveness of the tests or significantly lowering the costs, for example, would allow doctors to detect more mutations for a lower cost, making single-test strategies more effective. In addition, how the costs are distributed among patients, society, and the payer also could affect the choice of a strategy. Strategy N has the lowest cost per CF birth avoided, but the societal cost is higher because neither the payer nor the patient bear the full cost of screening. Based on the principle of moral hazard, we might expect patient demand for CF screening to exceed its societal value.[11] Similarly, factors such as

Table 13.1
Base-Case Analysis for 16 Alternative CF-Carrier Screening Strategies

Strategy	CF Births	CF Abortions	CF Miscarriages	Non-CF Births	Non-CF Abortions	Non-CF Miscarriages	CF Births Avoided (rel. to A)	Total Cost ($)	Cost per CF Birth Avoided (rel. to A) ($)
A	195	0	5	487,305	0	12,495	0	1,530,313,000	—
B	57	142	1	487,302	0	12,498	138	1,623,710,000	676,000
C	8	191	0	486,787	340	12,673	187	1,641,185,000	594,000
D	40	159	1	487,300	0	12,499	155	1,674,352,000	930,000
E	6	194	0	486,737	358	12,705	189	1,694,522,000	867,000
F	39	160	1	487,300	0	12,499	156	1,627,544,000	625,000
G	8	192	0	486,789	338	12,673	187	1,647,277,000	626,000
H	57	142	1	487,302	0	12,498	138	1,582,937,000	381,000
I	57	142	1	487,302	0	12,498	138	1,606,318,000	550,000
J	33	166	1	487,044	170	12,586	162	1,593,161,000	387,000
K	40	159	1	487,300	0	12,499	155	1,609,657,000	512,000
L	40	159	1	487,300	0	12,499	155	1,632,701,000	661,000
M	23	177	1	487,019	179	12,602	172	1,621,475,000	530,000
N	49	150	1	487,301	0	12,499	146	1,583,972,000	367,000
O	49	150	1	487,301	0	12,499	146	1,607,352,000	527,000
P	32	167	1	487,045	169	12,586	163	1,593,807,000	391,000

The figures represent the results of a strategy applied to a cohort of 500,000 pregnancies that have survived 16 weeks gestation. Birth outcomes are rounded to the nearest 1 and costs are rounded to the nearest 1,000.

Figure 13.3
Societal Cost-Effectiveness of 16 Alternative Screening Strategies

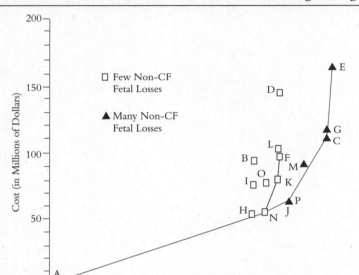

Each strategy is represented by a point reflecting the number of CF births avoided compared with a no-screening alternative and the additional societal cost for that strategy, also compared with a no-screening strategy. The line connects strategies representing an efficient frontier: No other strategies can achieve a greater reduction in CF births at a comparable or lower cost than strategies on this frontier. Strategies to the upper left of the frontier are less efficient at preventing CF births than strategies on the frontier. However, many of the efficient strategies also result in a large number of unaffected pregnancies being lost to spontaneous or therapeutic abortion. The line connecting A, N, K, and F creates a new frontier that excludes strategies that result in significant loss of unaffected pregnancies.

specificity, the chance that the individual tested is not the biological father, and the number of pregnancies the couple plans after screening also have an impact on costs and effectiveness. None of these factors, however, affects the relative rankings of the strategies.

Differing Goals

Most systematic approaches to health policy target few and relatively uncontroversial goals. For example, policies toward childhood immunization, prostate cancer screening, dietary fat reduction, and the like have as explicit goals the reduction of disease and disability, the promotion of health, or related goals easy to share. Typically, these policies become controversial only when these clinical goals conflict with other goals to reduce costs.

Genetic carrier screening for the purposes of reproductive planning leads to clinical outcomes that are more controversial. Even if the goal of CF carrier screening is to reduce the number of children born with this condition, many would want to balance that goal with their view of the outcomes of miscarriages or terminations of unaffected pregnancies. Balancing these outcomes raises issues concerning abortion, eugenics, contraception, and reproductive choice—issues that can incite or challenge strong feelings.[12]

Concerns specific to abortion in its strictest sense could be removed from consideration if the screening were performed exclusively in the preconception setting and were used to make decisions regarding alternatives to natural reproduction. For example, couples found to be at risk together might undergo artificial insemination, egg donation, or preimplantation diagnosis.[13] Or, carrier screening could be used to direct the selection of marriage partners as is common in the Mediterranean to reduce the incidence of thalassemia[14] or in some orthodox Jewish communities to reduce the incidence of Tay Sachs disease.[15]

These considerations are essential in policy analyses because the evaluation of clinical strategies requires an understanding of what these strategies are trying to accomplish. Policies to increase childhood immunization have a single clinical goal, which is to improve the health of children. Any policy involving reproductive planning in the prenatal setting will have an effect on six different clinical outcomes (affected vs. unaffected × delivery vs. miscarriage vs. termination). Our evaluation of these policies will depend on how we feel about each of these outcomes.

How does one measure the value of avoiding a delivery that would have resulted in the birth of a child with CF? Presumably, if the parents attach a positive value to the birth they would not terminate a pregnancy even at high risk. Conversely, a couple that chooses to terminate such a pregnancy reveals a set of values for which the birth of an affected child would be worse than an abortion. Such a decision would not imply, however, that should a child with CF be born to these parents, having that child survive is worse than having that child die. Most children with CF are deeply loved by their families. More likely the decision to terminate a pregnancy is based on an expectation that the abortion will be followed by a new pregnancy and a second chance at delivering an unaffected child.

In theory, for a specific couple or a specific individual one could engage in an exercise to assess the value, in monetary or nonmonetary terms, of each of the six outcomes in the context of an overall reproductive plan spanning several pregnancies. Such an exercise might help individuals make choices, which is the purpose of policy analysis applied to the individual case. But at the population level, great individual variation in values is likely, so it is virtually certain that no general policy could be ideal for everyone. In the case of conventional screening for breast cancer, all are likely to agree that more years of good health are better than fewer, though they probably do not agree on how much better they are, and at how much cost in money, pain, or disfigurement. But as hard as it is to set a national policy for breast cancer screening, it is probably impossible and not very useful to set a uniform policy for genetic screening where values are likely to be even more varied.

Prescriptive and Descriptive Approaches

The genetic screening model is a conventional, prescriptive approach to performing decision analysis. Tests are not done if they cannot, with at least some sequence of possible test results, lead to termination of the pregnancy. Also, once a strategy is chosen, the patient "follows directions."

But actual motivation and compliance can be far more complicated. For some, the motivation for screening may be to seek reassurance that they are not carriers.[16] We can imagine that these people know all along that they would not terminate, regardless of the test results. Some couples may prefer to delay full consideration of what they will do should they learn they are carriers. They might so underestimate the chances of receiving bad news that they do not fully consider what they might do under these circumstances. When the test turns out badly, they confront the decision as a reality for the first time, and do not terminate. Others may change their mind in the course of a pregnancy. What seems like a good strategy in the abstract becomes less attractive in reality. And some couples may use the information to prepare for the birth of an affected child.

All of these reasons lead to not terminating. At the individual level, a careful analysis would include both a full exploration of couples' true motives for testing and an estimate of how similar couples have or have not chosen to follow through on their stated intentions. This analysis would yield probability estimates for chance outcomes on the decision tree. These chance outcomes would replace decision branches that call for termination on the conventional decision tree.

At the population level, divergence of patients from the prescriptive assumptions can have serious implications for the measured cost-effectiveness of screening strategies. The cost of Strategy N is $367,000 per CF birth avoided, assuming that couples will terminate the pregnancy after a positive result. Studies have shown that perhaps only 20 percent to 50 percent will terminate a pregnancy under these conditions.[17] If only a third of couples terminate, the cost per CF birth avoided rises to approximately $1.1 million.

On the other hand, most couples who plan to have children will have more than one. CF carrier screening information is reusable, and so the overall cost-effectiveness of carrier screening improves as the costs are distributed over more pregnancies per couple. If CF carrier screening were performed only for individuals who are sure to terminate a pregnancy found to be at risk, and if these couples planned two children, then CF births could be prevented at a cost of approximately $183,000 each. This figure compares favorably with the expected medical costs of caring for an individual with CF.

Conclusions

Both prescriptive and descriptive approaches have a role in policy analysis. If one wants to predict the actual clinical and economic outcomes across a population given alternative strategies, the descriptive approach—accounting as it does for the way real people make real decisions—is preferred. But the prescriptive approach is preferred if one wants to give advice to a couple about the best way to proceed given their personal goals. The prescriptive approach yields the outcomes one expects of a strategy followed to completion. Our hybrid approach is prescriptive in the sense that it suggests a best policy, but it also balances people's intentions with their likely adherence to these intentions.

We have discussed three behavioral phenomena in decision making that must be recognized. The three phenomena are (1) *valuing options that offer early reassurance,* (2) *valuing the ability to avoid or delay making difficult tradeoffs,* and (3) *changing one's mind.* These phenomena have implications not only for broader societal decisions but also for management decisions, in which managers often hire advisors, perform analysis, and use the results in the decision process.

For example, managers often pay to set up studies, empanel committees, and hire consultants. Should they be spending corporate funds just for temporary reassurance, if the results have no effect on the ultimate decision? Should they spend money simply to delay inevitable decisions? Should they escape accountability for changing their mind after pursuing a strategy that makes sense only if they don't change their mind?

Among the managerial implications of our research:

- *Be clear about the purpose.* What is the purpose of the test and how will it be used? Will different outcomes change your ultimate decisions or will you proceed in the same direction regardless of the test results? If the test will not affect the ultimate decision, in many cases it will not justify the cost. The most important issue, it seems, is to be clear from the outset about the goals of the testing or analysis.
- *Value options.* On the other hand, creating future options can enhance flexibility and this added flexibility, or option value, may well be justified, both in managerial and in medical decision making. The consideration of strategic, or real, options for management decisions[18] has much in common with the use of empiric therapy in medicine. Real options thinking frees managers to think about the options that will be opened and the benefits derived from keeping these options open for the future. Empiric therapy in medicine frees clinicians from making firm decisions all at once; they can try a therapeutic approach knowing that they can modify it later based on initial results and subsequent changes in preferences.
- *Recognize behavioral factors.* Often the stated reasons for testing and analysis are not the only reasons. Testing that is designed merely to put off a difficult decision or create flexibility in a situation in which efficiency is needed can be expensive and counterproductive in a

management context. In addition, policy makers and managers who are designing testing protocols need to consider carefully the many reasons why decision makers may request these tests and create checks within the system to ensure that the testing actually serves some societal or organizational goal. Individuals in such systems may order tests for their own peace of mind when that does not necessarily serve the broader goals of those paying for the testing. Finally, managers can look for these behavioral factors at play as they evaluate the decisions of others.

As we have seen in the case of CF carrier screening, the cost-effectiveness of screening depends greatly on the goals and plans of the individuals who seek screening. When measured against a goal of reducing the number of children born with CF, carrier screening is expensive unless couples enter a screening program with the intention of terminating affected pregnancies. Carrier screening is more cost effective when couples follow this path, particularly when couples are screened prior to pregnancy and anticipate two or more pregnancies.

As complicated as these models may be, they are less complex than the actual clinical decisions faced by patients and health care professionals. Difficulties in modeling in the end reflect the complexity of the underlying clinical situation. As the use of genetic screening tests moves beyond the walls of specialized centers accustomed to these issues, policy analyses are likely to become more important as guides for practicing clinicians. Those who develop these analyses need to make sure that the implications of important assumptions are understood by the clinicians who will use them. At the same time, clinicians will need to enhance their understanding of what these models truly mean, and how they address underlying clinical, ethical, and economic issues.

CHAPTER 14

VALUES AND DECISIONS

JULIE IRWIN
University of Texas

JONATHAN BARON
University of Pennsylvania

People feel strongly about certain issues such as the environment and sometimes try to reflect this strength of conviction by refusing to trade off one benefit for another. Unfortunately, this stance is often, if not always, impossible to honor, and people often end up violating their stated "protected values," even though they may feel badly about doing so.

243

I love my car; I hate the bus. Yet I vote for candidates who promise to tax gasoline to pay for public transportation. I send my dues to the Sierra Club to protect areas in Alaska I shall never visit . . . [And I support the work of the American League to Abolish Capital Punishment although, personally, I have nothing to gain one way or the other. (If I hang, I will hang myself.) And of course,] I applaud the Endangered Species Act, although I have no earthly use for the Colorado squawfish or the Indiana bat. The political causes I support seem to have little or no basis in my interests as a consumer, because I take a different point of view when I vote and when I shop. I have an "Ecology Now" sticker on a car that drips oil everywhere it is parked.

—Mark Sagoff[1]

How do values for issues such as environmental quality, access to health care, or fair labor practices affect specific decisions? You may value the environment in the abstract, but what impact does that value have on decisions that impact the environment? When people hold strong values, they often state that they would refuse to compromise these values, no matter what the benefit for doing so. These "protected values" provide a clear-cut way for people to avoid making harmful trade-offs, but unfortunately, they are so extreme that they are impossible to satisfy across all situations. Also, people are likely to violate these protected values in practice, especially when they are in a purchasing context (e.g., buying an improvement or pricing an object). As the authors comment, these protected values are sometimes "strong opinions, weakly held."

In selecting an automobile, are customers more concerned about the air bags or the stereo system? It depends on how you ask the question. Ask it one way and concern for safety makes air bags paramount. Certainly few drivers would explicitly agree to risk their lives and those of their passengers merely to have a superior stereo. But if the question is asked in another way, a first-rate sound system actually could take precedence over the air bag. For instance, we have shown that people are willing to pay more for items such as stereos, but will demand more money to give up items such as air bags.[2] As this example illustrates, the relationship between values (what people care about) and decisions (what people choose) is not always simple.

We argue that people do express their moral values in their decisions, but also that they apply their values inconsistently, depending on the context. (See Chapter 17 for a discussion of how people make decisions differently in public versus private contexts.) They often trade general values, such as the environment, off financial gain. They may value the idea of organic farming but balk at the idea of paying more for organic carrots at the supermarket. They may value cleaner air but not support the introduction of more expensive but cleaner gasoline. At other times, they may behave in ways wholly consistent with their general values. People try to guard against inconsistencies by creating protected values, values that will never be traded off for another gain, but even these values can fade in certain contexts. One of our primary interests is identifying the contexts that encourage or discourage people from expressing their deeply held general values.

Values play a role in both business and policy decisions. Governments measure values by asking people about their willingness to pay for environmental improvements as input for decisions that affect the environment and about their willingness to trade off health and longevity as input for health policy decisions.

Marketing researchers measure values to increase market share or the effectiveness of social marketing campaigns. In health, the trade-off often is between length and quality of life, or between both of these and other economic goods. In environmental decisions, the trade-off is often between preservation of the natural environment and other goods.

Private businesses typically are concerned with values of the same sort. Health insurers are faced with trade-offs between providing better care and saving money. Producers of consumer goods often find that consumers are willing to pay a premium for goods that are less harmful to the environment or to animals, as illustrated by the viability of markets for free-range chicken, dolphin-safe tuna, and the resistance to purchases of endangered fish species such as swordfish. Social marketing attempts to promote a public good (e.g., avoiding illegal drug use, preventing forest fires) by using promotional techniques.

Inconsistencies in how people apply values can have serious implications for policy making as well as for corporate decisions. Will taxpayers be willing to foot the bill for aggressive environmental standards? Are they willing to pay for more health care if it takes away from other services? If a company launches a green product, will customers buy it? Both government and business decision makers face a conflict between satisfying the stated values of customers and constituents and responding to their (often inconsistent) behavior. Satisfying people's values is no guarantee of either electoral or marketplace success. Managers and policy makers need a better understanding of when and why values and decisions may be inconsistent. We argue that people do in fact express their moral values in their decisions; they just do not do so consistently across decision type (or survey question). A better understanding of how and why these inconsistencies operate will help managers and policy makers to better predict the trade-offs that people are willing to make.

HOW VALUES AFFECT DECISIONS

Much of social and political science is concerned with finding out and explaining what matters to people. To capture the concept of *mattering,* academics have developed a number of overlapping terms and subconcepts such as value, utility, desire, preference, and attitude. There are subtle differences in these terms. (See box.) The choice of one term over another is partially determined by tradition. Philosophers and economists often discuss utility, but rarely if ever mention attitudes, while social psychologists study attitudes exclusively, with little consideration of utility.

When governments and businesses measure values, in our sense, they require quantitative measures of what a value is worth. For instance, what are people willing to give up for the value's satisfaction? They want to know how much a consumer is willing to pay (out of her limited budget) for an organic carrot, not how she feels about organic carrots on a 7-point scale. In this regard, value measurement is similar to measurement of economic value as practiced by economists.

The difference is that economists traditionally rely on market *behavior* rather than how individuals *feel* about a specific concern (e.g., a clean environment). To understand people's values for organic foods, economists study the market prices of organic carrots. When they ask about the value people place on the natural environment, their first temptation is to look at what people spend on trips to look at natural objects such as natural parks. Our approach also is concerned with specific trade-offs, but we are

What Are Values?

Values are distinct from preferences, utility, desires, and attitudes.* The distinctions are by no means universally agreed upon, but we propose some distinguishing characteristics, in hopes of better clarifying what we mean by "value":

- *Values* are criteria for evaluating states of affairs—for example, the criteria used to judge figure skating performances or business proposals. Values are criteria that are explicitly and reflectively endorsed by the holder. For instance, in Olympic figure skating, national origin of the skater may in fact influence judgments, but most judges do not reflectively endorse it, so it is not a value in the present sense. Reflective endorsement implies that values are the result of thought. Values are important because they are our best judgments of the goodness of outcomes. Insofar as governments or other organizations seek to produce good outcomes, the ultimate judgments of those outcomes are values.

- A *preference* is a tendency to choose one type of thing over another. A consumer may choose between two shampoos, for instance, or a parent may weigh having side-impact air bags against having an upgraded audio system when considering a new car. The decision in each case would be a "preference" but may or may not reflect underlying general values. People's preferences often contradict their values. When this inconsistency is called to their attention, they feel badly about it.

- *Verbalizations* also do not perfectly express values. People may lack insight into their own standards, just as an art buyer may know what she likes but not be able to say why. Even the task of evaluation itself, such as assigning ratings to objects, may not fully capture underlying values, since responses may be influenced by extraneous factors. For example, when people are asked about their willingness to pay for a safety device, they may think more about the cost of the device than about their value for the safety it provides. We give some additional examples of how trivial contextual aspects of the evaluation task may influence responses later in this chapter. Many of the experiments reported here rely on verbal or numerical expressions of value, but we must remember the limitations of this response mode and be cognizant of the ways in which response mode can affect the response.

(continued)

247

What Are Values? (Continued)

- *Utility* is a quantitative measure of the extent to which our values have been honored, which allows their effects to be compared on a single common scale. It is a measure of goodness. Economic theory is concerned with this metric because utility provides a unidimensional measure of value maximization. Utility is implicit in the idea of tradeoffs. We may think of safety as priceless, but if we are truly willing to pay only $500 extra for a car with air bags that reduce the chance of death and serious injury from a car accident we have implicitly put a price on the value of safety. We have, in effect, said that the utility of increased safety when driving a car is equal to the utility of $500, thus putting money and car safety on the same scale

- A *desire,* in contrast, is a felt pull to have certain things happen; we can desire things over which we have no control, and have desires that go against our values (e.g., for bad things). Infants and nonhuman animals have desires but (most likely) not values; their preferences are driven by their desires.

---

* E. Anderson, *Value in Ethics and Economics* (Cambridge, MA: Harvard University Press, 1993); J. Baron, "Norm-Endorsement Utilitarianism and the Nature of Utility," *Economics and Philosophy,* 12 (1986), pp. 165–182; J. Griffin, *Well-Being: Its Meaning, Measurement, and Moral Importance* (Oxford: Clarendon Press, 1986).

---

unwilling to rely solely on market behavior. For one thing, behavior and values may conflict. For another, people may not have any behavioral way of expressing certain values, such as the value they place on the mere existence of natural resources that they never desire to see.

When faced with a particular decision, we are called upon to figure out what general values are implicated and then weigh these values to maximize utility. This process is difficult when the implicated values are emotional[3] or if two or more values conflict in a way that is not easily resolved. (See Chapter 2.) Decisions with ethical content almost always involve trade-offs of values, especially if the decision includes monetary cost. For instance, consumers sometimes weigh ethical attributes against quality or price, as when they decide whether to buy products not tested on animals, products with recycled content, and/or products not made from endangered woods.

The process by which they integrate these components can be fraught with inconsistencies and emotion.[4]

People have time and attention constraints and are limited in their ability or desire to spend an enormous amount of effort on a particular decision. Even with unlimited resources, people may not have the experience to consistently and thoroughly trade off values and maximize utility.[5]

SOURCES OF INCONSISTENCIES IN DECISION MAKING

A range of studies has shown that people are inconsistent in identifying their preferences, even across seemingly minor changes in the way the questions are asked.[6] Inconsistencies in preference do not occur randomly, but rather are sensitive to and shaped by the context of the decision. Many studies have shown that the context of decisions robustly and consistently affects preference.[7] Among the contexts that affect the application of values are:

- *Sequential versus simultaneous.* If options are presented one at a time, decision makers may be more likely to trade off values than if they see all options simultaneously. In a study in which people traded off air quality against consumer goods, for instance, respondents preferred the consumer goods when they were pricing the items one at a time, but preferred the air quality when they chose among the items presented together.[8] This general finding has been replicated in other domains such as health care.[9] It appears that people often satisfy what they *should* do when they make comparative judgments (i.e., focus on their values) but satisfy what they *want* when they make one-at-a-time judgments (i.e., focus on their desires).[10] In other words, people have conflicting desires and values and the way options are presented guides them toward one or another of these choices.[11]

- *Buying versus selling.* People are more focused on values such as environmental quality,[12] health care,[13] fair labor practices,[14] and charitable tie-ins[15] when they are asked to give up or sell something than if they are buying or obtaining it. Buying (obtaining) is more driven by issues such as concerns with quality and saving money. Selling (giving up) is more driven by emotions such as guilt and responsibility,[16] reflecting general ethical values. The implication is that people may not express their general ethical values when they decide how much to give to charity, whether to pay for an environmentally friendly consumer good, or whether to vote for a political candidate who will raise taxes to fund educational reform. But, if charitable goals are not met, if the environment worsens, if the schools deteriorate, then the judgments of these losses are more affected by general values and people are likely to become very upset.

This inconsistency is caused in part by people's tendency to free ride by not paying their share for public goods but demanding their share in compensation should the goods disappear. The difference is robust even above and beyond the effect of free riding, however, and appears even for private goods. For instance, people are remarkably unwilling to pay for the removal of radon from their house (which is the homeowner's responsibility) but they would demand a great deal of compensation to accept a house that contains a high degree of radon. Likewise, imagine the amount of compensation someone might demand for the removal of smoke alarms from her house, as opposed to the amount people are willing to pay for smoke alarms.

- *Pricing versus rating.* Decision makers also tend to weigh values more heavily when they are rating options rather than pricing them. In a series of five studies, we used prices and ratings to determine how much subjects were willing to pay for consumer products consistent with their moral values.[17] In four of the studies, decision makers were asked to trade off costs and other features against moral values. They had to choose among hypothetical desks, which varied in price ($350–$550), composition, and (in some studies) quality. At the *worst* level, the desk was made of wood from pristine tropical rain forests that were disappearing because of logging. At the *best* level, the wood came from tree farms, where trees were replaced as they were cut. The intermediate level mixed the two kinds of wood. We examined ratings and pricing decisions based on examining individual options and comparing pairs of options. The main result, consistent across all studies, is that rating is more sensitive than pricing to the composition of the wood. In other words, when values are thought of in explicitly monetary terms, they are more likely to be sacrificed.

On the average, people were only willing to pay a trivial $11.42 more for desks that came from tree farms rather than from pristine tropical rain forests. However, they rated the desks from tree farms a 6 (out of 9) and those from pristine tropical rain forests a 3 (out of 9), a significant difference. More complicated statistics showed that the relative weight (importance) for the rain forest wood versus the cost of the desk favored the wood in ratings (53% versus 47%) and the cost in pricing (35% versus 65%), *for the same people.*

In a study involving health insurance for abortions, subjects varied in their opinion about abortion coverage, from the view that it should never be covered to the view that it should be covered up to the third trimester of pregnancy. Again, we found that rating was more sensitive to this morally loaded value than was pricing. We think that pricing responses are more influenced by *what things are worth* in the marketplace rather than by how much the consumer values them.[18] It is possible that consumer behavior is especially driven by pricing concerns because preferences in the marketplace usually are expressed by explicitly paying for the goods. Thus, our results may help explain why consumer behavior may not be as reflective of moral values as one might hope or expect them to be.

PROTECTED VALUES

People often draw a line in the sand to create values that are protected from trade-offs.[19] These protected values (PVs) are considered absolute and inviolable. Many of these values concern natural resources, such as species and pristine ecosystems, and health issues such as feeding the hungry and protecting children's welfare. People with these PVs do not think these values should be sacrificed for any compensating benefit, no matter how small the sacrifice or how large the benefit. In other words, the values should be protected from trade-offs.

The unbending nature of PVs creates challenges for policy makers seeking to evaluate the trade-offs among values. For example, a policy might reduce environmental pollutants but increase costs for companies. In practical terms, we cannot spend all our resources on protecting the environment, saving human lives, protecting human rights, or any one thing. We must make trade-offs. And these trade-offs should respect individual attitudes toward the relative importance of the goods at issue. A natural (and defensible) way to make these trade-offs is to base them on individual values for the goods that are traded off, such as by using averages across all the individuals affected. Cost-benefit analyses are one way to do this.

PVs render cost-benefit analyses difficult, if not impossible. If we try to find the average willingness to pay in increased taxes to save a forest, but some people say that the forest has infinite value, the average will be infinite, regardless of what others say. Increased expenditures on one good will involve sacrifices of other goods, such as human life and health, and other people might claim absolute values for these. If that happens, no decision is possible based on trying to measure values. Even if only one side of the equation has an absolute value, we could almost never honor it in practice.

This presents two problems: (1) the possibility that one person could dominate a decision by expressing an absolute value and (2) the possibility that people with conflicting absolute values could induce a policy standstill. These problems can happen with any measure of value that allows expression of protected or absolute values.

Characteristics of Protected Values

Protected values have distinctive characteristics that affect how they are applied in decision making. They are the following:

- *Independent of consequences.* Protected values concern rules about actions, irrespective of their consequences, rather than the consequences themselves. First, people who endorse such values (in questionnaires) think the values should be followed even when the actions have only a marginal impact. People who have PVs for forests, for example, say that they would not buy stock in a company that destroys forests, even if their purchase would not markedly affect the share price and would be unlikely to affect anyone else's behavior with respect to the forests.[20] This is an *agent relative* obligation, a rule for the people holding the value that applies to their own choices but not (as much) to their obligations with respect to others' choices. So it is better for them not to buy the stock, even if not buying it means that someone else will buy it.

- *Insensitive to quantity.* People who hold a PV for forests tend to say that it is just as bad to destroy a large forest as a small one. They say this more often than they say the same thing for violations of values that are not protected.

- *Applied to acts.* PVs tend to apply to acts, not omissions, which means people who hold PVs show an omission bias. Omission bias is the tendency to weight an action more than an inaction, even though the outcomes of both are the same.[21] So, it would be an omission bias to refuse to destroy forest A (an action) to prevent the destruction of other, larger, forests that would occur if forest A is left undestroyed (an inaction). It is not the destruction that matters to people protecting the value so much as the act of destroying. Having a PV means people show more of this sort of omission bias than do people without a PV.[22]

How Protected Are They?

How seriously do people take their endorsement of PVs? Surely, people who endorse PVs violate them in their behavior, but these violations do not imply that the values are irrelevant for social policy. People may want social decisions to be based on the values they hold on reflection, however they behave. When people learn that they have violated some value they hold, they may regret their action rather than revising the value.

But a deeper concern is that people sometimes abandon their values deliberately. This may be because these values are not well constructed and so only appear to be strongly held because they have not been put to the test. Values probably are constructed from other values, and from knowledge that people accrue about particular issues. In this way, values are like concepts, which are constructed from knowledge and experience. If values are seen as constructed, we can ask whether they are constructed well, just as we can ask whether concepts are formed well. It is possible that PVs result from the same kind of lack of knowledge or reflection that leads to incorrect or over generalized concepts.[23]

People may agree with the claim that "all apples are red" without pausing to consider counterexamples. Likewise, they may endorse the statement that "no benefit is worth the sacrifice of a pristine rain forest" without thinking much about possible benefits (a cure for cancer or malaria, for example). Or, when people say that they would never trade off life for money, they may fail to think of extreme cases, such as crossing the street (hence risking loss of life from being hit by a car) to pick up a stack of money, or failing to increase the health-care budget enough to vaccinate every child against all diseases or screen everyone for colon cancer.

If PVs are unreflective in this way, then they should yield to simple challenges, as illustrated by the following experimental studies.[24] The first experiment found that PVs do sometimes respond to challenges in the form of a request to think of counterexamples.[25] A second experiment found that people do not appear to have thought much about what happens when PVs conflict with one another. For example, what should we do when we must choose between protecting endangered species and saving human lives? Such a choice might arise if a dam were proposed for crop irrigation in a poor country where people are dying from malnutrition. The research found that people tend to deny that conflicts between protected values actually exist. They do not think that such choices ever need to be made. This, we think, is wishful thinking, but it does seem to indicate that these protected values may be less likely to be carefully scrutinized. The last two experiments asked what happens when harm (that goes against a PV) is probabilistic, and when it varies in amount. For example, when a program has a very low probability of destroying a couple of acres of a pristine forest, people are willing to trade off even if they have a PV for forests. If (as we found), PVs are not honored when the probability and magnitude of harm is extremely low, this finding suggests a way in which we can measure trade-offs. It may also suggest that PVs are, in a sense, unreflective. When people say that a value is absolute and inviolable, they seem to subconsciously have in mind a violation of a certain magnitude and probability. In other words, even when holding protected values people have some threshold for when it is appropriate to hold this value and when it is appropriate to trade it off.

In sum, PVs appear to be labile and amenable to challenge. One strategy for eliciting values might be to ask how people make trade-offs with small amounts, and then extrapolate to larger amounts.[26] A remaining question is whether people would find such extrapolation acceptable.

We think of PVs as strong opinions, weakly held. They are strong in the sense that they express infinite trade-offs. Holders of these values assert that they are so important that they should not be traded off for anything. This assertion, however, yields to a variety of challenges. After yielding, of course, the value may still be strong in the sense that a large amount of benefit is required to sacrifice the value.

CONCLUSIONS AND IMPLICATIONS

People hold values that inform their decisions, including decisions in the marketplace and those concerning public policy. These values can be inconsistently expressed across contexts, which is why preferences do not always reflect deeply held values. One way in which people try to ensure that their preferences reflect their values is by forming rules such as, "this value will never be traded off against another value." These protected values are useful because they ensure that values will be kept in mind in every decision, but they are harmful to policy makers and managers because they make trade-offs impossible and conflicts between competing absolute values impossible to resolve. There is no possibility for trade-offs between people who are absolutely opposed to abortion and others who are absolutely in favor of it. There is no compromise between an environmental activist who believes every tree must be saved and the CEO of a logging operations business.

Given these insights, how can managers, policy makers, and other decision makers effectively respond to protected values and incorporate them into their analyses? Among the strategies:

- *Shape the context.* Given that different ways of presenting decisions (such as rating vs. pricing) can have significant implications for how values are interpreted, those posing questions to decision makers should be very careful how these questions are presented. As considered further in Chapter 8, the way questions are framed has a significant impact on choices. Consider, for example, showing the options simultaneously rather than (or in addition to) sequentially, presenting an opportunity for gain rather than (or in addition to) a loss, or asking for pricing rather than (or in addition to) ranking. These differences can lead to very different interpretations of the values in question.

- *Challenge protected values by asking about conflicts.* Often you can test the strength of unchallenged values by asking people to imagine conflicts with other PVs, or to imagine small amounts of an undesirable feature and low probabilities of harm from it. Such probing might be useful in negotiations that involve apparent protected values on both sides.

- *Recognize that extreme positions such as zero tolerance are untenable.* Because PVs are rarely completely protected, it may be wise to acknowledge this by avoiding extreme positions. If you say you will never do something, you may have to go back on your word. It may be very difficult to actually hold onto that value when it is traded off against other highly regarded values. These expectations can go especially awry when people have protected values for risks. People appear to have an aversion to risk information that isn't certain.[27] The truth is that we all are at some nonzero (but very small, usually) risk for any possible harm. It is unlikely that a meteor will hit us, that we will be poisoned by pesticides, that our cell phones will give us brain cancer, but there is never zero risk. The terms *zero tolerance* and *zero risk* are often repeated in politics. Politicians may claim that they will not tolerate any risk from a local threat, thus indicating that this threat will not be traded off for any benefit, no matter how small the risk and how great the benefit. The term zero tolerance has been prevalent lately in relation to violence, especially in schools. In the name of zero tolerance (i.e., zero possibility of school violence), schools have implemented rigid policies, such as searching students' lockers and expelling students on first offenses, that may in fact eliminate violence. If taken to an extreme, these policies may cause other sorts of harm to the schools and students.

- *Understand the marketing value of protected values.* Some of the bravado in the expression of protected values is pure marketing. Although protected values may be untenable in the long run, in the short run they can provide an easy mechanism for expressing a strong value—as politicians and corporations recognize. PVs often are expressed by companies as part of their marketing positioning or expression of their corporate values. Expressions of corporate values often are stated in the extreme language of protected values, such as "No animal testing, ever"; "Has never contained x and never will." It is not clear whether these sorts of claims work, but their prevalence suggests that people naturally regulate their individual preferences using extreme rules such as protected values. Furthermore, they expect those in charge to do so as well.

Values will continue to play an important role in the way people make decisions. The values of citizens must be considered in broad policy decisions and the values of customers must be recognized in marketing decisions. By recognizing how the context of the decision affects the application of values, one can more effectively present questions involving values. By accepting that protected values are not always as protected as people think, one can probe more thoroughly to determine how these values might be traded off. Finally, managers and policy makers need to avoid being blocked by protected values so they can achieve trade-offs that benefit the entire population or relevant group of customers.

CHAPTER 15

PROTECTIVE DECISIONS: FEAR OR PRUDENCE

HOWARD C. KUNREUTHER
The Wharton School

Being prepared has its payoff, but the irony is that people are often willing to pay for prudent protection such as home theft prevention only *after* disaster strikes.

We should be careful to get out of an experience only the wisdom that is in it.
—Mark Twain

Early and provident fear is the mother of safety.
—Edmund Burke (Speech 1792)

Although we are all aware that unfortunate events or accidents are a part of life, there is a tendency for most people to believe that they will not happen to them. Many home owners in hazard-prone areas do not invest in protective measures to reduce the chances of damage from an earthquake or flood. A surprisingly large number of businesses may not back up their computerized data should their existing system crash or their hardware be destroyed by a fire. Even small investments, such as starter cables, are often purchased only after one experiences a dead battery and is stranded on the road. Decisions about these types of low-probability, high-risk events are particularly problematic. Instead of actually evaluating the probabilities of the events, decision makers tend to treat them as all-or-nothing propositions. They vacillate between the idea of "it can't happen to me" and the sense of inevitability of a reoccurrence when the event actually does happen. The author examines some of the reasons for this phenomenon and then explores strategies for overcoming this tendency, including public-private partnerships.

The two examples that follow suggest the challenges that firms and individuals face in deciding on whether to undertake protective measures for their home.

EXAMPLE 1: PREPARING FOR AN EARTHQUAKE

The Richter Company is a small industrial firm that has been in business in Northridge, California, since 1974. When deciding to locate in this part of the country, the owners of the company (a fictitious company based on the experience of real firms) were aware that the region was earthquake-prone. Still they had not undertaken simple protective measures such as anchoring furniture to keep it from toppling over during an earthquake. They had not backed up their computer data nor arranged for emergency power should an earthquake occur. Furthermore, they had not bought earthquake insurance.

The company's laissez-faire attitude changed after the very severe 1994 Northridge earthquake. Richter was fortunate to suffer only minor damage, but decided to purchase earthquake insurance coverage after the event. Managers anchored their furniture and backed up their computer data. Richter took these actions even though managers were fully aware that seismologists reported that the chances of another earthquake in the area was lower than it was prior to 1994 due to the relief of stress in the fault line running through Northridge.

EXAMPLE 2: REDUCING THE CHANCES OF A THEFT

Art Safely and Bob Carefree each have two-year leases on apartments in the same building in West Philadelphia. At a recent Crime Watch meeting that both Art and Bob attended, they were given a briefing on the chances of apartment thefts in the area and how the purchase of a dead-bolt lock would reduce the likelihood of a break-in. Art is very fearful of crime and decided to purchase the dead-bolt lock; Bob is much less concerned and decided not to. They both had the same data on the costs of the dead-bolt lock and the risks of a theft. The value of the contents of their apartment did not differ appreciably. It appears that Art's fear of crime was primarily responsible for him investing in the dead-bolt lock while Bob's lack of concern led him not to take this protective action.

Both of these stories suggest that factors not easily quantifiable, such as past experience or fear and anxiety, have an important influence on decisions on whether or not to invest in protective measures. Research shows that people often treat these decisions with excessive fear or prudence—and have a hard time carefully evaluating these choices.

This chapter first examines how individuals should decide whether a protective action is worthwhile and in what ways actual choices differ from these predictions. It then focuses on prescriptive measures for improving the decision-making process. Are there ways to encourage consumers and managers to invest in cost-effective protective measures in advance of a low-probability, high-consequence event? If it is difficult to provide information or economic incentives so people will voluntarily take these steps, then public-private partnerships may be necessary.

HOW DECISION MAKERS SHOULD DECIDE ABOUT PROTECTION

The normative model in the case of protective measures requires a comparison between the expected benefits of the investment relative to its cost. Decision makers are assumed to maximize the expected utility or expected net benefit of the decision.

For example, consider the Richter Company's earthquake insurance decision. In deciding whether to purchase earthquake insurance, the Richter Company would consider the probability of a loss, the cost of protection, the size of the loss without protection, and the duration of the protection. Suppose the annual probability of a severe earthquake is $1/100$.[1] Suppose the loss to the property and contents of the Richter plant from an earthquake is $900,000 and the firm has the option of purchasing an insurance policy that would provide it with $600,000 worth of coverage if an earthquake occurred, reducing its loss to $300,000. Then the Richter Company can compute the expected benefits of purchasing an insurance policy:

Expected benefits = 1/100 ($900,000) − 1/100 ($300,000) = $6,000

If the insurance premium is less than $6,000, then the cost of the policy is less than the expected benefits to Richter and the firm should purchase coverage.

In 1947, the mathematician-economist team of John von Neumann and Oscar Morgenstern showed that an individual who satisfies a reasonable set of axioms should choose the alternative that maximizes her expected utility. If the individual or firm is risk neutral, as in this example, then this criterion for optimal decision making is the same as maximizing expected benefits minus expected costs.

Extending the Analysis

There are several different ways that this initial analysis can be extended to provide a more complete model of the decision-making process:

- *Risk aversion.* If the Richter Company is risk averse, then it will want to pay more than $6,000 for $600,000 worth of earthquake insurance. Risk aversion implies that the extra amount of utility from receiving another \$1 decreases as one's total wealth increases. For example, the extra utility of increasing total wealth from \$10,000 to \$10,001 is greater than an increase from \$10,001 to \$10,002. If a person is consistently risk averse, this relationship holds for any wealth level and any fixed increase to one's wealth. For any given premium, the Richter Company will be more interested in purchasing insurance, as it becomes more risk averse.

- *Multiperiod protective decisions.* Now consider the case where the Richter Company could reinforce its plant in Northridge, California, so that it is more earthquake resistant. This mitigation measure involves a one-time, upfront investment, but yields benefits over many years. Given the time value of money, an appropriate discount rate must be applied to reflect the opportunity costs of the investment to compare with the savings from earthquake damage. In other words, one should choose the alternative that maximizes one's discounted expected utility.[2]

- *Multiattribute model.* The above analyses were all based on a single attribute—money—either expended or saved. In reality there may be other factors, some of which are qualitative and thus have an impact on a person's decisions. For example, if the contents of a house are destroyed or stolen, there may be damaged or lost objects that have sentimental value that cannot be measured in monetary terms. The disruption of production by an earthquake and emotional costs on the employees from the insecurity of working in an unprotected building may be important to Richter in making its decisions. To deal with these factors, one may want to introduce other attributes into the analysis to reflect these nonmonetary features of a loss. In general, as one incorporates these other factors into the picture, protection becomes more attractive.

- *Sensitivity analysis.* Many of the estimates of costs and benefits are highly uncertain in determining the relative attractiveness of insurance or loss-reduction measures. Hence, it is often useful to undertake sensitivity analyses to determine how important it is to accurately estimate specific values. For example, a dead-bolt lock may be an attractive protective measure over a wide range of theft probabilities and/or loss of contents. If this is the case one does not need precise risk estimates to make a final decision.

CHALLENGES FACING DECISION MAKERS

These adjustments to the model begin to suggest some of the ways that decision makers normally process information differently from the expected utility model. When behavioral factors are introduced into the picture, they produce unexpected results. They help us to understand why Richter failed to protect itself against earthquakes when it made more sense from a benefit-cost perspective, and why the company bought the protection when it could not be justified from this type of formal analysis. Similarly, they also help explain why Safely and Carefree had very different responses to the same threats from neighborhood crime. What is it about human decision makers that make them diverge from the model? The key factors that make protective decisions challenging are discussed next.

Difficulty Evaluating Low Probabilities

Several studies show that individuals rarely seek out probability estimates in making their decisions, and often do not use the information.[3] In one study, researchers found that only 22 percent of subjects sought out probability information when evaluating several risky managerial decisions. Even when another group of respondents was given precise probability information, less than 20 percent mentioned the word "probability" in their verbal protocols.[4]

When consumers are asked to justify their decisions about whether or not to purchase warranties for items such as stereos, computers, and VCRs, they rarely list the probability that the product needs repair as a reason for purchasing this protection.[5] This information is relevant for deciding how much to pay for the warranty if one were utilizing a normative model of choice.

Why do people have such difficulty dealing with probabilistic information for small likelihood events? They need a context in which to evaluate the likelihood of an event occurring.[6] For example, people may have difficulty gauging how concerned to feel about a 1 in 100,000 probability of death without some comparison points. Most people just do not know whether 1 in 100,000 is a large risk or a small risk.

This evaluation can be improved by providing reference points. In one study individuals were presented with either a probability or an actuarially fair insurance premium characterizing the risks associated with the discharge of a hypothetical toxic chemical, Syntox. The chemical had the potential of causing fatalities to individuals living near the fictitious ABC chemical plant located on the outskirts of an urban center in New Jersey.[7] As a reference point, respondents also were given the probability of death from a car accident. Finally, the participants were asked a set of questions regarding how risky they perceived the facility to be (see Box).

People were not able to distinguish between low, medium, and high probabilities in judging the riskiness of the facility. Surprisingly, the study also found that subjects did not respond to insurance premiums as a signal of risk. You might think that because most people are familiar with insurance policies, they should know that premiums tend to reflect risk. While they may not be able to think meaningfully about what a 1 in 100,000 chance of death means, they certainly know what $15 means. Yet there was no difference between the perceived risk of the ABC chemical plant, whether the annual premiums paid for coverage against fatalities from the release of Syntox were $15, $1.50 or 15 cents.

While comparing premiums did not help in the risk assessment process, offering comparisons to other risks did. When respondents were presented with a description of high- and low-probability automobile accident scenarios to compare with a chemical accident, they more accurately classified the safety of the ABC plant as one varied either the probability of a Syntox release or the annual insurance premium. It thus appears that fairly rich context and information needs to be made available to people for them to be able to judge differences between low-probability events.

Simplified Models of Choice

Another challenge in making protective decisions is that instead of seeing a range of probabilities and risks, people tend to simplify the choice into a simple yes or no.[8] Prior to disasters, the low risk is rounded to zero as decision makers believe, "It can't happen to me." After disasters, the risk is rounded

Scenarios for ABC Chemicals Company with Syntox Discharge and Auto Accident Comparison

The ABC Chemicals Company is a large firm that has a plant in a community on the outskirts of an urban center in New Jersey. A chemical labeled Syntox, used in production at the plant, will be regulated under the Environmental Protection Agency's Clean Air Act Amendments. Syntox is the only toxic chemical used at the plant. As is required in the regulations, ABC Chemicals has determined that the worst conceivable accident at the plant would occur if its entire inventory of Syntox were accidentally released into the atmosphere in a very short time period. If this did occur, a plume of toxic vapors would form that could cover any home in the community, depending on how the wind blows. This vapor would only affect a few homes in the community.

An insurance company has estimated the probability of a discharge of Syntox causing deaths in the community surrounding the plant. The insurance company made the risk assessment to determine what premium it should charge ABC Chemicals to provide $1 million coverage to each resident of the community against death from the discharge of Syntox. Insurance companies charge a higher premium to cover an individual if they believe the risk the individual faces is high; they charge a lower premium if they believe the risk is low.

Half of the respondents then read one of three scenarios based on the following text (which varied as shown in brackets):

1. As background for assessing the risks of Syntox, the probability of an individual dying in a car accident is 1 in 6,000 per year.

2. The estimated probability of an individual in the community dying from a discharge of Syntox is 1 in 1 million per year. [or 1 in 100,000 or 1 in 10 million]

3. A regulatory agency has determined that for both car accidents and Syntox discharges, these probability estimates are accurate.

The other respondents read one of three scenarios (which varied as shown by the brackets):

1. As background for assessing the risks of Syntox, a fair premium for providing $1 million coverage against each death in a car accident is $245 per year.

2. A premium of 15 cents [or $1.50 or $15] per year for each resident of the community is the fair and appropriate one to charge for providing $1 million coverage against each death from a discharge of Syntox.

3. A regulatory agency has determined that for both car accidents and Syntox discharges, these premiums are fair and appropriate.

266

up to one, "It will happen to me." In reality, though, the risk is the same—actually lower sometimes, as we saw in the Richter Company earthquake example.

Decision makers often use "threshold models" as a way of simplifying their lives. In a laboratory experiment on purchasing insurance, many individuals bid zero for coverage, apparently viewing the probability of a loss as sufficiently small that they were not interested in protecting themselves against it.[9] Similarly, many homeowners residing in communities that are potential sites for nuclear waste facilities have a tendency to dismiss the risk as negligible.[10] Prior to the Bhopal Chemical disaster, firms in the industry rated the chances of such an accident as so low that it was not worth worrying about.

It is easy to see why the it-will-not-happen-to-me strategy violates the tenets of expected utility theory. Instead of weighing the outcome from an event by its perceived probability of occurrence, those who utilize a threshold model do not even consider the consequences from such events. They essentially treat them as impossible, and hence have no reason to invest in protective measures. After the event, however, the potential for loss is much more concrete, so people tend to treat it not just as possible but probable.

High Discount Rates or Myopia

Because people have short time horizons in planning for the future, they may not fully weigh the long-term benefits from investing in loss reduction measures.[11] This is part of the reason that people are reluctant to incur the high immediate cost of energy-efficient appliances in return for reduced electricity charges over time.[12] There is even less interest in investing in protective measures where there is only a small chance that the person will benefit from having taken such action.

In one study, subjects indicated the maximum they were willing to pay for protective measures such as investing in a dead-bolt lock for their apartment, purchasing a steering wheel club, and strengthening their homes against earthquakes.[13] By varying the number of years that each of the measures provided protection, we could determine how much more the person was willing to invest in the item as a function of time. If a person was willing to pay $50 for a dead-bolt lock if he planned to live in his apartment for one year then he should be willing to pay up to $91.65 if he had a two-year lease and an annual discount rate of 20 percent. If one learned how much the person was willing to pay for the protective measure as a function of time, then one could work backwards and compute the implied annual discount rate, which was consistent with these dollar figures.

Table 15.1 indicates that individuals tend to follow three different decision strategies in determining their maximum willingness to pay for risk protection. Strategy 1, labeled Relatively Low Discounting, includes all people whose annual discount rate is less than 20 percent. These individuals are consistent with a discounted expected utility model.

Relatively few individuals behave in this manner. The Myopic Behavior group consists of those whose implied annual discount rate is greater than 20 percent. Their willingness to pay does not increase very much as time is increased, thus implying their use of short time horizons. The third group does not change its willingness to pay as one changes the number of years that the protective measure will be useful. This implies an infinite discount rate. This behavior appears to indicate that the individual believes there is a fair price for the item that should not be affected by time of use. Most people fall into this third category.

Table 15.1
Percentage of Subjects Willing to Pay for Protective Measures

	Change (Years)	Relatively Low Discounting (%) r ≤ .20	Myopic Behavior (%) r > .20	No Change in Willingness to Pay (%)
Lock	1–2	18 ($r = .14$)	34 ($r = .72$)	47
	2–3	9 ($r = .11$)	33 ($r = .77$)	58
	1–3	30 ($r = .12$)	35 ($r = .67$)	35
Club	1–2	25 ($r = .1$)	35 ($r = .72$)	40
	2–3	10 ($r = .12$)	31 ($r = .79$)	49
	1–3	21 ($r = .1$)	38 ($r = .69$)	41
Quake	5–10	14 ($r = .1$)	41 ($r = .72$)	45
	10–20	27 ($r = .13$)	34 ($r = .67$)	71
	5–20	30 ($r = .12$)	38 ($r = .74$)	32

Source: Kunreuther, Onculer, and Slovic (1998)
r = Average implied annual discount rate within that category.

In the case of investing in an earthquake protective measure, the constant willingness to pay even when time horizons changed could be explained if these individuals believed that the value of their property would increase to reflect the cost of the protective measure. However, none of the subjects used this argument to justify their decisions. In the case of the investment in a dead-bolt lock to protect their apartment from theft, this rationale would not hold since the renters could not take the lock with them when leaving the apartment.

When subjects were asked to specify what reasoning they utilized in determining how much they would be willing to pay for the dead-bolt lock, few suggested that they were utilizing a discounted expected utility model. Most subjects referred to the selling price—focusing on the cost of the product rather than the value of the protection—when asked how they determined their maximum willingness to pay.[14]

Role of Affect and Emotions

There is now a growing body of evidence that affect and emotions play an important role in people's decision processes for choices when there are uncertain outcomes.[15] In the context of investing in protective measures, people are more willing to purchase insurance the more affection they have for an object.[16] The expected utility model does not predict this behavior. Rather, these findings appear to be explained by a "consolation hypothesis," according to which, people perceive insurance compensation as a token of consolation.

A simple example illustrates the importance of affection on the decision as to how much to pay for shipping insurance on an antique clock:

> Suppose that you are about to move to a new city. Your company will pay for all the moving expenses. Among the things you ask the moving company to ship is an antique clock. There is some chance that the clock may get lost in shipment. The moving company does not provide insurance, but you can purchase insurance from an independent company yourself. Buying insurance will not affect the chance of loss, but if you buy insurance and the clock is lost, you will receive $100 in compensation. The clock no longer works and cannot be repaired. It has literally no market value.

Half of the respondents then read a high-affection description:

> However, it has a lot of sentimental value to you. It was a gift from your grandparents on your 5th birthday. You grew up with it. You learned how to read time from it. You have always loved it very much.

The remaining half of the respondents read a low-affection description of the clock:

> It does not have much sentimental value to you. It was a gift from a remote relative on your 5th birthday. You didn't like it very much then, and you still don't have any special feeling for it now.

Both groups of participants were then asked to indicate the maximum amount they were willing to pay for the shipping insurance. They were given 11 choices, ranging from $0 to $50 or more. On average, those in the high-affection condition were willing to pay about twice as much ($22.24) for insurance as those in the low-affection condition ($10.51). This result supports the consolation hypothesis. Presumably, those who loved the clock would feel greater pain if the clock was lost and therefore would be in greater need of consolation. This is true even when the clock has no monetary value and cannot easily be replaced.

In protective decisions, fear is often a powerful emotional factor. Art Safely's fear of crime is what makes him more willing to invest in a deadbolt lock. The Richter Company's fear of another earthquake, now that it has experienced the first one, also may contribute to its decision. The impact of emotions on decisions is discussed in more detail in Chapter 2 and strategies for a more detached and reflective approach are explored in Chapter 6.

MAKING BETTER PROTECTIVE DECISIONS

We have seen how difficulties in evaluating low probabilities, a focus on short time horizons, and how emotions like fear and love interfere with the ability to make well reasoned decisions about protection against risks. Given this description of how people make protective decisions and their deviations from normative models, how can we improve the choice process? Some combination of the following options may be helpful:

- *Present probabilities using concrete comparisons.* Remember, people have great difficulty evaluating low-probability risks, but they do a better job when these risks are presented in concrete form. They might not know what a one-in-a-million risk means, but they can better interpret the figure when it is compared to the risk of an automobile accident. People need to see these decisions in the contexts of risks that they understand. Comparisons of risks are much more effective in helping decision makers focus than translating the risks into dollar values on insurance premiums. Presenting the information in this form can help decision makers better assess the risk.
- *Avoid microscopic numbers.* People also are willing to pay considerably more to reduce the risk of some adverse events if the likelihood is depicted as ratios rather than very tiny probabilities.[17] For example, saying that the risk of an event occurring when one is protected is half of what it is when one is not protected elicits a far stronger reaction than saying the risk is reduced from .000006 without protection to .000003 with protection.

  Adjusting the time frame also can affect risk perceptions. For example, if the Richter Company is considering earthquake protection over the 25-year life of its plant, managers are far more likely to take the risk seriously if they are told the chance of at least one earthquake is more than 1 in 5 during the entire period rather than 1 in 100 in any given year.[18] Similarly, people are more willing to wear seatbelts if they are told they have a .33 chance of an accident over a 50-year lifetime of driving rather than a .00001 chance each trip.[19]

  Studies have shown that even just multiplying the single-year risk—presenting it as 10 in 1,000 or 100 in 10,000 instead of 1 in 100—makes it more likely that people will pay attention to the event.[20] Most people feel small numbers can be easily dismissed, while large numbers get their attention. One challenge for future research is to determine ways to present information to individuals so that they understand the meaning of low and high probabilities.
- *Use private-public partnerships.* Private insurers, financial institutions, and other private sector groups alone are unlikely to be able to address these challenges in risk management. Rather, a combination of public and private involvement may be much more desirable. First, private

sector firms such as insurers and banks can offer incentives to purchase protection in the form of loans and other financial vehicles. For example, if the Richter Company has to spend $15,000 to make its plant more earthquake proof and save $200,000 in property damage from a severe quake, it might have trouble justifying the decision in the short run. If the risk of a severe quake each year is $1/100$, the expected reduction in annual loss is just $2,000, which would be reflected in an equivalent reduction in its annual insurance premium. But the $15,000 investment wouldn't pay for itself in the 2- to 5-year payback period required by Richter management.

How could one encourage the managers of the Richter plant to make the investment? If Richter could finance the protection with a 20-year loan with an interest rate of 10 percent, it would now face an annual payment of $1,700 (with an annual $2,000 reduction in its insurance premium). This means that Richter comes out ahead $300 per year, the bank earns a reasonable interest rate, and the insurer will experience lower claims following the next earthquake and hence reduce its risk of insolvency.

Even with financial incentives, there may be a need for public policy measures. When a building collapses it may break a pipeline and cause a major fire that would damage other property not affected by the earthquake in the first place. Losses from these and other externalities would not be covered by Richter's insurance policy. A well-enforced building code that requires cost-effective mitigation measures would help reduce these risks.

As we have seen, protective decisions offer particular challenges for decision makers and policy makers. Due to misperceptions of the risks and simplified decision rules companies and individuals often overprotect or underprotect against low-probability, high-consequence events. With care, when we recognize these limitations, we can help decision makers make choices that come closer to meeting a set of optimality criteria.

CHAPTER 16

LEARNERS OR LEMMINGS: THE NATURE OF INFORMATION CASCADES

FELIX OBERHOLZER-GEE
The Wharton School

Sometimes following the crowd makes sense, but only if the herd is headed in the right direction.

The fact disclosed by a survey of the past that majorities have been wrong must not blind us to the complementary fact that majorities have usually not been entirely wrong.

—Herbert Spencer

In uncertain environments, we often look to others for guidance about decisions. It is reassuring for an operations manager to purchase from the #1 supplier or for a consumer to buy the most popular brand. This can be an effective way to learn from others about what works. Managers are said to be in an "information cascade" if they rely on conventional wisdom and adopt solutions that others have developed. Information cascades are often an effective way to save resources and focus on unique managerial problems. Unfortunately, they also sometimes lead to the wrong answer. Like lemmings, managers may follow one another into the sea. Using a hiring decision and a real estate transaction as his examples, the author shows when it is risky to follow the crowd. The quality of information is often key. For instance, European firms discriminate against the unemployed much more heavily than U.S. firms due to informational differences in the two labor markets. Hence it would be wrong to export the nondiscriminatory U.S. employment practices to Europe.

Suppose you are a member of a personnel committee seeking to hire a division manager. One of the applicants appears to be exactly the person whom you have been looking for. He has the kind of expertise that is indispensable in your line of business, and he successfully led a somewhat smaller division for several years. However, his resume indicates that he has been unemployed for almost two years. At an earlier meeting, the candidate explained that he was invited to many job interviews but that he could not find the kind of challenge that he was looking for. Everyone in the committee agrees that since this candidate has not worked in two years he is a risky choice. On the other hand, his experience seems just about right for your firm. How would you decide? Would you be willing to hire this manager?

Consider a second situation: Suppose your firm expands its operations in China and wishes to acquire additional office space outside Guangzhou. The property that you saw last week would be just about perfect for your needs—a two-story building in a bustling industrial area with easy access to major transportation routes. However, the report of a local real estate agent mentioned that the building had been vacant for more than two years. The agent and building engineers assure you that there is nothing wrong with the property. Still, it seems odd that a building would be vacant for such a long time in an area that is renowned for its tight real estate market. Would you recommend that your firm purchase the building?

INFORMATION CASCADES

When facing decisions such as these—where there is high uncertainty and they are too complex or costly to fully analyze—managers often rely on rules of thumb and intuition.[1] One way managers deal with uncertainty is to learn from other decision makers. The decisions of other firms and managers often reveal information on how difficulties can be mastered. This information appears to be particularly valuable if *everyone has arrived at the same solution.* The assumption that a solution is likely to be correct if everyone else adopted it seems innocent enough. If many decision makers *independently* arrive at the same conclusion, we have good reason to believe that they are right. This rationale is often used to convince consumers of the quality of products and services. Many products are advertised as the one that "Americans use most," the "leading brand" or simply "#1." In pointing out that most individuals keep buying a particular product, we hope to convince consumers that this product is in fact among the best.

But this type of reasoning can be misleading. It can lead to *information cascades,* in which managers do not make decisions based on their own information and experience.[2] Instead, they simply copy the decisions that others have made, assuming that someone along the way has carefully studied the issue at hand. Often, no one has. Information cascades occur in many settings, including the stock and insurance markets, in real estate transactions, as well as in hiring decisions.[3]

There are three reasons why managers should be aware of information cascades:

1. When appropriate, simply copying the decisions of others saves time and other valuable resources. In many instances, the optimal decision is to follow the crowd. However, it is important to understand when

this is not the case and when acquiring more information would be appropriate.

2. As information cascades are often built on limited information, a change in the underlying parameters can lead to dramatic changes in the behavior of other managers and competing firms. What is seen as the dominant solution today can be viewed as entirely foolish tomorrow. It is valuable to be prepared for such changes.

3. Different global markets not only show differences in consumers' tastes but also informational differences that affect the nature of information cascades. As companies operate in increasingly global markets, managers should think carefully before applying a uniform policy for making decisions. It is likely that "following the crowd" means something substantially different in Philadelphia than in Paris or Baku.

THE NATURE OF INFORMATION CASCADES

The hiring decision and real estate decision in the previous section illustrate the type of environment where information cascades emerge. In general, cascades are likely in a situation of:

- *Uncertainty.* We do not know if the job applicant is qualified. Similarly, the building may or may not turn out to be suitable for our purposes.
- *Observable public actions.* We can observe how other firms and managers have decided. We know that no other firm hired the division manager and, obviously, the real estate agent has so far not been successful at selling the property.
- *Unobservable private information.* While we know the outcome, we are left in the dark as to why firms made those decisions. Did they offer the manager a job but he turned it down? Did they perform some test that the candidate failed? Did a former employer make an unfavorable recommendation? The same holds for the real estate transaction. Did other prospective buyers find out that the property was contaminated? Was it just bad luck that the real estate agent did not sell this property?

This combination of *uncertainty, publicly observable actions,* and *unobservable private information* may lead to information cascades. The decisions that others have made provide valuable information that should enter our own judgment. If many of these decisions are identical, they will dominate any information that we might be able to produce. The optimal decision-making rule then says: "Do not buy the property if it has been on the market for *x* number of months." "Do not hire an unemployed manager if he has been out of a job for more than *y* years." Once managers follow these types of rules, they are in an information cascade.

The Underlying Mechanism

The underlying mechanism of information cascades can best be illustrated with a numerical example. Suppose 50 percent of all job applicants are qualified for a particular job. Before hiring an applicant, firms invite the candidates for an interview and conduct a test. In 80 percent of all cases, the test correctly reveals if the candidate is qualified. Before his very first interview, we would assume that there is a 50 percent chance that the candidate is up to the job. Now suppose we know that the candidate had an interview with another firm that tested him. This firm concluded that he was not qualified and turned him down. How should we incorporate this information into our own decision?

Optimal decision making requires the updating of beliefs using a rule that is known as Bayes' rule.[4] In our case, the probability (Pr) that a person who failed the test is nonetheless qualified is given by:

$$\frac{\text{Pr qualified candidate fails the test}}{\text{Pr qualified candidate fails the test} + \text{Pr unqualified candidate fails the test}}$$

The numerator is 20 percent because the test correctly reveals the type of candidate (qualified/unqualified) in 80 percent of all cases. The denominator sums to one. Thus, seeing that another firm has turned down our candidate, we conclude that the probability that this person is qualified decreases from our initial estimate of 50 percent to 20 percent. The heavy line in Figure 16.1 shows the decline in this probability for an increasing number of failed tests when the tests are 80 percent accurate.

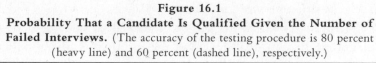

Figure 16.1
Probability That a Candidate Is Qualified Given the Number of Failed Interviews. (The accuracy of the testing procedure is 80 percent (heavy line) and 60 percent (dashed line), respectively.)

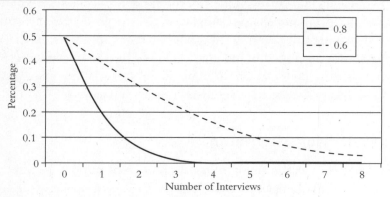

In this case, after three strikes, the candidate is out. The probability that this candidate is qualified becomes negligible after he has been turned down three times. This is an example where uniform decisions of firms dramatically change the beliefs of subsequent decision makers. Given that interviews are costly, recruiting managers are likely to be better off if they do not invite a candidate who has failed three tests. The rational strategy here is to follow the crowd and not hire this person. An information cascade emerges after round 3.

Managers rarely have such clear-cut information from a systematic test with a known probability of success. Yet the accuracy of the information is crucial. The point at which managers should copy the decisions of others depends critically on the quality of information. The dashed line in Figure 16.1 is drawn assuming the interviews identify qualified candidates not in 80 percent of all cases but only in 60 percent. This has a rather dramatic effect on the likelihood that a candidate is qualified. Even after eight failed interviews, this probability is still greater than 3 percent. While this may not be sufficiently high to warrant an interview, it is still considerably higher than if the test was 80 percent accurate.

This example illustrates two characteristics of information cascades that are important for managerial decision making. First, information cascades may rest on very little information. In our base case, the cascade emerged after three failed tests. After the third interview *no new information is added* because subsequent human resource managers all rely on the signals that the first three produced. Our intuition generally tells us that a candidate who has been unemployed for 300 periods is less likely to be qualified than a person who has failed in three interviews. This intuition is incorrect. If information cascades produce unemployment, the duration of unemployment contains *no information* because it is based on merely following the crowd. If no firm finds it profitable to invite the candidate in question after round 3, he is as likely to be qualified in the fourth period of his unemployment as in the three-hundredth period.

INTERNATIONAL DIFFERENCES IN HIRING PRACTICES

As illustrated in the previous example, the quality of the information available affects the cascading of information. An employment test with 80 percent accuracy produces a different cutoff than one with 60 percent accuracy. Firms need to adjust their rules and procedures to the quality of signals that prevail in different markets. These differences are often pronounced in international settings, in which very different information environments prevail. At the opening of the chapter, we considered whether it is appropriate to hire a job candidate who had been unemployed for two years. The answer, it turns out, is country specific. It is more likely to be "no" in Europe, and more likely to be "yes" in the United States.

To examine these differences, I conducted a study of job searches by administrative assistants in Switzerland and the United States. For the purposes of our discussion, there are two key differences between the United States and most European labor markets. First, hiring conditions are more favorable for unemployed candidates in Switzerland than in the United States. In Switzerland, as is common in many European countries, employees are required by law to give two to three month's notice before they can leave their current job. One effect of this regulation is that it creates a competitive advantage for the unemployed. If a new job opens up, individuals who are out of work can start working immediately while the employed need to respect the notice periods. The theory of information cascades predicts that such initial advantages lead to *earlier cascades,* that is, managers refuse to interview candidates after a shorter duration of unemployment. Human resource managers understand that the unemployed enjoy an initial advantage. Thus, while not finding a job for more than six months may not mean much in the United States, not being employed after six months *given these favorable circumstances* becomes a more negative signal in Switzerland.

The second difference is that Swiss employers receive much more information than their U.S. counterparts. While a U.S. firm is typically given a one-page resume, job applicants in Switzerland send in detailed descriptions of their previous work experience along with letters of recommendation by all former employers. Many applicants also provide information on their grades in school and during apprenticeship. Moreover, recruiters in Switzerland generally call up their colleagues to inquire about the past performance of job applicants. In contrast to the United States, where human resource managers are reluctant to provide such information for legal reasons, HR staff in Switzerland freely share this type of information across firms. To the extent that this helps firms in Switzerland to evaluate job candidates, subsequent interviewers may place much more weight on these prior decisions, given that they are based on more extensive information. As Figure 16.1 suggests, these signals of higher quality lead to earlier cascades.

A Field Experiment

To test the theoretical predictions, I conducted a field experiment.[5] I invited four administrative assistants to have me carry out their job search for them. These individuals worked for firms that had just announced that they would go out of business. All four planned to look for a job that was similar to their present position. Two worked in New York City, two in Zurich. I sent out their resumes to firms that advertised job openings in the *New York Times* (190 different ads) and in the *Zurich Tages-Anzeiger* (320 ads). For several weeks, I responded to all job openings in the section titled Administrative Assistants. If firms invited a person for an interview, I passed that information on to my subjects. In the course of the experiment, each individual went to numerous interviews and all of them eventually accepted a job.

In exchange for having me conduct their job search, subjects allowed me to exaggerate the duration of their unemployment.[6] In the experiment, each firm received applications from two of the administrative assistants. One cover letter correctly stated that the applicant was still employed. The other letter mentioned (incorrectly) that the candidate had been unemployed for some time. I randomly varied the duration of unemployment between 1 and 8 quarters. This experimental setting allows me to control for the quality of the signals that the firms receive. The results of this study are presented in Figure 16.2.

The outcome of this experiment is consistent with the theory of information cascades. In the United States, clerical workers who have been unemployed for up to two years are not discriminated against at all. (The slight disadvantage after eight quarters of unemployment shown in the graph is not significantly different from zero.) Keeping the quality of job applicants constant, the duration of unemployment does not influence the probability of being invited for a job interview. The situation in Switzerland is entirely different. In the early phases of unemployment, those without a job enjoy a statistically significant advantage over the employed. The probability that an unemployed administrative assistant would be invited to

Figure 16.2
Probability of Being Invited to a Job Interview—Differences between Employed and Unemployed Job Applicants

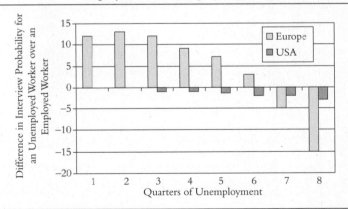

an interview is more than 10 percentage points higher than the probability for a person with a job.

To better understand this result, I conducted a survey among 766 Swiss managers asking them why they would prefer to hire a person who was short-term unemployed. The managers rated four different answers on a scale ranging from 1 = Not important to 6 = Very important. Figure 16.3 gives the mean ratings.

As expected, firms in Switzerland prefer to hire the short-term unemployed because this group can take up work immediately. The mean rating for this answer is significantly higher than the means for the other three possibilities.

While the short-term unemployed enjoy preferential hiring, firms in Switzerland heavily discriminate against the long-term unemployed. As Figure 16.2 illustrates, a person who is unemployed for two years is 15 percentage points less likely to be interviewed than an employed person. For an administrative assistant in Switzerland, it does not make much sense to apply for a job once she has been without work for two years. The chances that she will actually be invited for a job interview are almost nonexistent.

Figure 16.3
Why Do Managers Prefer to Hire the Short-Term Unemployed?

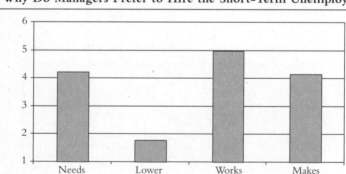

The answers presented to the respondents read as follows: (1) "Swiss firms prefer the unemployed candidate because this person needs the job"; (2) "Swiss firms prefer the unemployed candidate because this person will accept a lower wage"; (3) "Swiss firms prefer the unemployed candidate because this person is able to take up work immediately"; (4) "Swiss firms prefer the unemployed candidate because this person knows how difficult it can be to be unemployed. For this reason, the unemployed will make an extra effort to succeed on the job."

After two years of unemployment, it appears that firms copy the decisions of other firms and stop considering these candidates for job openings. An information cascade has emerged. It is important to keep in mind that this observation cannot be explained by differences in resumes that employed and unemployed candidates send in since they were identical in the experiment. In other words, *given identical resumes,* the long-term unemployed find it impossible to get invited to interviews.

The theory of information cascades suggests that firms stop interviewing the long-term unemployed because they interpret unemployment duration as a signal for low productivity. I wanted to know if this interpretation is consistent with the views of managers in Switzerland. In the survey mentioned earlier, I presented four possible reasons for not hiring a long-term unemployed applicant. The 766 managers rated these answers on a scale ranging from 1 = Not important to 6 = Very important. Figure 16.4 gives the mean ratings for all options.

The answer that is suggested by the theory of information cascades is rated significantly higher than any other answer in Figure 16.4. It appears

Figure 16.4
Why Do Managers Prefer Not to Hire the Long-Term Unemployed?

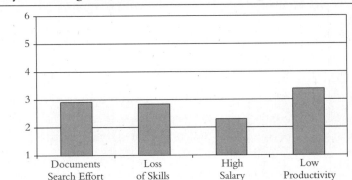

The wording of the questions was as follows: (1) "Swiss firms believe that a person who was unemployed for the past two years only applies for the job to document her search efforts, not because she is seriously looking for a job." (In Switzerland, unemployed workers need to document their job search to qualify for unemployment benefits.); (2) "Swiss firms believe that a person who was unemployed for the past two years lost some of her professional skills and is not familiar with recent developments"; (3) "Swiss firms believe that a person who was unemployed for the past two years probably asks for a very high salary"; (4) "Swiss firms believe that a person who was unemployed for the past two years is probably not very productive. If she were productive, she would have been hired by another firm."

that managers do indeed read long durations of unemployment as a signal for low productivity.

The international differences in this experiment show why it may be inappropriate to export firm-level decision rules to geographically dispersed markets with different institutional backgrounds. If U.S. decision rules were applied in Europe, managers might overestimate the potential of applicants. If European rules were applied in the United States, they might underestimate their potential. While the signal "two years unemployed" does not mean much in the U.S. labor market, European managers are much more likely to infer that the applicant is not sufficiently productive. This difference is not due to cultural differences but is created by European regulations that favor the short-term unemployed.

We find similar negative inferences in the U.S. labor market after a longer period of unemployment or in different market conditions. For example, a U.S. worker is more likely to suffer from unemployment stigma if he lost his job in a tight labor market.[7] Again, the same forces are at work: Not being able to find a job during an upswing in the business cycle generates stronger signals than remaining unemployed during a recession. And the stronger signal produces an earlier information cascade. Hence, we see more discrimination if the unemployed applicant has lost his job in good times.

LESSONS FOR MANAGERS

In an information cascade, you make assumptions based on very little information. This can be a very efficient strategy, particularly in environments of high uncertainty or when gathering information is costly (interviewing every applicant, for example). By following the crowd on some decisions, you can devote resources to decisions where more information can be used productively.

But you need to choose your cascades wisely. Information cascades are based upon the assumption that other decision makers have made careful decisions. This may not always be the case. By understanding these cascades, you can better determine when to follow the crowd or do your own thorough analysis. Among the lessons from my studies of information cascades:

- *Challenge conventional wisdom.* In information cascades, intuition is often misleading. The longer an information cascade lasts, the more credible seems the underlying information: "If a property has been on the market for eight years, something has to be not quite right." But this type of reasoning may be misleading if no new information is added in the course of a cascade. Thus, a property that has been on the market for eight years is as likely to be of good quality as a property for which an information cascade has just started.

- *Follow the crowd when efficiency is important.* When the efficiency of the decision process is more important than its accuracy, it often makes sense to use the perspectives of the crowd as shorthand for underlying information. For example, if your firm is receiving many job applications, the duration of unemployment might be a useful first filter to narrow the field. You will cut some well-qualified applicants in the process. You should, however, be aware that this shorthand is not completely accurate. In cases where the quality of the decision is far more important than efficiency, you need to think independently to assess the true quality of the candidate or property.

- *Make a good first impression.* Information cascades also affect how other decision makers respond to your actions. Suppose your firm introduces a new product. If consumer enthusiasm for this product is easy to detect (in the case of a new car, for example), consumers also will infer the quality of the car from the number of these cars that they see on the street. In such cases, initial demand is critical. Once consumers have decided that "no one seems to think that x is a good new car" and an information cascade has set in, the battle is lost. Thus, marketing investments should be concentrated in the beginning for this type of product. Similar mechanisms apply to financial markets. Investors may be more likely to subscribe to an initial public offering if they see that many others do so.[8]

- *Beware of sudden changes.* Because decision makers follow the crowd in information cascades, these decisions are much less stable than uniform behavior from independent decision making. Changes in the behavior of one player may trigger changes in the behavior of many others. This occurs because in cascades decisions are conditional upon observing what others do. Bank runs may be viewed as information cascades in which those who panic early send signals regarding the liquidity of the bank to other depositors.[9] Stock market movements can be interpreted in a similar fashion.[10]

- *Adapt rules to global markets.* As the hiring example has made clear, firms need to adapt their rules to the quality of the information signals that prevail in different markets. In the United States, it does not appear to be useful to base hiring decisions on unemployment duration. European managers seem to be convinced that the opposite is the case. The theory of information cascades suggests that there is no right or wrong here. Differences in managerial behavior are due to differences in the information conditions in the two markets. Global firms would do well to acknowledge such differences and to adopt their rules and practices to the quality of the signals.

Information cascades are a fact of life in decision making. Everyone participates in them at times—swept away by the crowd instead of following independent thinking. The most important thing is to be aware of them. They are most likely to lead to problems when you assume your inferences about the decisions made by others are reality. For example, we infer that because employees have not been hired in several years, they are not productive workers. The reality is that they have simply not been employed, which may be for a wide range of reasons (including, perhaps, several bad interviews early in the process that launch the cascade).

The key is to make these information cascades more transparent. You need to challenge these assumptions, particularly in cases in which the decision is very important. If the manager you are looking at is a key hire and all other indications are good, you'd be foolish not to hire the person on the basis of a long period of unemployment. If the house is exactly what you are looking for, then the fact that it has been on the market for a long time should not be a reason to reject it. (In fact, it may help you negotiate a more favorable price.) This information on length of time in the market isn't a sign that you need to walk away, but it may be a sign that you need to probe more deeply into the record and see what it really means. Does the employee's work record show poor performance? Is there a hidden problem with the property? If you are aware of information cascades, you can decide when you need to follow the crowd or march to your own drummer.

CHAPTER 17

SPLIT PERSONALITY: INCONSISTENCIES IN PRIVATE AND PUBLIC DECISIONS

MARK V. PAULY
The Wharton School

People are willing to implicitly trade safety against cost all the time in personal decisions—such as the author's decision to take a family vacation by car to save the cost of a less-risky airplane flight. But people tend to be much less willing to make these trade-offs in public decisions about issues such as health-care coverage.

Conscience is the inner voice that warns us that someone may be looking.
                                                    —*H.L. Mencken*

When making health-care and insurance decisions, people often make very different decisions in public and private settings. Why would Oregon voters publicly choose a Medicaid plan that is far more costly, relative to its benefits, than what researchers proposed as optimal? On the other hand, why would a parent privately choose to drive rather than fly on a family trip to save a few dollars when air travel is safer—effectively trading off family health and safety for cold cash? The author explores the split between the public and private decisions of individuals, and examines reasons for this division. He discusses how decision makers are influenced by the perception of the value of the coverage, the impact of the decision on their reputations, and the way costs and benefits are distributed.

In the early 1990s, voters in Oregon were engaged in a debate over what types of medical services should be covered under the state's basic Medicaid program and recommended for other private insurance programs. Researchers analyzed the problem and proposed a rational model. They weighed the cost per person versus improvement in health for various preventive and curative services. (The cost represented the expenditures on medical services, and the improvements in health were measured by a type of quality-adjusted survival index.) Researchers recommended high priority for coverage for those services that were very effective relative to their cost, and recommended against spending limited state resources on services that did only a small amount of good at a high cost.

The real world was not so simple. When citizens groups reviewed this ranking of priorities, they substantially altered the recommendations. The most important alteration was a reclassification of virtually all of the preventive services to a much higher priority. This set of services included all of those recommended by the U.S. government's Task Force on Preventive Care, but also a number of services that the task force had declined to recommend because of inconclusive evidence on effectiveness or because of low measured health effectiveness relative to cost. Specifically, the Oregon citizen groups, with eventual concurrence by the legislature, recommended coverage of a whole range of preventive services as having higher priority than a set of curative services that had ranked higher on cost-effectiveness.

Moreover, the set of preventive services was assigned higher priority than some treatment services that saved lives or avoided morbidity at lower cost per life saved or illness avoided. Should Oregon ever need to cut its Medicaid budget, some treatment services would be dropped before the preventive ones, even though researchers had determined that these treatment services were more cost effective. These citizens groups collectively chose prevention over treatment, even at high cost relative to outcome. Why did these groups and their elected representatives make this seemingly irrational decision? And more important for the purposes of this discussion, would they have made the same decision if it were their own money they were spending on themselves?

Trade-offs between preventive and curative medical care spending, and between the cost of insurance premiums and other consumption, are unavoidable, but so are many other trade-offs in life. What makes this one especially difficult, conflicting, and confusing is that it involves health as well as money. As we shall see, even the most flint-eyed decision maker often speaks, feels, and acts in a confusing fashion when it comes to trade-offs involving health risks, health insurance, and preventive care. What is more, people often are influenced by the collective opinion of others, and sometimes by collectively chosen programs, in making these choices.

Oregon policy makers offer an example of how people trade health for money in public decisions. Consider a more private example of trade-offs. When my three children were young, our family made semiannual visits to my parents' house in Cincinnati. The question was always: Drive or fly? Setting aside questions of available time, the trade-off involved money versus both survival and convenience. The 10-hour drive from eastern Pennsylvania to Ohio is more dangerous and less convenient than flying, but is unequivocally cheaper. When time permitted, we drove, even though five airline tickets would have shocked, but not devastated, our budget.

Had I been challenged publicly on why I was deciding to risk my own life and that of my family to save money, I would not have had an adequate reply (other than to point to the large number of expensive family cars with Pennsylvania license plates we saw on the Interstate in Ohio). I, like many others, privately chose cost savings over risk prevention.

SPLIT PERSONALITY

Public and private choices often are inconsistent, and in direct opposition to one another. Oregon voters chose what some would regard as too much prevention, while I chose what some would regard as too little. There is no obvious explanation to rationalize these choices.

In modeling human decision making, economists generally assume people will maximize their expected utility. We assume that they will make the choice that appears to offer them the highest benefit relative to the cost. In health care, the model has to be modified slightly because health is not a commodity that can always be bought at a competitive price (or, sometimes, at any price).[1] Unlike other commodities that might be considered in a utility model, health is affected by the random occurrence of illness or accident. It may not be possible to buy additional health at any price, much less at a constant price. (It also may not be possible to sell excess health.) As a further complication, definitions of health are not clearly defined. Do we mean longevity, and/or the ability to perform certain functions, or (most plausibly) both the quantity and the quality of life? The model has to be modified to account for measures of both utility and health.

Do individual consumers make decisions in accord with this modified textbook utility function when deciding on the amount and type of insurance to buy, or whether to obtain preventive and curative care? The answer is, yes and no.

The actual *private* behavior of individuals and firms sometimes (though not always) comes reasonably close to the textbook model. But their *public* behavior may be quite different. To judge from individuals' own comments and the pace at which adaptations occur, people appear uncomfortable with these private choices. Policies adopted in social and political settings often reflect this discomfort. This impact of social pressures on private choices leads to decision processes in health care that are often different from the textbook model.

So why do we act this way? What is the explanation for this split personality? In the remainder of this chapter I will review recent research and offer new theories to document and explain the inconsistencies. These inconsistencies between public and private decisions can be attributed to three concepts: perception, reputation, and distribution.

DEBATING DEDUCTIBLES

The split between public and private opinions shows up in the issue of insurance deductibles. Should insurance be catastrophic (with a large deductible) or offer first dollar coverage? While deductibles make sense according to expected utility models, people generally do not like them. Publicly, they fight against deductibles, but privately, they settle for them.

Deductibles make sense. If insurance generates administrative costs proportional to benefits paid, optimal coverage is full coverage above a deductible.[2] If we add the fact of moral hazard in health insurance, a deductible is beneficial because it reduces total costs of care. Compared to receiving care totally free of charge, the out of pocket payment a deductible represents will cause people to avoid or postpone some medical services. Indeed, empirical estimates show that a moderate health insurance deductible of about $300 per person per year virtually pays for itself, in the sense that it reduces total expenses by nearly $300. Even above this level, a deductible is rational in the textbook analysis. The marginal utility of losses that are small relative to wealth is virtually constant, so there is no substantial additional risk from raising the deductible, but there is money saved.

Despite this strong theoretical argument for deductibles, there has been and remains considerable controversy about the use of deductibles in health insurance. My reading of what happens is as follows: Consumers' advocates and health advocates dislike deductibles, even for the middle class. Many consumers do eventually choose health plans with deductibles (especially when they do not like restrictive managed care), but only slowly and only with guilt, under the pressure of rising premiums. But there is a continual appeal to the desirability of limiting deductibles, and strong hostility to proposals to increase them above modest amounts. In their private decisions, consumers choose higher deductibles, as shown by several studies:

- When faced with a choice between a high deductible and low deductible policy at appropriate relative premiums, there is some evidence that people do choose the high deductible policy.[3] Both the explicitness of choice and the framing of the problem may have contributed to this result.
- Studies of the demand for insurance show that when the tax subsidy is lower, people choose policies with less coverage (higher out of

pocket payments), in the form of deductibles, co-insurance, and ex-
clusion of some low cost, high moral hazard services.[4] For example,
they will choose policies with less coverage for outpatient psy-
chotherapy, eyeglasses and routine vision care, and expensive non-
generic drugs.
- Finally, even under managed care insurance where use is conditioned
by financial incentives and rules for doctors, the most rapidly growing type of plan is a point-of-service plan—an HMO with a network
of managed care doctors that imposes a deductible (and co-insurance)
for out-of-network use.

To a considerable extent, however, consumers continue to express hostility against these cost-containing devices. After all, they expose consumers to financial risk and induce them to avoid care that might have
improved their health. In an informal sense, the use of patient cost sharing seems lower than it ought to be. We might therefore judge such behavior to be the result of some sort of erroneous or misinformed decision
process.

If we turn to government for correction of such irrational behavior, we
run into a problem: the same sort of bias against deductibles that individuals express with regard to their own behavior appears, often in an even
stronger form, in public policy discussions and in some actual public sector
choices in democratic governments.[5]

Reasons for Avoiding Deductibles

Why do people show this split in opinions and actions on deductibles? One
reason may be the difficulty of admitting that you are potentially sacrific-
ing health for money, especially for your family. The "principle" that life
is of infinite value is appealing to most people, and in an individual decision their own life is obviously identified. I drive my family to Grandma's
house when airfares rise, but I cannot admit that I am thereby trading their
lives (and my own) for money. Of course, I am a better-than-average dri-
ver as 90 percent of the population believe themselves to be.

In health insurance, there appear to be two primary sources of discomfort. First is the intuitive recognition, based on the principle of moral

hazard, that a higher deductible will discourage us from using health-care services. If the value of health care is alleged to be infinite, or even very great, then we don't want to choose an option that will give us less of it—or at least we don't want to look like we desire that option.

We now know beyond a shadow of a doubt that higher out-of-pocket payments cause everyone to use less care.[6] Lower income people use less care when they have to pay, but so do higher income people; in fact, the percentage impact of cost sharing is roughly similar regardless of income. However, the care foregone because of cost includes services that physicians would judge as both inappropriate (useless or harmful) or appropriate (beneficial), but it does not appear that the lost care appreciably affects health.[7] This might indicate that consumers sacrifice care that is of lesser value to them, based on their perceptions of their own health risks, which may differ from others in the population. But we have no external evidence to judge whether these perceptions are correct. The second reason for the discomfort about deductibles is more strictly financial. It is a judgment that insurance with a large deductible will only pay benefits rarely, whereas one with first dollar coverage will allow almost everyone to get some of their premium back. The notion that insurance is more valuable if there is a larger probability of some positive benefit is a common misconception.

Given these concerns, what do individuals actually choose? Virtually all indemnity insurances contain a deductible; there is no "first dollar" indemnity insurance left, and almost all PPO plans also have a deductible for out-of-network use. However, there also is strong evidence that people try very hard to avoid deductibles. The most common way of doing so in the past decade for people under the age of 65 has been to choose an HMO or some other type of managed care plan. These plans rarely contain deductibles, although they are likely to contain co-payments (usually in fixed dollars per unit) for drug prescriptions, doctor or emergency room visits, and the like.[8]

There is a countervailing force for using HMOs to avoid deductibles—the limitations of HMO coverage. We now know that there is also substantial risk when using a managed care network. The plan may refuse to supply beneficial care. To address this issue, consumers are adding on point of service or preferred provider organization features, plans with moderate deductibles for the use of providers outside the network.

Political Choices

While insurance in the private sector has moved modestly toward managed care plans with greater deductibles, the public sector has not followed suit. Medicare insurance, changed only slightly since the 1966 plan, has a negligible deductible for outpatient care, but a deductible of about $700 for inpatient care. The strangest feature of Medicare coverage is that it places an upper limit on the amount of benefits to be paid; coverage starts diminishing after 59 days in the hospital and disappears entirely after a long stay or a large number of lifetime days.

Federal policy makers proposed changes to this design feature when they introduced the Medicare Catastrophic Insurance Plan in the 1980s. The original version of that plan would have raised premiums by a modest amount but extended benefits to long hospital stays.

Journalists and the general public roundly criticized this proposal on the grounds that few people would collect these extra benefits. So to get the bill passed, coverage of prescription drugs (with a deductible!) was added, existing deductibles were left intact, and premiums were raised substantially.

A year after passage of the bill, it was repealed, because elderly beneficiaries (especially those with higher income who had to pay higher premiums) complained that the cost they were required to pay in additional premiums was greater than the additional benefit they would expect to receive. The passage and repeal of this act makes the point that reliance on the government to correct mistakes or biases in individual choices in this area is unwise.

Attempts to Sanitize Deductibles

More recently, policy makers have attempted to sanitize the deductible through the use of medical savings accounts.[9] Suppose the person is currently purchasing (or his or her employer is purchasing on his or her behalf) a plan with a low or zero deductible. The person substitutes a catastrophic health plan (CHP) for the original policy, thereby saving on premiums but paying for more health care out-of-pocket. Does it make much of a difference if the premium savings are put in an earmarked account, called a medical savings account (MSA), which could not be used for nonmedical expenses for a year, compared to just depositing them in a conventional savings account? In the traditional theory of rational decision making, I think the answer to this rhetorical question would be "not much." And yet advocates of these plans labeled the accounts "self-insurance," and claimed that they offered more protection than a conventional catastrophic plan. (Of course, savings balances in general provide protection, whether earmarked or not.)

Legislation to set up such accounts, complete with favorable tax treatment for the deposits in them and the interest earned on them, was passed in 1997. Because of fears about underuse of preventive care (see below) and adverse selection, the accounts were limited to firms with 50 or fewer employees and capped at 750,000 persons. The short-term verdict on this attempt to make deductibles more palatable appears to be somewhat unfavorable. As the experiment neared its end in 1999, fewer than 100,000 persons had bought MSAs. Even those already buying catastrophic coverage were slow to convert to this subsidized form. Both the experimental nature of the plan and its administrative complexity have slowed acceptance.

It seems that the prejudice against a deductible remains. The attempt to soften the effect of a deductible by disguising it as a return of premium has not proved popular. Of course, we do not know whether that is because consumers prefer the more transparent form of catastrophic insurance or because they are not attracted to plans that reward them for low use even when covered by a fig leaf in the form of an MSA.

PERPLEXING PREVENTIVE CARE

Decision making regarding preventive care is similarly conflicted between public and private desires. Traditional or indemnity insurance usually did not cover preventive care unless required by state regulation. The argument was that the use of a preventive service (say, a once-a-year screening exam) did not represent an uncertain risk, and was fully under the control of the insured. It was far more efficient, insurers argued, for people to pay out of pocket for those services, thus avoiding the paperwork or administrative costs of processing a claim.

This makes sense. If I am the type of person who desires an annual colonoscopy, I will probably schedule one regardless of coverage. The procedure has monetary, inconvenience, and discomfort costs. If the preventive care is not covered by my insurance, the procedure reduces my wealth because I pay the out-of-pocket cost. If my insurance covers it, the cost of the procedure plus the administrative cost of processing a claim adjusts my premium and so also reduces my wealth. A person who would have been willing to pay for the procedure out of pocket should not rationally want to have it covered by their insurance. And yet there is strong social pressure, and some market appeal, for insurance that covers preventive care. Why?

One way to answer this question is to imagine three groups of individuals. The first will use the service whether or not it is covered. The second will use the service only if it is covered by insurance. The third will not use preventive care in any case. The argument for coverage is that there are many in the second group but few in the first or third groups.

For example, suppose a flu shot costs $10, but (for high-risk people over 50) it would save, on average, much more than $10 per person in doctor visits and drug costs associated with the flu. Suppose that if insurance did not cover the cost of the shots, 40 percent of people would get them. (This is approximately the proportion in practice.) Presumably, some did not get the flu shot because of its $10 cost, but others did not bother for other reasons: inattention, inconvenience, and fear of shots. If insurance covered the cost of the shot, more people would get it, but the key question is: How many more? Suppose that the percentage would rise to 60 percent from 40 percent. Some of the newly inoculated would avoid the flu, and save the insurer money, but the insurer would have to pay for flu shots for the 40 percent who would have bought them anyway, to gain the additional 20 percent. The point is that covering shots, however much they may save on other medical costs, will do a lot more good if those newly induced to use preventive care—the second group—is large.[10]

And yet this question of how much of a difference coverage of preventive care makes is rarely asked; the discussion is usually only in terms of the difference preventive care makes. Preventive care is widely believed to be desirable even if people have to be induced to use it through artificially low prices (or if almost everyone would have paid for it anyway). This attitude—that everyone should use preventive care—exists even though people privately report no preferences for preventive over curative care.[11]

Most preventive care does not reduce total cost, according to the empirical evidence. There are a small number of preventive interventions, largely pediatric inoculations, which appear to improve health and save enough in future expected costs to offset the upfront costs—compared to a situation with no vaccinations. But most preventive care does not save money. Yet public pressure for this coverage continues to be strong.

Over time, coverage of preventive care has (like auto seat belts) switched from being an option to being a marketing device. Managed care in the form of HMOs always covered (and spotlighted) such maintenance services. There are several plausible explanations for this shift in emphasis. First, the costs of curative care probably grew faster than the cost of preventive care, as hospital expense growth in the 1980s and early 1990s outran growth in physician spending overall. Second, recognition grew that if preventive care could reduce future curative costs, even modestly, then offering nearly full coverage of curative care provided incentives to underuse preventive care.[12] Finally, coverage of preventive care paradoxically may attract lower risk people to a health plan, since people in the midst of an episode of serious illness are not likely to seek general preventive care.

Why the Passion for Prevention?

Why does the public choice differ from the private choice? The reason may lie in the distribution of benefits. Health care insurance distributes premiums from the total population in favor of the majority of individual policy holders. Consider the following example. Suppose an average of $1,000 per person could be spent on either of two types of health insurance coverage—coverage of a costly catastrophic illness that affects only one in 20 people per year, or coverage of a preventive service that is of significant value to (and would be used by) slightly more than half the population. Suppose that all risk-averse people value the catastrophic insurance coverage at $1,300 per person. In contrast, suppose the smaller number who attach significant value to the preventive service each value it at $1,800. The efficient outcome is clear: cover the catastrophic illness (worth $1,300 to the average person) and not the preventive service (worth about $900, or $0.5 \times \$1,800$) on average. However, if all people pay the same insurance premium for either addition to coverage ($1,000), the majority is likely to prefer to cover the preventive care. To them, it would yield a higher gross benefit ($1,800) than would covering the catastrophic illness ($1,300). Others who do not value the preventive service will prefer the efficient outcome, but they will be in the minority.

This kind of inefficient majority rule equilibrium is common in models of public choice. It may help to explain public preferences for prevention relative to treatment. The key insight is that, among the great majority of the population in moderately good health, there are few beneficial cures that most or all would expect to use. By contrast, preventive measures are usually desired by the great majority in moderately good health, but are usually of less value to those already at higher risk. Preventive care thus becomes an ideal vehicle for a large coalition to get others to pay for services of selective benefit when insurance is publicly financed or community rated. That these services are certain to be used, and thus certain to benefit the members of the dominant coalition, only adds to the appeal of the lets-you-pay-for-my-preventive-care strategy.

This public choice explanation is surely not the only reason why the self-selected Oregon citizens groups put preventive care at the top of their priority list. Yet it is at least as plausible an explanation as other attempts to rationalize those choices as reflecting some type of special ethical preferences.[13]

However, in addition to such political games, it does seem that the social approbation of greater use of preventive care—even when it is not warranted on efficiency grounds—is ubiquitous and universal. It may simply reflect a nagging feeling that people should value their health more highly than they actually do. However, it might also reflect a desire to avoid a kind of externality. For example, others may be adversely affected when someone gets a preventable illness. If my neighbor is not fully insured for curative care, I might prefer that he spend more on preventive care rather than expect me to subsidize him if he gets sick. This desire may encourage greater use of affordable (even if not cost-effective) preventive services.

Finally, people may prefer preventive care to avoid regret or recrimination. For example, cases of tetanus are very rare in developed countries, yet the practice of getting a new tetanus shot after a cut or puncture wound is very common. Perhaps people are thinking of the regret they would feel if their cut turned out to be the one in a million that resulted in tetanus. The risk of death or injury in driving to (and sitting in) the emergency room may more than offset the risk of the illness—but few would feel regret for an accident on the way to the hospital.

CONCLUSIONS

As we have seen in the discussions of health-care deductibles and preventive care, public and private behavior can often diverge. In general, private behavior more closely follows expected utility models while public decisions often move in the opposite direction. People avoid deductibles publicly but accept them privately. They want their insurance companies to pay for preventive care even when it might be more cost effective for them to pay for it themselves.

There are three reasons for this divergence:

1. Misperceptions of Value

Individuals often have misperceptions of the value of health insurance or of preventive care. We can find examples of both underpurchase and overpurchase, relative to the benchmark of a person maximizing a risk-averse utility function.

The underpurchase of health insurance (as evidenced by the 43 million Americans with no health insurance whatsoever) may be an indication that many people misperceive the risks. The concentration of the uninsured in the lower income portion of the population suggests that moral hazard, the availability of charity care or care in public hospitals, or unusually high administrative costs also contribute to this phenomenon.

There may, however, be a residual amount of misperception of the usual type—people underestimate the probability that they will have medical expenses and so even fail to consider the potential value of health insurance. The fact that millions of low income people who are eligible for free Medicaid insurance do not enroll themselves and their families may be an indication that they underestimate the value of this coverage.

With preventive care, we find the same phenomenon. On the one hand, many people overestimate the value of preventive care and underestimate the value of curative care. On the other hand, even highly effective types of preventive care, such as pediatric immunizations, are neglected by some families for whom they would be free of cost.

There are nonmonetary costs that might discourage a rational, risk-averse person from buying insurance or preventive care if the benefit from either were small relative to the price, so we can never be absolutely certain that misperception is present. Still, there is some evidence that in health insurance and prevention some people display the same kind of persistent under protection against low-probability, high-loss events that they do in other situations. This is interspersed with occasional bouts of excess caution that lead to purchases of nearly useless dread disease insurance and the tetanus booster shots. (See Howard Kunreuther's discussion in Chapter 15 for further insights on this yo-yo phenomenon.)

Government regulations apparently are not the antidote to these misperceptions. Governments of the people and by the people tend to put into law the misperceptions of their citizens. The fate of the Medicare Catastrophic legislation shows that the misperceptions that confuse consumers also confuse the political process. At this point, we do not have a definitive theory of public choice equilibrium when citizens have misperceptions about health insurance and preventive care. The assumption that "correction" is always politically feasible is surely unrealistic, but we do not know when collective choice might make things better (or when it might possibly make them worse). Caution about suggesting remedies would seem to be the best strategy.

2. Reputation

People seek respect (or the avoidance of disrespect) for their decisions about health care coverage. They want to avoid the appearance that they are increasing the risk of death or injury for themselves or their family in return for lower prices or more money to spend on other, less important items of consumption. In the privacy of my car on the way to Ohio, my reputation is fairly safe (as long as my family does not attack the decision). As a member of a citizens group establishing health care policies, my reputation is much more exposed.

People may thus speak publicly in ways that preserve their reputations even when their actual personal behavior is highly consistent with trading off health for money. In situations in which collective or community interests are present, this desire to appear politically correct may have a much stronger effect on the options proposed and chosen.

It is virtually certain that some of this kind of motivation influenced voters' choices of covered services in Oregon—although the self-selection of "citizens groups" also may have played a part. Here again we know that the desire for approbation is present and affects the outcome, but we are not able to generalize about those effects.

3. Distribution

Finally, distribution of benefits also affects public decisions. Insurance is fundamentally a redistributive mechanism—taking from those who do not make claims to give to those who do. In ideal markets, competitive insurance charges the same premium to everyone with the same expected expenses, but charges different premiums to those with different levels of expected expenses. However, when insurance is financed by or subsidized by taxation, as is the case with Medicare or Medicaid, there are possibilities to use the political system to redistribute funds from some risk classes to others.

Part of the political support for preventive care may be based on this kind of process. If a majority of people will benefit from better coverage for preventive care but the entire population (including those who do not benefit) will pay premiums or taxes, there may be a temptation to favor such coverage. Coverage of preventive care does, after all, offset what would otherwise be certain expenses from those who would otherwise have paid for the preventive care, so it is an effective vehicle for redistribution. Those who are already ill with an identified condition may paradoxically be less likely to use or benefit from preventive care than those who are still healthy—and so the healthy may be able to get the unhealthy to share in the cost of their preventive care.

It is surprising that public insurance plans such as Medicare do not provide more preventive benefits than they now do, given the possibilities for redistribution. Perhaps this is due to the overall reluctance of politicians to raise taxes for any reason.

Management Implications

How can managers and policy makers identify, understand and manage these public-private conflicts?

- *Watch for public-private divergence.* In your own decisions, in any case involving both public and private decisions, look at the question through both lenses. For a public decision, especially when there are reputational issues at stake, consider whether you would make the same decision in a private situation. Also, look at whether the decision really provides the highest expected utility.
- *Expect that people will not do as they say.* By understanding this inconsistency between public and private decisions, you may be better able to anticipate behavior. People may call for a certain option in public, but be willing to accept a very different option if they can do so privately. Customers may publicly call for more environmentally friendly cars and gasoline, but privately decide at the pump and car dealership that these values are not worth the cost. (For further discussion of the inconsistency of applying values, see Baron and Irwin in Chapter 14.) Will people actually follow their public positions in private decisions? Is there a way to allow decision makers to save their reputations but still make the decision you advocate? When negotiating or making customer offers, awareness of these differences can help you better decide how to shape and communicate options.
- *Look for redistribution mechanisms.* The redistribution of funds from premiums to a certain group in the population can affect decisions. When there is a perception that a larger organization—the company, government, or pool of the insured—will foot the bill, people make very different decisions than when they are paying out of their own pockets. If you are making policy for the government or setting up systems, pay close attention to the impact of these redistribution mechanisms.

There will probably always be inconsistencies between our public and private selves, particularly when it comes to such emotional issues as health care coverage. This divergence will affect decision-making processes throughout our society. By better understanding this phenomenon, and its causes, we can be more effective at managing it.

NOTES

Chapter 1

1. Nick Leeson with Edward Whitley, *Rogue Trader: How I Brought Down Barings Bank and Shook the Financial World* (Boston: Little, Brown and Company, 1996), p. 40.
2. See note 1, p. 28.
3. Stephen Fay, *The Collapse of Barings* (New York: W.W. Norton, 1996), p. 77.
4. See note 3, pp. 79–80.
5. See note 3, p. 78.
6. See note 3, p. 125.
7. See note 3, p. 68.
8. Allan Sloan, "Helping Banks Lose Their Barings," *Newsweek*, 125, 11 (March 13, 1995), p. 51.
9. See note 3, p. 80.
10. See note 3, p. 68.
11. See www.businessweek.com/1997/b3539141.htm.
12. Dow Jones News Service, January 3, 1996.
13. See note 1, frontispiece.

Chapter 2

1. Mary Frances Luce, John W. Payne, and James R. Bettman, "Emotional Trade-off Difficulty and Choice," *Journal of Marketing Research*, 36 (May 1999), pp. 143–159.
2. John W. Payne, James R. Bettman, and Eric J. Johnson, *The Adaptive Decision Maker* (Cambridge, MA: Cambridge University Press, 1993).
3. John W. Payne, James R. Bettman, and Mary Frances Luce, "When Time Is Money: Decision Behavior under Opportunity Cost Time Pressure," *Organizational Behavior and Human Decision Processes*, 66, 2 (May 1996), pp. 131–152.
4. James R. Bettman, Mary Frances Luce, and John W. Payne, "Consumer Choice Processes: An Adaptive, Constructive View," *Journal of Consumer Research*, 25 (December 1998), pp. 187–217.

5. Deborah Frisch and Robert T. Clemen, "Beyond Expected Utility: Rethinking Behavioral Decision Research," *Psychological Bulletin,* 116 (July 1994), pp. 45–46.

6. See note 4.

7. Philip E Tetlock,, Randall S. Peterson, and Jennifer S. Lerner, "Revising the Value Pluralism Model: Incorporating Social Content and Context Postulates," in *The Psychology of Values: The Ontario Symposium on Personality and Social Psychology,* Vol. 8, ed. Clive Seligman, James M. Olson, and Mark P. Zanna (Mahwah, NJ: Erlbaum, 1996), pp. 25–51; Robert E. Lucas Jr. "Adaptive Behavior and Economic Theory," *Journal of Business,* 59 (October 1986), pp. S401–S426; Daniel McFadden, "Rationality for Economists," working paper (Berkeley, CA: University of California, Department of Economics, 1997); Charles R. Plott, "Rational Individual Behavior in Markets and Social Choice Processes: The Discovered Preference Hypothesis," in *The Rational Foundations of Economic Behavior,* ed. Kenneth J. Arrow et al. (New York: St Martin's, 1996), pp. 225–250.

8. R.N. Shepard, "On Subjectively Optimum Selection among Multiattribute Alternatives," in *Human Judgments and Optimality,* ed. M.W. Shelley and G.L. Bryan (New York: Wiley, 1964), pp. 257–281; Robin M. Hogarth, *Judgment and Choice* (2nd ed.) (New York: Wiley, 1987), pp. 257–281.

9. Alan P. Fiske and Philip E. Tetlock, "Taboo Trade-Offs: Reactions to Transactions That Transgress the Spheres of Justice," *Political Psychology,* 18 (June 1997), pp. 255–297.

10. In Chapter 17 of this book, Mark Pauly discusses the particular problematic trade-off of health versus money.

11. W.R. Dubourg, M.W. Jones-Lee, and Graham Loomes, "Imprecise Preferences and the WTP-WTA Disparity," *Journal of Risk and Uncertainty,* 9, 2 (1994), pp. 115–133; John Loomis, George Paterson, Patricia Champ, Thomas Brown, and Beatrice Lucero, "Paired Comparison Estimates of Willingness to Accept versus Contingent Valuation Estimates of Willingness to Pay," *Journal of Economic Behavior and Organization,* 35, 4 (1998) pp. 501–515; Gwendolyn C. Morrison, "Resolving Differences in Willingness to Pay and Willingness to Accept: Comment," *American Economic Review,* 87, 1 (1997), pp. 236–240.

12. Jason F. Shogren, Seung Y. Shin, Dermot J. Hayes, and James B. Kliebenstein, "Resolving Differences in Willingness to Pay and Willingness to Accept," *American Economic Review,* 84, 1 (1994), pp. 255–270.

13. Richard S. Lazarus, *Stress and Emotion: A New Synthesis* (New York: Springer, 1999).

14. Susan Folkman and Richard S. Lazarus, "Coping as a Mediator of Emotion," *Journal of Personality and Social Psychology,* 54 (March 1988), pp. 466–475.

15. Mary Frances Luce, James R. Bettman, and John W. Payne, "Attribute Identities Matter: Subjective Perceptions of Attribute Characteristics," forthcoming *Organizational Behavior and Human Decision Processes.*

16. Mary Frances Luce, James R. Bettman, and John W. Payne, "Choice Processing in Emotionally Difficult Decisions," *Journal of Experimental Psychology: Learning, Memory and Cognition,* 23 (March 1997).

17. Mary Frances Luce, "Choosing to Avoid: Coping with Negatively Emotion-Laden Consumer Decisions," *Journal of Consumer Research,* 24 (March 1998), pp. 409–433.

18. See note 16, pp. 384–405.

19. Elizabeth H. Creyer, James R. Bettman, and John W. Payne, "The Impact of Accuracy and Effort Feedback and Goals on Adaptive Decision Behavior," *Journal of Behavioral Decision Making,* 3 (January–March 1990), pp. 1–16.

20. James R. Bettman, Eric J. Johnson, Mary Frances Luce, and John W. Payne, "Correlation, Conflict, and Choice," *Journal of Experimental Psychology: Learning, Memory, and Cognition,* 19 (July 1993), pp. 931–951.

21. See note 2.

22. Irving L. Janis and Leon Mann, *Decision Making: A Psychological Analysis of Conflict, Choice, and Commitment* (New York: Free Press, 1977).

23. See note 6.

24. See note 4.

25. Leonard J. Savage, "The Theory of Statistical Decision," *Journal of the American Statistical Association,* 46 (March 1951), pp. 55–67; Graham Loomes and Robert Sugden "Regret Theory: An Alternative Theory of Rational Choice Under Uncertainty," *Economic Journal,* 92 (December 1982), pp. 805–824.

26. Amos Tversky, "Contrasting Rational and Psychological Principles of Choice," in *Wise Choices: Decisions, Games, and Negotiations,* ed. Richard J. Zeckhauser, Ralph L. Keeney, and James K. Sebenius (Boston, MA: Harvard Business School Press).

27. Jane Beattie,, Jonathan Baron, Jack C. Hershey, and Mark D. Spranca, "Psychological Determinants of Decision Attitude," *Journal of Behavioral Decision Making,* 7 (June 1994), pp. 129–144.

28. Jonathan Baron, "The Effects of Normative Beliefs on Anticipated Emotions," *Journal of Personality and Social Psychology,* 63 (August 1992), pp. 320–330.

29. Daniel Kahneman and Jackie Snell, "Predicting Utility," in *Insights in Decision Making: A Tribute to Hillel J. Einhorn,* ed. Robin M. Hogarth (Chicago: University of Chicago Press, 1990), pp. 295–310.

30. Wesley A. Magat, W. Kip Viscusi, and Joel Huber, "A Reference Lottery Metric for Valuing Health," *Management Science,* 42 (August 1996), pp. 1118–1130.

31. Jonathan Baron and Mark D. Spranca, "Protected Values," *Organizational Behvaior Decision Research and Human Decision Processes,* 70 (April 1997), pp. 1–16.

32. W. Kip Viscusi, Wesley A. Magat, and Joel Huber, "An Investigation of the Rationality of Consumer Valuations of Multiple Health Risks," *Rand Journal of Economics,* 18, 4 (1987), pp. 465–479.

Chapter 3

1. See, for example, Richard Bellman, "The Theory of Dynamic Programming," *Bulletin of the American Mathematical Society,* 60 (1954), pp. 503–516.

2. In his later writings Bellman even questioned this use as well, noting that managers sometimes rely on its prescriptions to excess, using it to avoid assuming personal responsibility for decisions that, in fact, lie outside the computational domain of decision theory.

3. Robert J. Meyer and Yong Shi, "Learning to Choose among Inherently Risky Alternatives: Intuitive Solutions to the One-Armed-Bandit Problem," *Management Science,* 41, 5 (1995), pp. 817–834.

4. Colin F. Camerer, Eric J. Johnson, Talia Rymon, and Sankar Sen, "Cognition and Framing in Sequential Bargaining for Gains and Losses," in *Proceedings of the International Conference on Game Theory,* ed. K. Binmore, A. Karman, and P. Tani (Cambridge, MA: The MIT Press, 1993).

5. Richard Thaler, "Toward a Positive Theory of Consumer Choice," *Journal of Economic Behavior and Organization,* 1 (1980), pp. 39–60; Richard Thaler, "Savings, Fungibility, and Mental Accounts," in *The Winner's Curse: Paradoxes and Anomalies of Economic Life,* ed. R. Thaler (New York: The Free Press, 1992), pp. 107–121.

6. Robert J. Meyer, Rajiv Tyagi, and John Walsh, "An Experimental Analysis of Dynamic Pricing in Markets with Uncertain Demand," working paper, Department of Marketing, The Wharton School of Business, 1997.

7. Barbara Hayes-Roth and Frederick Hayes-Roth, "A Cognitive Model of Planning," *Cognitive Science,* 3 (1979), pp. 275–310.

8. Perhaps the most well-known example of this is the psychologist Richard Herenstein's work on what he called "melioration effects"—a phenomenon that he used to explain the difficulty we often have ridding ourselves of addictive behaviors. Richard J. Herrnstein and Drazen Prelec, "Melioration: A Theory of Distributed Choice," *Journal of Economic Perspectives,* 5 (summer 1991), pp. 137–156.

9. Daniel Kahneman and Amos Tversky, "On the Psychology of Prediction," *Psychological Review,* 80 (1973), pp. 237–251; see note 6.

10. See note 9.

11. Richard E. Nisbett, *Rules for Reasoning* (Hillsdale, NJ: Erlbaum, 1993).

12. Joseph W. Alba, Susan M. Broniarczyk, Terence A. Shimp, and Joel E. Urbany, "The Influence of Prior Beliefs, Frequency Cues, and Magnitude Cues on Consumers' Perceptions of Comparative Price Data," *Journal of Consumer Research,* 21 (December 1994), pp. 219–235.

13. Lauren B. Alloy and Naomi Tabachnik, "Assessment of Covariation by Humans and Animals: The Joint Influence of Prior Expectations and Current Situational Information," *Psychological Review,* 91 (January 1984), pp. 112–149; J.R. Bettman, E.H. Creyer, D.R. John, and C.A. Scott, "Covariation Assessment in Rank Order Data," *Journal of Behavioral Decision Making,* 1 (1988), pp. 239–254.

14. Joseph W. Alba and J. Wesley Hutchinson, "Knowledge Calibration: What Consumers Know and What They Think They Know," *Journal of Consumer Research,* 27 (September 2000), forthcoming; Joseph W. Alba, J. Wesley Hutchinson, and John G. Lynch, "Memory and Decision Making," in *Handbook of Consumer Behavior,* ed. Thomas S. Robertson and Harold H. Kassarjian (Englewood Cliffs, NJ: Prentice-Hall, 1991), pp. 1–49; Steven Hoch and John Deighton, "Managing What Consumers Learn from Experience," *Journal of Marketing,* 53 (April 1989), pp. 1–20.

15. See note 9.

16. Ward Edwards, "Conservatism in Human Information Processing," in *Formal Representation of Human Judgment,* ed. B. Kleinmuntz (New York: Wiley, 1968).

17. David M. Grether, "Bayes Rule as a Descriptive Model: The Representativeness Heuristic," *Quarterly Journal of Economics* (1980), pp. 537–557.

18. Dipankar Ghosh, "Throwing Good Money After Bad," *Management Accounting,* 77 (1995), pp. 51–54.

19. See note 14.

20. J.P. Gilbert and F. Mosteller, "Recognizing the Maximum of a Sequence," *Journal of the American Statistical Association,* 61 (1966), pp. 35–73.

21. See note 6.

22. Another interpretation is that subjects acted as if the effectiveness of protection levels was governed by a step function where it was effective, but only if the investment was beyond a certain (higher) level.

23. We might note that a number of computer industry analysts have recently expressed fears that firms might draw this exact same conclusion from the recent Y2K episode—rather than drawing the conclusion that their investments helped stave off problems, firms might conclude that there was never a problem to begin with—and be less prone to heed warnings in the future; Marcia Stepanek, "The Y2K Bug Repellent Wasn't a Waste," *Business Week* (January 15, 2000), p. 35.

24. John D. Sterman, "Modeling Managerial Behavior: Misperceptions of Feedback in a Dynamic Decision Making Experiment," *Management Science,* 35 (1988), pp. 321–339.
25. Joseph W. Alba and J. Wesley Hutchinson, "Dimensions of Consumer Expertise," *Journal of Consumer Research,* 13 (March 1987), pp. 411–454.
26. See note 25.

Chapter 4

1. For comprehensive reviews of the extensive literature existing regarding variety-seeking behavior see Leigh McAlister and Edgar A. Pessemier, "Variety-Seeking Behavior: An Interdisciplinary Review," *Journal of Consumer Research,* 9 (December 1982), pp. 311–322; Barbara E. Kahn, "Consumer Variety-Seeking Among Goods and Services," *Journal of Retailing and Consumer Services,* 2, 3 (1995), pp. 139–148; Hans Van Trijp, *Variety-Seeking in Product Choice Behavior: Theory with Applications in the Food Domain,* Thesis Landbouwuniversiteit Wageningen, The Netherlands, 1995.
2. C. Coombs and G.S. Avrunin, "Singled Peaked Preference Functions and Theory of Preference," *Psychological Review,* 84, 2 (1977), pp. 216–230.
3. F. Hansen, *Consumer Choice Behavior* (New York: The Free Press, 1972); P.S. Raju, "Optimal Stimulation Level: Its Relationship to Personality, Demographics, and Exploratory Behavior," *Journal of Consumer Behavior,* 7 (1972), pp. 272–282.
4. Elizabeth C. Hirschman, "Innovativeness, Novelty Seeking, and Consumer Creativity," *Journal of Consumer Research,* 7 (1980), pp. 283–295.
5. Joel Huber and David J. Reibstein, "The Relationship Between Attitude Measures and Choice Frequency," in *Attitude Research Plays for High Stakes,* ed. J.C. Maloney (Chicago, IL: American Marketing Association, 1978).
6. Peter H. Farquhar and Vitahala R. Rao, "A Balance Model for Evaluating Subsets of Multiattribute Items," *Management Science,* 5 (January 1976), pp. 528–539.
7. Edgar Pessemier, "Stochastic Properties of Changing Preferences," *American Economic Review,* 68, 2 (1978), pp. 380–385.
8. Daniel Kahneman and Jackie Snell, "Predicting Utility," in *Insights in Decision Making: A Tribute to Hillel J. Einhorn,* ed. R.M. Hogarth (Chicago: University of Chicago Press, 1990); Simonson Itamar, "The Effect of Purchase Quantity and Timing on Variety-Seeking Behavior," *Journal of Marketing Research,* 27 (May 1990), pp. 150–162; John Walsh, "Flexibility in Consumer Purchasing for Uncertain Future Tastes," *Marketing Science,* 14 (1995).
9. Barbara E. Kahn and Donald R. Lehmann, "Modeling Choice Among Assortments," *Journal of Retailing,* 67 (fall 1991), pp. 274–299.

10. R.J. Herrnstein, "Behavior, Reinforcement and Utility," *Psychological Science,* 1 (July 1990a), pp. 217–224; R.J. Herrnstein, "Rational Choice Theory," *American Psychologist,* 45 (March 1990b), pp. 356–367; R.J. Herrnstein, G.F. Loewenstein, D. Prelec, and W. Vaughan, "Utility Maximization and Melioration: Internalities in Individual Choice," *Journal of Behavioral Decision Making,* 6 (1993), pp. 149–185.

11. B.E. Kahn, R. Ratner, and D. Kahneman, "Patterns of Hedonic Consumption Over Time," *Marketing Letters,* 8, 1 (1997), pp. 85–96.

12. George Loewenstein and Drazen Prelec, "Preferences for Sequences of Outcomes," *Psychological Review,* 100 (1993), pp. 91–108.

13. Daniel Kahneman and Amos Tversky, "Prospect Theory: An Analysis of Decision Under Risk," *Econometrica,* 47, 2 (1979), pp. 363–391.

14. Daniel Kahneman and Jackie Snell, "Predicting a Changing Taste: Do People Know What They Like?" *Journal of Behavioral Decision Making,* 5 (1992), pp. 187–200; Donald A. Redelmeier and Daniel Kahneman, "Patients' Memories of Painful Medical Treatments: Real-Time and Retrospective Evaluations of Two Minimally Invasive Procedures," *Pain,* 66, 1 (July 1996), pp. 3–8.

15. Rebecca K. Ratner, Barbara E. Kahn, and Daniel Kahneman, "Choosing Less-Preferred Songs for the Sake of Variety," *Journal of Consumer Research* (June 1999), pp. 1–15.

16. Jeffrey Inman, "High Satiety: The Role of Sensory-Specific Satiety in Consumer Variety Seeking," *Association of Consumer Research Conference,* Columbus, Ohio, October 1999.

17. Leigh McAlister and Edgar A. Pessemier, "Variety-Seeking Behavior: An Interdisciplinary Review," *Journal of Consumer Research,* 9 (December 1982), pp. 311–322; Barbara E. Kahn, "Consumer Variety-Seeking Among Goods and Services," *Journal of Retailing and Consumer Services,* 2, 3 (1995), pp. 139–148.

18. B.E. Kahn, D. Morrison, and G. Wright, "Aggregating Individual Purchases to the Household Level," *Marketing Science,* 5 (summer 1986), pp. 260–268.

19. R.K. Ratner and B.E. Kahn, "A 'Consumption Norm': Social Pressure to Choose Variety," working paper, The Wharton School, 1999.

20. Dan Ariely and Jonathan Levav, "Taking the Road Less Traveled and Less Enjoyed: Collective Variety Seeking and Personal Dissatisfaction," working paper, Duke University, Fuqua School of Business, Marketing Department, 1999.

21. Alice M. Isen, "Positive Affect, Cognitive Processes, and Social Behavior," in *Advances in Experimental Social Psychology,* ed. Leonard Berkowitz, 20 (New York: Academic Press, 1987), pp. 203–253.

22. Barbara E. Kahn and Alice M. Isen, "The Influence of Positive Affect on Variety-Seeking Behavior Among Safe, Enjoyable Products," *Journal of Consumer Research* (September 1993), pp. 257–270.

23. D.J. Mitchell, B.E. Kahn, and S.C. Knasko, "There's Something in the Air: Effects of Congruent and Incongruent Ambient Odor on Consumer Decision-Making," *Journal of Consumer Research*, 22 (September 1995), pp. 229–238.

24. Satya Menon and Barbara E. Kahn, "The Impact of Context on Variety-Seeking in Product Choices," *Journal of Consumer Research*, 22 (December 1995), pp. 285–295; Satya Menon and Barbara E. Kahn, "Cross-Category Effects of Stimulation on the Shopping Experience: An Application to Internet Shopping," working paper, University of Pennsylvania, Philadelphia, 1997.

25. G. Hofstede, *Culture's Consequences* (Newbury Park, CA: Sage, 1990); H. Markus and S. Kitayama, "Culture and the Self: Implications for Cognition, Emotion, and Involvement, *Psychological Review,* 98, 2 (1991), pp. 224–253.

26. Susan M. Broniarczyk, Wayne D. Hoyer, and Leigh McAlister, "Consumers' Perceptions of the Assortment Offered in a Grocery Category: The Impact of Item Reduction," *Journal of Marketing Research,* 35 (May 1998), pp. 166–188.

27. Stephen Hoch, Eric T. Bradlow, and Brian Wansink, "The Variety of an Assortment," working paper, University of Pennsylvania, Philadelphia, Marketing Department, 1999.

28. Stephen Hoch, Eric T. Bradlow, and Brian Wansink, "The Variety of an Assortment," working paper, University of Pennsylvania, Philadelphia, Marketing Department, 1999; Andrea Morales and Barbara E. Kahn, "The Combo Meal Effect: How to Increase Variety without Really Trying," *ACR Conference Presentation,* October 1999.

29. Cynthia Huffman and Barbara E. Kahn, "Variety for Sale: Mass Customization or Mass Confusion?" *Journal of Retailing,* 74, 4 (1998), pp. 491–513.

Chapter 5

1. Daniel Kahneman and Amos Tversky, "Subjective Probability: A Judgment of Representativeness," *Cognitive Psychology,* 3 (1972), pp. 430–454.

2. Thomas Gilovich, Robert Vallone, and Amos Tversky, "The Hot Hand in Basketball: On the Misperception of Random Sequences," *Cognitive Psychology,* 17 (July 1985), pp. 295–314.

3. Paul Meehl, *Clinical versus Statistical Prediction* (University of Minnesota Press: Minneapolis, 1954).

4. The study is based on data that Robert Blattberg and I originally collected. Robert. C. Blattberg and Stephen J. Hoch, "Database Models and Managerial Intuition: 50% Model and 50% Manager," *Management Science,* 36 (1990), pp. 887–899; Stephen J. Hoch, "Models and Experts in Combination," in *The Marketing Information Revolution,* ed. R.C. Blattberg, R. Glazer, and J.D.C. Little (Cambridge, MA: Harvard University Press, 1990).

5. The numerical entries in the table represent the R^2 of each of the different forecasting methods. R^2 is the percent of variance explained, a measure of predictive accuracy ranging from 0% (zero predictive validity) to 100% (perfectly accuracy). The model fits are from a cross-validation analysis where the model parameters were estimated on one subset of data and then used to forecast on another independent subsample of the data in order to avoid overfitting.

6. Stephen J. Hoch and David A. Schkade, "A Psychological Approach to Decision Support Systems," *Management Science* (January 1996), pp. 51–64.

7. Specifically, each person's individual predictive accuracy (R^2) was divided by the predictability of the decision environment in which they operated (high $R^2 = .8$, low $R^2 = .2$) in order to facilitate comparison across groups. Obviously it is easier to be accurate in the high as opposed to low predictability environment.

8. "Data Mining for Fool's Gold," *Computerworld* (January 12, 1997).

9. "Turning Datamining into a Management Science Tool: New Algorithms and Empirical Results," *Management Science* (2000, in press).

Chapter 6

1. M. Feinberg and J. Tarrant, *Why Smart People Do Dumb Things* (New York: Fireside Books, 1995).

2. J. McGrath, "Groups: Interaction and Performance Time," (Englewood Cliffs, NJ: Prentice Hall, 1984).

3. G. Hofstede, *Culture's Consequences: International Differences in Work Related Values* (Beverly Hills, CA: Sage, 1980); H. Bontempo Triandis, R. Villareal, M. Asai, and N. Lucca, "Individualism and Collectivism: Cross-Cultural Perspectives on Self-Ingroup Relationships," *Journal of Personality and Social Psychology,* 54 (1988), pp. 323–333.

4. G. Lowenstein and J. Elster, *Choice over Time* (New York: Sage, 1992).

5. K.A. Jehn and E. Weldon, "Conflict Management in Bicultural Teams: Cultural Dimensions and Synergistic Problem Solving," in *Economic Cooperation in Northeast Asia,* ed. K. Jeong (Seoul, Korea: University of Korea Press, 1997), pp. 27–54.

6. S. Crainer and N. Campbell, "Only Patience Pays in China," *Management Today* (December 1986), pp. 68–69.

7. M. Van Oldenborgh, "Court with Care," *International Business* (April 1995), pp. 20–22.

8. J. Cunningham, "Success in Corporate and Entrepreneurial Organizations in Singapore," *Journal of Small Business Management,* 33 (1995), pp. 80–86.

9. T. Chang, "Joint Ventures with Vietnam," *National Public Accountant,* 39 (1994), pp. 20–23.

10. J. Fisher, "A Culture of Contribution," *Executive Excellence,* 14, 16 (1997); G. Grune, "Patience Plus Perspective: Keys to Successful Marketing in the 90's," *Executive Speeches,* 5 (1991), pp. 1–5; R. Henkoff, "Inside America's Biggest Private Company," *Fortune,* 126 (1992), pp. 82–90; P. Morgan, "Central Skills of Successful General Managers," *Practising Manager,* 8 (1987), pp. 13–15; M. Murray, "Four Perspectives for Success," *Executive Speeches,* 2 (1987), pp. 4–7; M. Rashid and J. Dar, "Current Managerial Styles and Effective Managers," *Management Services,* 38 (1994), pp. 16–17; L. Sukay, "Bottom Line: Management," *Oil and Gas Investor* (February 1994), pp. 8–10; D. Vittitow, "Ten Action Steps for Vital Boards," *Nonprofit World,* 10 (1992), pp. 13–14; B. Wisdom and D. Denton, "Manager as Teacher," *Training and Development,* 45 (1991), pp. 54–58.
11. K. Hardy, "Implementing Marketing Strategy," *Business Quarterly,* 55 (1991), pp. 33–35; B. Reimann, "Philosophers of the Strategic Renaissance," *Planning Review,* 21 (1993), pp. 49–53.
12. F. Leclerc, B.H. Schmitt, and L. Dube, "Waiting Time and Decision Making: Is Time Like Money?" *Journal of Consumer Research,* 22 (1995), pp. 110–119.
13. J. Dowd and W. Meyercord, "The Patience Bank," *Quality Progress,* 25 (1992), pp. 61–63; E. Furash, "Strategy Pays," *Journal of Lending and Credit Risk Management,* 79 (1997), pp. 7–12; James P. O'Shaughnessy, "High Yields, High Rewards," *Barrons,* 72, 42 (October 19, 1992), p. 16.
14. See note 5.
15. Kathleen M. Eisenhardt, "Making Fast Strategic Decisions in High-Velocity Environments," *Academy of Management Journal,* 32, 3 (September 1989), pp. 543–576.
16. S. Blount and G.A. Janicik, "Getting and Staying In-Pace: The In-Synch Preference and Its Implications for Work Groups in Organizations," in *Research on Managing Groups and Teams in Organizations,* Vol. 4, ed. M.A. Neale, E. Mannix, and H. Sondak (Greenwich, CT: JAI Press, 2001).
17. Sybil B. Eysenck and H.J. Eysenck, "Scores of Three Personality Variables as a Function of Age, Sex, and Social Class," *British Journal of Social and Clinical Psychology,* 8, 1 (1969), pp. 69–76.
18. See note 4.
19. A.W. Kruglanski and D.M. Webster, "Group Members Reactions to Opinion Deviates and Conformists at Varying Degrees of Proximity to Decision Deadline and of Environmental Noise," *Journal of Personality and Social Psychology,* 61 (1991), pp. 215–225.
20. R. Tung, "Strategic Management Thought in East Asia," *Organizational Dynamics,* 22 (1994), pp. 55–65; K. Weigelt, "Eastern Philosophy, Basketball and Management," working paper, University of Pennsylvania, 1999.

21. See note 20, Weigelt, 1999.
22. See note 20, Tung, 1994.
23. B. Voss, "Japan: Model, Myth, or Mistake?" *Journal of Business Strategy,* 14 (1993), pp. 49–54.
24. A. Tsuda, "JIT and the Warrior Manager," *Manufacturing Systems* (October 1986), pp. 52–53.
25. See note 16.
26. *The Book of Leadership and Strategy,* trans. Thomas Cleary (Shambhala, 1992, p. 65).
27. Sun Tzu, *The Art of War,* trans. Zhang Huimin (Panda Books, 1996, p. 134).
28. L. Doucet and K. Jehn, "Analyzing Harsh Words in a Sensitive Setting: American Expatriates in Communist China," *Journal of Organizational Behavior,* 18 (1997), pp. 559–582.
29. K. Jehn, "Human-Machine Interfaces and Conflict: A Study of NASA Mission Control," in *Research on Managing Groups and Teams,* ed. M. Neale and E. Mannix (London: JAI Press, 2000).
30. Miyamoto Musashi, *The Book of Five Rings,* p. 18.
31. K. Jehn and E. Weldon, "Managerial Attitudes toward Conflict: Cross-Cultural Differences in Resolution Styles," *Journal of International Management,* 3 (1997), pp. 291–321.
32. K. Jehn and P. Shah, "Interpersonal Relationship and Task Performance: An Examination of Mediating Processes in Friendship and Acquaintance Groups," *Journal of Personality and Social Psychology,* 72 (1997), pp. 775–790; P. Shah and K. Jehn, "Do Friends Perform Better than Acquaintances?: The Interaction of Friendship, Conflict and Task," *Group Decision and Negotiation,* 2 (1993), pp. 149–165.
33. E. Weldon, K. Jehn, and P. Pradhan, "Processes That Mediate the Relationship between a Group Goal and Improved Group Performance," *Journal of Personality and Social Psychology,* 61 (1991), pp. 555–569.
34. M.H. Bazerman, *Judgment in Managerial Decision Making* (4th ed.) (New York: Wiley, 1998); J. Edward Russo and Paul J.H. Schoemaker, *Decision Traps: Ten Barriers to Brilliant Decision Making and How to Overcome Them* (New York: Simon & Schuster, 1990).
35. See note 28.

Chapter 7

1. These projects were developed and carried out with contributions by teams of researchers in the Risk Center, in cooperation with other Centers at Wharton. For additional information on these projects and other on-going work in risk and decision processes at the Center, consult our Web site: http://opim.wharton.upenn.edu/risk.

2. For a recent discussion of Wharton-based research on environmental trends affecting decision making, see Jerry Y. Wind and Jeremy Main, *Driving Change* (New York: The Free Press, 1998).

3. For a synthesis of research on the traditional models of decision making, see Paul R. Kleindorfer, Howard C. Kunreuther, and Paul J.H. Schoemaker, *Decision Sciences: An Integrative Perspective* (New York: Cambridge University Press, 1993).

4. There is already a rich literature on the structure and results of electricity trading that I will not review here. Organizations like the Edison Electric Institute in Washington, DC and the Electric Power Research Institute (EPRI) in Palo Alto have numerous publications devoted to this subject. For a brief introduction, see *Designing Competitive Electricity Markets,* ed. Hung-po Chao and Hillard G. Huntington (Boston: Kluwer Academic Publishers, May 1998).

5. These include centralized approaches to data mining and data warehousing, as described in *e-Business: Roadmap for Success,* ed. Ravi Kalakota and Marcia Robinson (Reading, MA: Addison-Wesley, 1999); and decentralized approaches to data acquisition and optimization such as those discussed in *Multi-agent Systems: A Modern Approach to Distributed Artificial Intelligence,* ed. G. Weiss (Cambridge, MA: MIT Press, 1999).

6. For a discussion of other uses of data warehousing and datamining in support of e-Business, see note 5.

7. For a readable introduction to new tools in artificial intelligence and their implications for complexity theory, see John H. Holland, *Hidden Order: How Adaptation Builds Complexity* (Reading, MA: Perseus Books, 1995).

8. Similar weather models and data infrastructure are being developed in support of catastrophe insurers and emergency response organizations. Recent news releases covering systems from major natural hazard risk modeling companies like Risk Management Solutions, Inc. and Applied Insurance Research have emphasized the sophistication of these applications. For example, in a recent ClariNet Business Wire release from July 14, 2000, the following announcement was carried. "Representatives of the world's largest insurance, reinsurance, and financial institutions were on hand for the unveiling in London today of AIR's Worldwide Weather, a new Web site providing leading edge historical weather and forecast data. The raw, cleaned and reconstructed weather data now available online through AIR Worldwide Weather provides a full range of timely data and forecast information for decision makers trading in the expanding weather derivatives marketplace."

9. See Stephen Hoch in Chapter 5 for a detailed discussion of the rationale for incorporating managerial judgment in forecasts such as these.

10. For a recent discussion of decision making under systemic complexity, see J. Gharajedaghi, *Systems Thinking: Managing Chaos and Complexity* (Boston: Butterworth-Heinemann, 1999).

11. See note 5. Mention of ERP should not pass without also noting the increased risks associated with running the operations of an enterprise through such an integrated system. Small data problems can become very large production or delivery problems when the results of the ERP are implemented. Notwithstanding these increased risks, the global ERP industry has grown from almost nothing in 1990 to over $50 billion in worldwide revenue in 1999. Clearly a large number of companies believe the risk is worth taking for the added efficiency benefits they believe will be forthcoming through the use of ERP.

12. For a discussion of other natural hazards and approaches to insurance and catastrophe modeling for these, see *Paying the Price,* ed. Howard Kunreuther and Richard J. Roth Sr. (Washington, DC: Joseph Henry Press, 1998).

13. Interestingly, such models have also begun to have a significant impact on the public sector and on regulation. In electric power, for example, it is routine at regulatory hearings to enter testimony based on such models as the benchmark or baseline for the effects of proposed regulation on rates and standards. Although the situation is not quite as advanced in catastrophe modeling, there too one sees significant increases in such modeling as part of regulatory hearings justifying premium structures or other issues. For modeling issues in electricity regulation, see, for example, Carl Pechman, *Regulating Power* (Boston, MA: Kluwer Academic Publishers, 1993). For a discussion of catastrophe modeling in insurance regulation, see Craig Taylor, Erik VanMarcke, and Jim Davis, "Evaluating Models of Risks from Natural Hazards," in *Paying the Price,* eds. Kunreuther and Roth (Washington, DC: Joseph Henry Press, 1998).

14. See the Weiss volume cited in note 5 for details on new approaches to decentralized optimization by artificial agents.

15. The importance of co-opetition for modern market economies is discussed more fully in Adam M. Brandenburger and Barry J. Nalebuff, *Co-opetition* (New York: Doubleday Books, 1997).

16. See, for example, Hubert Österle, Elgar Fleisch, and Rainer Alt, *Business Networking: Shaping Enterprise Relationships on the Internet* (New York: Springer-Verlag, 2000).

17. For a detailed description of one such exercise in the electric power industry, see Paul R. Kleindorfer, Dongjun Wu, and Chitru Fernando, "Strategic Gaming Models for the Electric Power Industry," *European Journal of Operations Research,* 130 (2001), pp. 156–168.

18. For details on a number of such experiments related to electric power markets, see Stephen J. Rassenti and Vernon L. Smith, "Deregulating Electric Power: Market Design Issues and Experiments," in *Designing Competitive Electricity Markets,* ed. Hung-po Chao and Hillard G. Huntington (Boston, MA: Kluwer Academic Publishers, 1998).

19. For a discussion of real options in the R&D area, see B. Kogut and N. Kulatilaka, "Options Thinking and Platform Investments: Investing in Opportunity," *California Management Review* (1994), pp. 53–71. For an interesting discussion of recent applications of real options thinking in the broader sense described in this paper, see Arnd Huchzermeier and Chris H. Loch, "Project Management under Risk: Using the Real Options Approach to Evaluate Flexibility in R&D," *Management Science* (forthcoming 2001).

Chapter 8

1. For further details see "Encyclopedia Britannica," Harvard Business School Case, N9-396-051, December 1995; and for an update, see "Bound for Glory?: The Venerable Encyclopedia Britannica Struggles to Survive in an Electronic Age," *Chicago Tribune Magazine* (March 1998).

2. *Handbook of American Business* (New York, Hoover, Inc., 1995), pp. 488–489.

3. Amos Tversky and Daniel Kahneman, "The Framing of Decisions and the Psychology of Choice," *Science,* 211 (1981), pp. 453–458.

4. Avi Fiegenbaum, Stuart Hart, and Dan Schendel, "Strategic Reference Point Theory," *Strategic Management Journal,* 17, 13 (March 1996), pp. 219–235.

5. J. Edward Russo and Paul J.H. Schoemaker, "Managing Overconfidence," *Sloan Management Review* (winter 1992), pp. 7–18.

6. For examples, see John D.W. Morecroft and John D. Sterman, *Modeling for Learning Organizations* (Portland, OR: Productivity Press, 1994).

7. Vincent P. Barabba, *Meeting of the Minds: Creating the Market-Based Enterprise* (Boston, MA: Harvard Business School Press, 1995).

8. Paul J.H. Schoemaker, "Scenario Planning: A Tool for Strategic Thinking," *Sloan Management Review* (Winter 1995), pp. 25–40.

9. Steven E. Prokesh, "Unleashing the Power of Learning: An Interview with British Petroleum's John Browne," *Harvard Business Review* (September–October 1997), pp. 147–168.

10. The Raychem Case was recounted to us by David Dye and Mike Rafko as part of an MBA project at Duke University. It is summarized here with their permission.

11. Howard Perlmutter: personal communication; see also Howard V. Perlmutter, "On Deep Dialog," working paper, Emerging Global Civilization Project, The Wharton School, 1999.

12. J. Edward Russo and Paul J.H. Schoemaker, *Decision Traps* (New York: Simon & Schuster, 1990), pp. 75–76.

Chapter 9

1. Define the attraction for strategy j, after period t's experience is incorporated, as $A^j(t)$, and define the payoff from strategy j in period t to be $\Pi(j,t)$. In the EWA theory, attractions are modified each period according to the formula,

$$A^j(t) = \frac{(\phi A^j(t-1) + \Pi(j,t))}{\phi(1-\kappa)+1}$$

if strategy j was chosen in period Δt, or

$$A^j(t) = \frac{(\phi A^j(t-1) + \delta\Pi(j,t))}{(\phi(1-\kappa)+1)}$$

if strategy j was not chosen. Attractions are then used to determine the chance of playing a particular strategy through an exponential "logit" formula. See Camerer and Ho (1999) for more details. The parameter ϕ is the change index, δ is the consideration (or imagination) index, and κ is the commitment index.

2. Reinforcement learning and belief-based learning are thus closely interrelated: belief learning is a kind of *general* reinforcement in which even unchosen strategies are strongly reinforced by what they would have earned. This surprising kinship came as a shock to theorists who had thought the two kinds of learning were fundamentally unrelated, like adventurers discovering that two wide rivers in different parts of a country spring from a common source. Having a single unified theory economizes by replacing two different tools with a single tool that can do what the other two could do.

3. Colin F. Camerer and Teck-Hua Ho, "Experience-Weighted Attraction Learning in Normal-Form Games," *Econometrica* (June 1999); John Van Huyck, Raymond Battalio, and Richard Beil, "Strategic Uncertainty, Equilibrium Selection and Coordination Failure in Average Opinion Games," *Quarterly Journal of Economics,* 106 (1991), pp. 885–909.

4. This behavior was called "satisficing" by the behavioral economist and Nobel laureate Herbert Simon. Simon's point was that people and organizations often behave this way, while our purpose is to help managers learn faster and understand how others learn.

5. John Maynard Keynes, *The General Theory of Employment, Interest and Money* (New York: Harcourt, Brace, 1936).

6. Colin F. Camerer, "Progress in Behavioral Game Theory," *Journal of Economic Perspectives* (July 1997), pp. 1–48.

7. R. Nagel, "Experimental Results on Interactive Competitive Guessing," *American Economic Review,* 85 (1995), pp. 1313–1326.

8. Thomas J. Sargent, *The Conquest of American Inflation* (Princeton: Princeton University Press, 1999).

9. Note that most money managers *underperform* the market (about 75 percent of actively managed mutual funds underperform the S&P 500 after fees are subtracted).

10. Teck-Hua Ho and Kuan Chong, "A parsimonious model of SKU choice: Familiarity-based choice and response sensitivity," Wharton School Department of Marketing, 1999, or www.marketing.wharton.upenn.edu/ideas/pdf /99-020.pdf.

Chapter 10

1. David Johnson, *Philadelphia Inquirer* (November 18, 1990), p. D1.

2. See note 1.

3. Interview, September 17, 1999.

4. Interview, September 18, 1999.

5. Laurie Weingart, Elaine Hyder, and Michael Prietula, "Knowledge Matters: The Effect of Tactical Descriptions on Negotiation Behavior and Outcome," *Journal of Personality and Social Psychology,* 70 (1996), pp. 1205–1217.

6. Bruce Barry and Richard Oliver, "Affect in Dyadic Negotiation: A Model and Propositions," *Organizational Behavior and Human Decision Processes,* 67 (1996), pp. 127–143.

7. Joyce Neu and John Graham, "A New Methodological Approach to the Study of Interpersonal Influence Tactics: A 'Test Drive' of a Behavioral Scheme," *Journal of Business Research,* 29 (1994), pp. 131–144.

8. Peter Carnevale and Donald Conlon, "Time Pressure and Strategic Choice in Mediation," *Organizational Behavior and Human Decision Processes,* 42 (1988), pp. 111–133.

9. Interview, September 13, 1999.

Chapter 11

1. "Bad-Faith Bargaining Claims Belong before NLRB," *The National Law Journal* (June 1, 1998), p. B19.

2. *Bonczek v. Carter-Wallace,* 1997.

3. T. Miller, "Sears Admits 'Mistakes' at Auto Service Centers," *The San Francisco Chronicle* (June 23, 1992), p. A1; "Sears Gets Handed a Huge Repair Bill," *Business Week* (September 14, 1992), p. 38; "Getting Your Car Fixed without Getting Fleeced," *Money* (December 1992), p. 138.

4. K. O'Connor and P. Carnevale, "A Nasty but Effective Negotiation Strat-
    egy: Misrepresentation of a Common-Value Issue," *Personality and Social
    Psychology Bulletin,* 23 (1997), pp. 504–515.

5. M. Schweitzer and R. Croson, "Curtailing Deception: The Impact of Direct
    Questions on Lies and Omissions," *The International Journal of Conflict
    Management,* 10 (1999), pp. 225–248.

6. P. Singer, *Practical Ethics* (2nd ed.) (New York: Cambridge University Press,
    1993).

7. Negotiators are often held responsible for misleading partial disclosures as
    well.

8. See note 4; M. Schweitzer, S. Brodt, and R. Croson, "Visual Access and
    Context-Dependent Lies: The Use of Deception in Videoconference and
    Telephone Mediated Negotiation," working paper, 2000.

9. R.J. Anton, "Drawing the Line: An Exploratory Test of Ethical Behavior in
    Negotiation," *The International Journal of Conflict Management,* 1 (1990),
    pp. 265–280; R.J. Lewicki and N. Stark, "What Is Ethically Appropriate in
    Negotiations: An Empirical Examination of Bargaining," *Social Justice Re-
    search,* 9 (1996), pp. 69–95; R.J. Lewicki, D.M. Saunders, and J.W. Minton,
    Essentials of Negotiation (Boston, MA: Irwin, 1997); R.J. Lewicki and R.
    Robinson, "Ethical and Unethical Bargaining Tactics: An Empirical Study,"
    Journal of Business Ethics, 17 (1998), pp. 665–682.

10. For a discussion of legal considerations of lying in negotiations, see R.G.
    Shell, "When Is It Legal to Lie in Negotiations?" *Sloan Management Re-
    view,* 32 (1991), pp. 93–101.

11. B. DePaulo, D. Kashy, S. Kirkendol, M. Wyer, and J. Epstein, "Lying in
    Everyday Life," *Journal of Personality and Social Psychology,* 70 (1996),
    pp. 979–995.

12. R.J. Lewicki, "Lying and Deception: A Behavioral Model," in *Negotiating
    in Organizations,* ed. M.H. Bazerman and R.J. Lewicki (Beverly Hills, CA:
    Sage, 1983).

13. A. Tenbrunsel, "Misrepresentation and Expectations of Misrepresentation in
    an Ethical Dilemma: The Role of Incentives and Temptation," *Academy of
    Management Journal,* 41 (1998), pp. 330–339.

14. T. Carson, "Second Thoughts about Bluffing," *Business Ethics Quarterly,*
    3 (1993), pp. 318–341.

15. See note 13.

16. M. Schweitzer and C. Hsee, "Stretching the Truth: Elastic Justification and
    Motivated Communication of Uncertain Information," working paper,
    1999.

17. P. Ekman, M. O'Sullivan, W. Friesen, and K. Scherer, "Face, Voice, and
    Body in Detecting Deceit," *Journal of Nonverbal Behavior,* 15, 2 (1991),
    pp. 125–135. M. Frank and P. Ekman, "The Ability to Detect Deceit

Generalizes across Different Types of High-Stake Lies," *Journal of Personality and Social Psychology,* 72, 6 (1997), pp. 1429–1439.

18. See note 8, Schweitzer, Brodt, and Croson, 2000.

19. B.M. DePaulo, J.I. Stone, and G.D. Lassiter, "Deceiving and Detecting Deceit," *The Self and Social Life,* ed. B.R. Schlenker (New York: McGraw-Hill, 1985), pp. 323–370; P. Ekman and W.V. Friesen, "Detecting Deception from Body or Face," *Journal of Personality and Social Psychology,* 219 (1974), pp. 288–298.

20. See M. Schweitzer and L. DeChurch, "Conflict Frame Adoption and the Use of Deception in Negotiations," working paper, 1999, for a recent discussion of framing in negotiations.

21. See note 5.

22. R.G. Shell, *Bargaining for Advantage* (New York: Viking Press, 1999).

23. C. Heath, R. Larrick, and G. Wu, "Goals as Reference Points," *Cognitive Psychology,* 38 (1999), pp. 79–109.

24. M. Schweitzer, L. Ordonez, and B. Douma, "The Dark Side of Goal Setting: The Role of Goals in Motivating Unethical Behavior," working paper, 1999.

25. See note 16.

26. See note 5.

Chapter 12

1. The *Wall Street Journal* has reported that organizational life is filled with "e-mail disaster" stories, many of them stemming from disclosures of sensitive or personal information to unintended audiences. Rebecca Quick, "Misdirected E-Mail Can Wreak Havoc, Especially at the Office," *Wall Street Journal* (January 14, 1999), p. A1; Ralph T. King, "Lehman Analyst's Misdirected E-Mail Offers a Glimpse Into Office Politics," *Wall St. Journal* (December 4, 1998), p. B5.

2. Sara Kiesler, "The Hidden Messages in Computer Networks," *Harvard Business Review* (January–February 1986), p. 47.

3. Researchers estimate that, in 1997, 40 percent of correspondence in day-to-day business and professional life was conducted using electronic mail. This estimate came from the U.S. Postal Service. See G.A. Marken, "Think Before You Click," *Office Systems,* 15, 3 (March 1998), pp. 44–46.

4. Lee Sproull and Sara Kiesler, *Connections: New Ways of Working in the Networked Organization* (Cambridge, MA: MIT Press, 1991), p. 40.

5. See note 4, p. 69.

6. See note 4, p. 69.

7. Z. Barsness and A.E. Tenbrunsel, "Technologically Mediated Communication and Negotiation: Do Relationships Matter?" Manuscript presented to

the *Annual Conference for the International Association for Conflict Management* (February 17, 1998).

8. N. Frohlich and J. Oppenheimer, "Some Consequences of E-Mail vs. Face-to-Face Communication in Experiments," *Journal of Economic Behavior and Organization,* 35 (1998), pp. 389–403.

9. Harvey Wichman, "Effects of Isolation and Communication on Cooperation in a Two-Person Game," *Journal of Personality and Social Psychology,* 16, 1 (1970), pp. 114–120; Peter J.D. Carnevale, "The Influence of Positive Affect and Visual Access on the Discovery of Integrative Solutions in Bilateral Negotiations," *Organizational Behavior and Human Decision Processes,* 37 (1986), pp. 1–13.

10. See note 4; Sara Kiesler, Jane Siegel, and Timothy W. McGuire, "Social Psychological Aspects of Computer-Mediated Communication," *American Psychologist,* 39, 10 (1984), pp. 1123–1134; Sara Kiesler, "The Hidden Messages in Computer Networks," *Harvard Business Review* (January–February 1986), pp. 46–60.

11. See note 10, p. 1130.

12. William Lucas, "Effects of E-Mail on the Organization," *European Management Journal,* 16, 1 (1998), pp. 18–30. See note 4.

13. See note 12, p. 20.

14. See note 4, p. 4.

15. Studies by Professor Albert Mehrabian of UCLA found that the literal meanings of the words used in a face-to-face conversation conveyed only about 7 percent of the total set of feelings and attitudes communicated between people. Tone of voice carried 38 percent of the contextual "load"; while some 55 percent of feelings and attitudes were discerned from cues such as posture, pacing, eye contact, and the like. Albert Mehrabian, *Nonverbal Communication* (Chicago: Aldine Press, 1972), p. 3.

16. D.A. Moore, T.R. Kurtzberg, and L.L. Thompson, "Long and Short Routes to Success in Electronically Mediated Negotiations: Group Affiliations and Good Vibrations," *Organizational Behavior and Human Decision Processes,* 77, 1 (1999), pp. 22–43.

17. G. Richard Shell, *Bargaining for Advantage* (New York: Penguin, 1999), pp. 186–187.

18. Robert Cialdini, *Influence: The Psychology of Persuasion* (New York: William Morrow, 1993), pp. 167–203.

19. Marjorie Sarbaugh-Thompson and Martha Feldman, "Electronic Mail and Organizational Communication: Does Saying 'Hi' Really Matter?" *Organizational Science,* 9, 6 (1998), pp. 685–698.

20. Thomas Oetzinger Jr., "With the Stakes High, a Lucent Duo Conquers Distance and Culture," *Wall Street Journal* (April 23, 1999), p. B1.

21. L. Adrianson and E. Hjelmquist, "Group Processes in Face-to-Face and Computer-Mediated Communication," *Behavior and Information Technology,* 10, 4 (1991), pp. 281–296; S. Weisband, S.K. Schneider, and T. Connoly, "Computer-Mediated Communication and Social Information: Status Salience and Status Difference," *Academy of Management Journal,* 38, 4 (1995), pp. 1124–1151.

22. See note 4, pp. 87–90.

23. See note 4, p. 97.

24. Scott McCartney, "The Deal-Breakers: How Renegade Pilots at American Airlines Upset the Union's Pact," *Wall Street Journal* (February 10, 1997), p. A1.

25. Striking staff members of an Israeli university used e-mail as a "secret weapon" that enabled them to maintain their unity, air issues during the conflict, and give continuous feedback to their negotiating team. Nava Pliskin, Celia T. Romm, and Raymond Markey, "E-Mail as a Weapon in an Industrial Dispute," *New Technology Work and Employment,* 12, 1 (March 1997), pp. 3–12.

26. Mary Parker Follet, "Constructive Conflict" in *Dynamic Administration: The Collected Papers of Mary Parker Follet,* ed. H.C. Metcalf and L. Urwick (New York: Harper, 1940), pp. 30–49.

27. R.T.A. Croson, "Look at Me When You Say That: An Electronic Negotiation Simulation," *Simulation and Gaming,* 30, 1 (1999), pp. 23–37.

28. Ann Davis, "For Dueling Lawyers, the Internet Is Unlikely Referee," *Wall Street Journal* (May 12, 1999), p. B1.

29. Stacey Higginbotham, "Next, Online Bids Over Jail Time?" *Business Week* (July 19, 1999).

30. S.S. Nagel and M.K. Mills, *Multi-Criteria Methods for Alternative Dispute Resolution: With Microcomputer Software Applications* (New York: Quorum Books, 1990).

31. A. Rangaswamy, J. Eliashberg, R. Burke, and J. Wind, "Developing Marketing Expert Systems: An Application to International Negotiations," *Journal of Marketing,* 53, 4 (1989), pp. 24–49 (discussing NEGOTEX system).

32. "Win Squared" is published by Arcadian Software in Escondido, California.

33. See http://www.smartsettle.com. The theoretical basis for this system can be found in E.M. Thiessen and D.P. Loucks, "Computer Assisted Negotiation of Multiobjective Water Resources Conflicts," working paper, School of Civil and Environmental Engineering, Cornell University, Ithaca, New York, 1992.

34. Our system and the tests we ran on it are described at more length in A. Rangaswamy and G.R. Shell, "Using Computers to Realize Joint Gains in

Negotiations: Toward an 'Electronic Bargaining Table,' " *Management Science*, 43, 8 (1997), pp. 1147–1163.

Chapter 13

1. For simplicity, we ignore the option of waiting beyond one week to make the decision, for example to see if an improved operation becomes available.

2. D. Kahneman and A. Tversky, "Prospect Theory: An Analysis of Decisions Under Risk," *Econometrica*, 47 (1979), pp. 263–291; D. Kahneman and A. Tversky, "Choices, Values, and Frames," *American Psychologist*, 39 (1984), pp. 341–350; and I. Ritov, J. Baron, and J.C. Hershey, "Framing Effects in the Evaluation of Multiple Risk Reduction," *Journal of Risk and Uncertainty*, 6 (1993), pp. 145–160.

3. A. Bastardi and E. Shafir, "On the Pursuit and Misuse of Useless Information," *Journal of Personality and Social Psychology*, 75 (1998), pp. 19–32.

4. It is further complicated in population-based decision analyses where each decision maker who is to be aided is an unnamed, randomly chosen, but nevertheless clearly affected, member of a group of decision makers for whom the analyst is attempting to choose a best policy. The analyst still must decide how much to acknowledge conflicting goals and the likelihood of people changing their minds. But the problem is not just deciding how to incorporate unknown or changing preferences. If a common, group decision must be made, the population's differing values and risk attitudes pose a challenge to the decision analyst who must choose a single, best policy for all. If a single, overall policy is not required, there may still be barriers to implementing individually tailored policies in the face of scale economies, such as for the costs of promulgating the policy or the costs of purchasing diagnostic equipment.

5. We acknowledge, but do not address in detail, decisions in which the analyst is a separate and possibly competing utility-maximizing agent.

6. U.S. Congress, Office of Technology Assessment. *Cystic Fibrosis and DNA Tests: Implications of Carrier Screening*, OTA-BA-532, Washington, DC: U.S. Government Printing Office (August 1992), Chapter 2.

7. D.A. Asch, J.C. Hershey, M.V. Pauly, J.P. Patton, M.K. Jedrziewski, and M.T. Mennuti, "Genetic Screening for Reproductive Planning: Methodological and Conceptual Issues in Policy Analysis," *American Journal of Public Health*, 86 (1996), pp. 684–690.

8. A.M. Garber and J.P. Fenerty, "Costs and Benefits of Prenatal Screening for Cystic Fibrosis," *Medical Care*, 29 (1991), pp. 473–489; T.A. Lieu, S.E. Watson, and A.E. Washington, "The Cost-Effectiveness of Prenatal Carrier Screening for Cystic Fibrosis," *Obstetrics and Gynecology*, 84 (1994), pp. 903–912.

9. N.J. Wald, "Couple Screening for Cystic Fibrosis," *Lancet,* 338 (1991), pp. 1318–1319.

10. Probability estimates were obtained by surveying the literature and consulting experts in obstetrics, genetics, and prenatal diagnosis. Cost estimates were also collected from a variety of sources. The estimate for the 6-mutation DNA test was constructed by calculating the cost for technical and professional personnel, reagents, equipment, royalties, and space. Estimates for the cost of midtrimester pregnancy termination, miscarriage, and delivery were calculated as 80 percent of charges using estimates from the Hospital of the University of Pennsylvania and surrounding centers. We assumed that 85 percent of deliveries would be vaginal and the remainder performed by cesarean section. We also included estimates for the cost of patients' time, genetic counseling time, prenatal diagnosis with amniocentesis, and the lifetime direct medical and nonmedical costs of CF. We used three different perspectives for the model: patient, payer, and society. For the patient perspective, we used estimates of charges and assumed that patients would bear 20 percent of medical charges as personal costs, and 100 percent of nonmedical costs such as transportation and time lost from work. Payer costs were assumed to be 80 percent of charges. Societal costs were assumed to be net costs independent of charges. For more details, see D.A. Asch, J.C. Hershey, M.L. Dekay, M.V. Pauly, J.P. Patton, M.K. Jedrziewski, F. Frei, R. Giardine, J.A. Kant, and M.T. Mennuti, "Carrier Screening for Cystic Fibrosis: Costs and Clinical Outcomes," *Medical Decision Making,* 18 (1998), pp. 202–212.

11. M.V. Pauly, "The Economics of Moral Hazard," *American Economic Review,* 58 (1968), pp. 531–539.

12. B.S. Wilfond and N. Fost, "The Introduction of Cystic Fibrosis Carrier Screening into Clinical Practice: Policy Considerations," *Milbank Quarterly,* 70 (1992), pp. 629–659.

13. A.H. Handyside, J.G. Lesko, J.J. Tarín, M.L. Winston, and M.R. Hughes, "Birth of a Normal Girl After In Vitro Fertilization and Preimplantation Diagnostic Testing for Cystic Fibrosis," *New England Journal of Medicine,* 327 (1992), pp. 905–909.

14. M. Angastiniotis, "Cyprus: Thalassaemia Program," *Lancet* (1990), pp. 119–120.

15. B. Metz, "Matchmaking Scheme Solves Tay-Sachs Problem," *Journal of the American Medical Association,* 258 (1987), pp. 2636–2639.

16. D.A. Asch, J.P. Patton, and J.C. Hershey, "Knowing for the Sake of Knowing: The Value of Prognostic Information," *Medical Decision Making,* 10 (1990), pp. 47–57; D.M. Berwick and M.C. Weinstein, "What Do Patients Value? Willingness To Pay for Ultrasound In Normal Pregnancy," *Medical*

Care, 23 (1985), pp. 881–893; J. Cairns, P. Shackley, and V. Hundley, "Decision Making with Respect to Diagnostic Testing: A Method of Valuing the Benefits of Antenatal Screening," *Medical Decision Making,* 16 (1996), pp. 161–168; C. Donaldson, P. Shackley, M. Abdalla, and Z. Miedzybrodzka, "Willingness to Pay for Antenatal Carrier Screening for Cystic Fibrosis," *Health Economics,* 4 (1995), pp. 439–452; W.A. Benish, "Relative Entropy as a Measure of Diagnostic Information," *Medical Decision Making,* 19 (1999), pp. 202–206.

17. G. Evers-Kiebooms, L. Denayer, and H. Van den Berghe, "A Child with Cystic Fibrosis: II. Subsequent Family Planning Decisions, Reproduction and Use of Prenatal Diagnosis," *Clinical Genetics,* 37 (1990), pp. 207–215; D.C. Wertz, J.M. Rosenfeld, S.R. Janes, and R.W. Erbe, "Attitudes Toward Abortion Among Parents of Children with Cystic Fibrosis," *American Journal of Public Health,* 81 (1991), pp. 992–996; J.R. Botkin and S. Alemagno. "Carrier Screening for Cystic Fibrosis: A Pilot Study of the Attitudes of Pregnant Women," *American Journal of Public Health,* 82 (1992), pp. 723–725.

18. A. Amram and N. Kulatilaka, *Real Options: Managing Strategic Investment in an Uncertain World* (Boston, MA: Harvard Business School Press, 1999).

Chapter 14

1. *The Economy of the Earth: Philosophy, Law and the Environment* (New York: Cambridge University Press, 1988).
2. Julie R. Irwin, "Buying/Selling Price Preference Reversals: Preference for Environmental Changes in Buying versus Selling Modes," *Organizational Behavior and Human Decision Processes,* 60 (1994), pp. 431–457.
3. See discussion by Luce, Payne, and Bettman in Chapter 2.
4. J.R. Irwin, "Introduction to the Special Issue on Ethical Tradeoffs in Consumer Decision Making," *Journal of Consumer Psychology* (1999).
5. E. Coupey, J.R. Irwin, and J.W. Payne, "Product Familiarity and the Expression of Preferences," *Journal of Consumer Research,* 24 (1998), pp. 459–468.
6. See, for example, P. Slovic and S. Lichtenstein, "Preference Reversals: A Broader Perspective," *American Economic Review,* 73 (1983), pp. 371–384; and J.W. Payne, J.R. Bettman, and E.J. Johnson, *The Adoptive Decision Maker* (New York: Cambridge University Press, 1993).
7. See, for example, S. Lichtenstein and P. Slovic, "Reversal of Preferences between Bids and Choices in Gambling Decisions," *Journal of Experimental Psychology,* 89 (1971), pp. 46–55.; J.R. Irwin, P. Slovic, S. Lichtenstein, and G.H. McClelland, "Preference Reversals and the Measurement of Environmental Values," *Journal of Risk and Uncertainty,* 6 (1993), pp. 1–13.

8. See note 5.

9. M.H. Bazerman, D.A. Moore, A.E. Tenbrunsel, K.A. Wade-Benzoni, and S. Blount, "Explaining How Preferences Change across Joint versus Separate Evaluation," *Journal of Economic Behavior and Organization,* 39 (1999), pp. 41–58.

10. See note 9. For an alternative but not incompatible explanation, also see C.K. Hsee, "The Evaluability Hypothesis: An Explanation of Preference Reversals between Joint and Separate Evaluation of Alternatives," *Organizational Behavior and Human Decision Processes,* 46 (1996), pp. 247–257.

11. J.R. Irwin, "Elicitation Rules and Incompatible Goals," *Behavioral and Brain Sciences,* 17 (1994), pp. 20–21.

12. See notes 1 and 2.

13. Gretchen B Chapman and Eric J. Johnson, "Preference Reversals in Monetary and Life Expectancy Evaluations," *Organizational Behavior and Human Decision Processes,* 62 (1995), pp. 300–317.

14. J.R. Irwin, "Loss Aversion and Guilt," working paper, 2000.

15. M. Strahilevitz, "The Effects of Product Type and Donation Magnitude on Willingness to Pay More for a Charity-Linked Brand," *Journal of Consumer Psychology,* (1999).

16. See notes 2 and 14.

17. J.R. Irwin and J. Baron, "Effect of Moral Values on Prices and Ratings," *Organizational Behavior and Human Decision Processes,* (in press, 2001).

18. J. Baron and N.P. Maxwell, "Cost of Public Goods Affects Willingness to Pay for Them," *Journal of Behavioral Decision Making,* 9 (1996), pp. 173–183.

19. I. Ritov and J. Baron, "Protected Values and Omission Bias," *Organizational Behavior and Human Decision Processes,* 79 (1999), pp. 79–94.

20. J. Baron and Spranca, "Protected Values," *Organizational Behavior and Human Decision Processes,* 70 (1997), pp. 1–16.

21. J. Baron and S. Leshner, "How Serious Are Expressions of Protected Values?" *Journal of Experimental Psychology: Applied* (in press).

22. See note 19.

23. J. Baron, "Semantic Components and Conceptual Development," *Cognition,* 2 (1973), pp. 189–207.

24. See note 21.

25. I. Ritov and J. Baron, "Reluctance to Vaccinate: Omission Bias and Ambiguity," *Journal of Behavioral Decision Making,* 3 (1990), pp. 263–277.

26. As suggested by Schelling, "The Life You Save May Be Your Own, in *Problems in Public Expenditure Analysis,* ed. S.B. Chace Jr. (Washington, DC: Brookings Institution, 1968) (pp. 127–175).

27. P. Slovic, B. Fischhoff, and S. Lichetenstein, "Facts and Fears: Understanding Perceived Risk," in *Societal Risk Assessment: How Safe Is Safe Enough?*, ed. R.C. Schwing and W.A. Albers Jr. (New York: Plenum Press, 1980).

Chapter 15

1. The likelihood of an earthquake is just as high whether insurance is purchased or not. This is equivalent to saying that there are no moral hazard problems. Moral hazard exists if the probability is higher after a person buys insurance. A classic example of moral hazard is when an individual drives more carelessly after she has purchased automobile insurance. Hence the chance of a car accident increases because insurance was purchased.
2. For a more detailed discussion of discounted utility theory and its relationship to other models of intertemporal choice. See G. Loewenstein and D. Prelec, "Anomalies in Intertemporal Choice," *Quarterly Journal of Economics,* 107 (1992), pp. 573–597.
3. C. Camerer and H. Kunreuther, "Decision Processes for Low Probability Events: Policy Implications," *Journal of Policy Analysis and Management,* 8 (1989), pp. 565–592; W. Magat, W. Viscusi, and J. Huber, "Risk-Dollar Tradeoffs, Risk Perceptions, and Consumer Behavior," in *Learning About Risk,* ed. W. Viscusi and W. Magat (Cambridge, MA: Harvard University Press, 1987), pp. 83–97.
4. O. Huber, R. Wider, and O. Huber, "Active Information Search and Complete Information Presentation in Naturalistic Risky Decision Tasks," *Acta Psychologica,* 95 (1997), pp. 15–29.
5. R. Hogarth and H. Kunreuther, "Decision Making Under Ignorance: Arguing with Yourself," *Journal of Risk and Uncertainty,* 10 (1995), pp. 15–36.
6. C. Hsee, "The Evaluability Hypothesis: An Explanation of Preference Reversals Between Joint and Separate Evaluations of Alternatives," *Organizational Behavior and Human Decision Processes,* 46 (1996), pp. 247–257; and C. Hsee, S. Blount, G. Loewenstein, and M. Bazerman, "Preference Reversals Between Joint and Separate Evaluations of Options: A Review and Theoretical Analysis," *Psychological Review,* 125 (1999), pp. 576–590.
7. H. Kunreuther, N. Novemsky, and D. Kahneman, "Making Low Probabilities Useful," *Journal of Risk and Uncertainty* (in press).
8. See Camerer and Kunreuther (note 3) for a more detailed discussion of this point.
9. G. McClelland, W. Schulze, and D. Coursey, "Insurance for Low-Probability Hazards: A Bimodal Response to Unlikely Events," *Journal of Risk and Uncertainty,* 7 (1993), pp. 95–116.

10. F. Oberholzer-Gee, "Learning to Bear the Unbearable: Towards an Explanation of Risk Ignorance," mimeo, Wharton School, University of Pennsylvania, 1998.

11. See note 2.

12. Jerry Hausman, "Individual Discount Rates and the Purchase and Utilization of Energy-Using Durables," *Bell Journal of Economics,* 10 (1979), pp. 33–54; and Willett Kempton and Max Neiman (eds.), *Energy Efficiency: Perspectives on Individual Behavior* (Washington, DC: American Council for an Energy Efficient Economy, 1987).

13. Howard Kunreuther, Ayse Onculer, and Paul Slovic, "Time Insensitivity for Protective Measures" *Journal of Risk and Uncertainty,* 16 (1998), pp. 279–299.

14. D. Schkade and J. Payne, "How People Respond to Contingent Valuation Questions: A Verbal Protocol Analysis of Willingness to Pay for an Environmental Regulation," *Journal of Environmental Economics & Management,* 26 (1994), pp. 88–109; J. Baron and P. Maxwell, "Cost of Public Goods Affects Willingness to Pay for Them," *Journal of Behavioral Decision Making,* 9 (1996), pp. 173–183.

15. For a summary of recent literature in this area, see M. Finacciane, L. Alhakami, P. Slovic, and S.M. Johnson, "The Affect Heuristic in Judgments of Risks and Benefits," *Journal of Behavioral Decision Making,* 13 (2000), pp. 1–17; G. Loewenstein, E. Weber, C. Hsee, and E. Welch, "Risk as Feelings," working paper, Carnegie Mellon University, Pittsburgh, PA (1999); and J. Baron, J. Hershey, and H. Kunreuther, "Determinants of Priority for Risk Reduction: The Role of Worry," *Risk Analysis* (in press).

16. Christopher Hsee and Howard Kunreuther, "The Affection Effect In Insurance Decisions," *Journal of Risk and Uncertainty,* 20 (2000), pp. 141–160.

17. E. Stone, F. Yates, and A. Parker, "Risk Communication: Absolute versus Relative Expressions of Low-Probability Risks," *Organizational Behavior and Human Decision Processes,* 60 (1994), pp. 387–408.

18. N. Weinstein, K. Kolb, and B. Goldstein, "Using Time Intervals Between Expected Events to Communicate Risk Magnitudes," *Risk Analysis,* 16 (1996), pp. 305–308.

19. P. Slovic, B. Fischhoff, and S. Lichtenstein, "Accident Probabilities and Seat Belt Usage: A Psychological Perspective," *Accident Analysis and Prevention,* 10 (1978), pp. 281–285.

20. P. Slovic, J. Monahan, and D.G. MacGregor, "Violence Risk Assessment and Risk Communication: The Effects of Using Actual Cases, Providing Instruction, and Employing Probability versus Frequency Formats," *Law and Human Behavior,* 24 (2000), pp. 271–296.

Chapter 16

1. Paul R. Kleindorfer, Howard C. Kunreuther, and Paul J.H. Schoemaker, *Decision Sciences: An Integrative Perspective* (New York: Cambridge University Press, 1993).

2. Abhijit Banerjee, "A Simple Model of Herd Behavior," *Quarterly Journal of Economics,* 107, 3 (1992), pp. 797–817; Sushil Bikhchandani, David Hirshleifer, and Ivo Welch, "A Theory of Fads, Fashion, Custom and Cultural Change as Informational Cascades," *Journal of Political Economy,* 100, 5 (1992), pp. 992–1026.

3. For example, in their study of disaster insurance purchases, Kunreuther et al. found that the most important variable influencing the decision to buy insurance was "knowing friends or neighbors who had bought a policy." Howard Kunreuther et al., *Disaster Insurance Protection: Public Policy Lessons* (New York: Wiley, 1978).

4. The general Bayes' rule is written as

$$\Pr(\Theta_i \mid x) = \frac{\Pr(\Theta_i)\Pr(x|\Theta_i)}{\displaystyle\sum_{i=1}^{n} \Pr(\Theta_i)\Pr(x|\Theta_i)}$$

Many readers will be familiar with Bayes' rule from applications in quality control.

5. Felix Oberholzer-Gee, "Unemployment Stigma as Information Cascades: Hiring Practices in Europe and in the United States," working paper, Wharton School, University of Pennsylvania, 2000.

6. I chose this method to make sure that the experiment did not inflict costs on the participating firms. To the extent that these firms care about unemployment duration at all, the actual duration of the subjects was always shorter than the duration stated in the cover letter.

7. Omori Yoshiaki, "Stigma Effects of Nonemployment," *Economic Inquiry,* 35, 2 (1997), pp. 394–416.

8. For a discussion of the consequences of these cascades for the optimal pricing of shares, see Ivo Welch, "Sequential Sales, Learning, and Cascades," *Journal of Finance,* 47, 2 (1992), pp. 695–732.

9. Douglas W. Diamond and Philip H. Dybvig, "Bank Runs, Deposit Insurance, and Liquidity," *Journal of Political Economy,* 91, 3 (1983), pp. 401–419.

10. Colin Camerer and Keith Weigelt, "Information Mirages in Experimental Asset Markets," *Journal of Business,* 64, 4 (1991), pp. 463–493; Daniel Friedman and Masanao Aoki, "Inefficient Information Aggregation as a

Source of Asset Price Bubbles," *Bulletin of Economic Research,* 44, 4 (1992), pp. 251–279.

Chapter 17

1. Mark V. Pauly, "Insurance Reimbursement," *Handbook of Health Economics,* eds. A. Culyer and J. Newhouse (Amsterdam: Elsevier, forthcoming).
2. The conventional arguments for the rationality of a deductible are well known. See, for example, C.E. Phelps, *Health Economics* (2nd ed.) (Reading, MA: Addison-Wesley, 1997).
3. J. Hershey, H. Kunreuther, J. Schwartz, and S. Williams, "Health Insurance Under Competition: Will People Choose What Is Expected?" *Inquiry* (1984), pp. 349–360.
4. J.P. Newhouse and the Health Insurance Experiment group, *Free for All?: Lessons from the RAND Health Insurance Experiment* (Cambridge, MA: Harvard University Press, 1993).
5. M.V. Pauly, H. Kunreuther, and J. Vaupel, "Public Protection against Misperceived Risks: Insights from Positive Political Economy," *Public Choice* (May 1984).
6. See note 4.
7. See note 4.
8. A.L. Hillman, M. Pauly, J. Escarce, K. Ripley, M. Gaynor, J. Clouse, and R. Ross, "Financial Incentives and Drug Spending in Managed Care," *Health Affairs,* 18, 2 (March–April 1999), pp. 189–200.
9. M.V. Pauly, *An Analysis of Medical Savings Accounts: Do Two Wrongs Make A Right?* (Washington, DC: AEI Press, 1994).
10. M.V. Pauly and P.J. Held, "Benign Moral Hazard and the Cost-Effectiveness Analysis of Insurance Coverage," *Journal of Health Economics,* 94 (1990), pp. 447–461.
11. P.A. Ubel, M.D. Spranka, M.L. Dekay, J. Hershey, and D.A. Asch, "Public Preferences for Prevention versus Cure," *Medical Decision Making,* 18 (April–June 1998), pp. 141–148.
12. See note 10.
13. D. Eddy, "Oregon's Methods: Did Cost Effectiveness Analysis Fail?" *Journal of the American Medical Association,* 266 (1991), pp. 2135–2141.

INDEX